ROBERT SMITH: *Architect, Builder, Patriot 1722-1777*

TO Fiske Kimball (1888-1955), *architect, historian and friend*

CHARLES E. PETERSON, FAIA, FAPT, FSAH

with Constance M. Greiff
and Maria M. Thompson

Foreword by Robert Venturi, FAIA

ROBERT SMITH

ARCHITECT, BUILDER, PATRIOT 1722-1777

THE ATHENÆUM OF PHILADELPHIA   2000

Published by

Charles E. Peterson Fellowship, The Athenæum of Philadelphia
East Washington Square, Philadelphia, PA 19106-3794

with additional funding from The Carpenters' Company of the City
and County of Philadelphia

LIBRARY OF CONGRESS CATALOGING-IN-PUBLICATION DATA

Peterson, Charles E. (Charles Emil), 1906-
Robert Smith: architect, builder, patriot, 1722-1777 / Charles E. Peterson with
Constance M. Greiff and Maria M. Thompson; foreword by Robert Venturi.—1st. ed.
    p. cm.
Includes bibliographical references and index.
ISBN 0-916530-17-5
1. Smith, Robert, 1722-1777.   2. Architects—United States—Biography.   3. Architecture,
Georgian—United States.   I. Smith, Robert, 1722-1777.   II. Greiff, Constance M.
III. Thompson, Maria M.   IV. Title.

NA737.S576 P48 2000
720'.92—dc21
[B]
                                                                00-057590

PRINTED AND BOUND IN ITALY

CONTENTS

FOREWORD

THIS HISTORICAL STUDY eloquently engages historical revelation and contemporary relevance, and it adds thereby to our knowledge of then and our understanding of now. And the richness of its content can be said to derive from the range of its dimensions embracing everyday details that acknowledge the significance of professional process, and overall theory that acknowledges the significance of architectural aesthetics.

Concerning details and process for instance: for a practicing architect of the late 20th century the issues revealed in this study that are technical (making the building stable as well as beautiful), financial (meeting the budget and getting paid), sociological (having the right connections for getting the job), political (keeping the job), along with those issues, at the same time, that involve positive relationships that can be rewarding among architects, builders, clients as they ultimately lead to personal satisfaction and aesthetic quality—become poignantly familiar. Here is confirmation of architecture as the ultimate medium that engages doing as well as creating in complex ways.

And then there is confirmed architecture as the most fragile of the visual arts—susceptible to alteration and demolition. Ironically brick walls within the context of evolving uses, urban development, and trends of fashion are more at risk than paper drawings hanging in galleries or deposited in archives. And it is this phenomenon which makes historical research in the case of Robert Smith most compelling.

And as significant as the fragility of a work of architecture is the fragility of the reputation of an architect—a phenomenon again demonstrated via Robert Smith—via his evolving degrees of recognition within the course of history as analyzed in this study.

Many artists have become victims of a cycle of taste that involves reaction against the art of the immediate past—as against Classical Georgian architecture during the subsequent periods of Romantic eclecticism in the case of Smith. But such a phenomenon is particularly prevalent and relevant today when the pace of the cycles of taste and consequent reactions intensifies as architecture becomes to a significant degree a component of hype/fashion via promotional journalism.

But perhaps the most significant lesson we can learn for today from the example of Robert Smith is that an architect and his architecture can be great but not original. There is no question that the style of Robert Smith's architecture is Classical Georgian and that he would have no problem acknowledging his works' conforming to a style—to the generic, conventional, vernacular dimensions that compose its vocabulary and content—to the style that was prevalent in his time.

Pattern books are mentioned throughout this book as explicit sources of Smith's architecture as are particular reference books including *Vitruvius Scoticus, The City and Country Builder's Treasury of Design, The Four Books of Architecture* of Palladio, *The British Carpenter* of Francis Price and *The Book of Architecture* of James Gibbs!

How ironical it is that a version of 19th-century Romantic eclecticism—the style or medley of historical-revival styles that succeeded and eclipsed the universal-Georgian style of Robert Smith—happens to thrive in the late 20th century via what is called signature architecture. Here again flourishes the Romantic concept of the artist as an original, heroic, constantly revolutionary genius who creates—creates individualistic expressionism above all. But, again multi-ironically, these "original" creations are consistently based on a symbolic source and specific vocabulary revived not from a remote historical style this time but from a recent kind of vernacular imagery evolving from the generic industrial architecture of the early 20th century—this in the Electronic Age.

Might architects of a Post-Industrial Age learn from the example of Robert Smith of a Pre-Industrial Age about an architecture explicitly generic and symbolic and valid for our Information Age? Might here be an explicit generic architecture ornamented, of course, not with a universal iconography like that of Roman-Classical orders applied via masonry articulation but ornamented with a multi-cultural iconography projecting moving/changing patterns, ornamental and/or graphic via electronic pixelation?

Viva Robert Smith as depicted in this book as a great architect of his time who created aesthetic tension within vernacular convention and as a significant architect for our time for learning from.

Robert Venturi

ACKNOWLEDGMENTS

THIS BOOK is the culmination of fifty years of interest and research into the life and work of America's foremost colonial architect-builder, Robert Smith. It is a first attempt to sum up his career, but almost certainly not the last. Documents in Philadelphia, and other places where Smith worked, will continue to shed new light on Smith and his contemporaries. Tedious, but needed, research in Philadelphia's real estate records should be extended, and may reveal hitherto unknown Smith buildings. It is hoped that most of the attributions made in this volume will be verified, but some eventually will be discarded. I wish my successors the patience and stamina needed to carry on.

Along the way many others, to whom I am grateful, have shared my interest and contributed their own findings. I wish I could name all of them. But many stand out.

Elizabeth Starr Cummin, a descendant of Robert Smith, provided much interesting information on his genealogy. It has always been my hope that knowledge of his family will lead to discovery of his drawings from the 1795 Columbianum exhibition tucked away in some descendant's attic. Beatrice Garvan tracked down Smith's ancestry and the date and place of his birth, based on a clue discovered by Willman Spawn.

The invaluable research of Wanda S. Gunning has added greatly to our knowledge of Smith. She unraveled the complicated tale of Smith's property dealings in Princeton. She also contributed a great deal to a number of topics, particularly references from the Samuel Hazard Letter Book (which provide important information on the Second Presbyterian Church); the Penn projects; and Smith's estate. Joseph Hammond pursued extensive research on many aspects of Smith's work, and also uncovered Smith's introduction of an advanced and distinctive type of truss, used in many of his churches. Nicholas Gianopulos and Suzanne M. Pentz, of Keast & Hood, generously shared their extensive knowledge of the structure of some of Smith's major designs: the steeple of Christ Church, Carpenters' Hall, and the roof trusses of St. Peter's and the Pine Street Presbyterian Church, all in Philadelphia, and the roof and cupola of Christ Church in Shrewsbury, New Jersey. Their firm's illuminating drawings of some of these projects add greatly to the interest of this book.

Travis McDonald, Jr., generously let us adapt his manuscript based on knowledge acquired while supervising reconstruction of the Public Hospital in Williamsburg, Virginia. This work owes a great deal to my secretary and assistant, Hilda Sanchez, who by now knows almost as much about Robert Smith as I do. In Scotland, David R. Smith was an informed and helpful guide to the history of Robert Smith's birthplace and boyhood home, and provided insight into what his education might have been.

Others, some of whom are no longer with us, whose contributions are gratefully acknowledged are: Susan Mary Alsop, Penelope Hartshorne Batcheler, Whitfield J. Bell, Jr., James S. Bishop, Carl and Jessica Bridenbaugh, Stanhope and Elizabeth Browne, Elizabeth Carroll-Horrocks, Hobart G. Cawood, Michael M. Chrimes, Jane Adams Clarke, Emily T. Cooperman, John L. Cotter, F. James Dallett, the Earl of Dalkeith, Scott deHaven, Evelyn Macauley Gambala, Bruce Cooper Gill, Frederick Stuart and Ann Gill, Roy E. Goodman, Louise Hall, Bernice Hamel, John Ingram, Charles Jackson, Thomas S. Keefer Jr., Dennis C. Kurjack, J. A. Leo Lemay, Colin McWilliam, Ehrman B. Mitchell, Caroline Morris, Lee H. Nelson, Paul Norton, David G. Orr, Richard W. Ostrander, John D. R. Platt, Edward M. Riley, Hannah Benner Roach, James R. Ross, Henry Savage, Sally Sells, Richard B. Sher, James Simpson, Carol Wojtowicz-Smith, Murphy Smith, Martin P. Snyder, Linda Stanley, Margaret B. Tinkcom, Anna Coxe Toogood, Nicholas B. Wainwright, Barbara Wriston, and Martin I. Yoelson.

A grant from the College of Fellows of the American Institute of Architects helped in the early stages

On 30 July 1983, the Friends of Robert Smith unveiled a commemorative tablet near what was believed to be his birthplace in Lugton, Dalkeith, Scotland. Those attending were, from left to right, Bobette Orr of the American Consulate, Edinburgh; Charles E. Peterson; Midlothian Councillor Sam Campbell; Councillor David R. Smith, former Provost [Mayor] of Dalkeith; Danny Molloy, Convenor, Midlothian Council; James R. Ross, Pipe Major, Pipes and Drums of the Delaware Valley. Courtesy Scottish County Press, Bonnyrigg.

of the publication process. But this volume would not have been possible without the generous support of The Athenæum of Philadelphia and the Carpenters' Company of the City and County of Philadelphia. Tireless assistance was provided by Dr. Roger W. Moss, Executive Director of The Athenæum, and Nicholas Gianopulos, chairman of the Carpenters' Company's Robert Smith Book Committee, whose other members were: Walter S. Riley, Treasurer; Hilda Sanchez, Secretary; John F. Larkin; George D. Batcheler, Jr.; Robert P. Breading; Charles W. Cook; Charles Dagit, Jr.; Neil P. Hoffman, Susan A. Maxman, and George P. Willman.

Finally I wish to thank my co-authors, Constance M. Greiff and Maria M. Thompson, whose additional research and organization brought this book to its present form.

Charles E. Peterson, FAIA, FAPT, FSAH

ROBERT SMITH: *Architect, Builder, Patriot* 1722-1777

INTRODUCTION: LIFE AND CAREER

WHEN ROBERT SMITH DIED in February 1777 ...his remains were interred in Friends burying ground, attended by many persons of character. By the death of this worthy and ingenious man, the public have sustained a very heavy loss, and his relations or acquaintances have to lament the sincere, steady, and affectionate friend. Several public buildings in this city, and its environs are ornaments of his great abilities.[1]

Smith's virtues and talents clearly were recognized by the citizens of his adopted city at the time. Nor was he quickly forgotten. When Owen Biddle brought out his builders' guide *The Young Carpenter's Assistant* in 1805, he featured an engraving of the tower and steeple of Christ Church, perhaps based on a Smith drawing. Six years later, a description of the Walnut Street Jail named Smith, and noted that it was "one of the many buildings for which Philadelphia is indebted to that excellent and faithful architect."[2] Within a few years, however, as new revival styles made inroads in what had been a predominantly Georgian city, Smith was largely ignored, although a few brief, and not entirely accurate, accounts of Smith's career appeared in nineteenth and early twentieth century publications.[3] Yet his buildings remained stubbornly in view, and some—Nassau Hall at Princeton University, the steeple of Christ Church and Carpenters' Hall in Philadelphia, the Mental Hospital at Williamsburg, Virginia—always were perceived as landmarks. But many of his other works were virtually forgotten.

More recently it has been recognized that Robert Smith was among the most important and skilled architect-builders in colonial America. His close contemporary, Peter Harrison of Newport (1716-1775), while also a competent designer, was a wealthy amateur, who gave away his architectural plans. Smith, however, sweated out the ardors of construction work, and struggled to maintain a successful professional career. Half a century ago it was possible to identify about twenty-two of his projects.[4] Subsequent research has raised that number to over fifty known and attributed works, discussed in the catalog entries in this volume. Others undoubtedly remain to be found. Tantalizing hints still appear. A drawing of the lost St. James Church in Lancaster, Pennsylvania, shows a tower and steeple, erected in 1760-1762, that look remarkably like those at Christ Church, Philadelphia. Hitherto, no documentation has been found naming Smith as the designer, but perhaps some future researcher will find the answer in as yet unexamined papers.[5]

Although it was recognized that Smith was Scottish, his origins were not known, and, given his name, it seemed possible that they never would be. There was speculation that he came to Philadelphia from Glasgow or that he was the same man as the Robert Smith who appeared in Chester County, Pennsylvania, records. Although the issue of the place of his birth was not solved, he could be identified from Quaker records as the man who married Esther Jones of Philadelphia Monthly Meeting shortly before the 23rd day of the 12th month of 1749 [23 February 1749/50], and whose death, at the age of fifty-five, was recorded on 11 February 1777.[6] Still, questions remained, and it was perhaps easier to say who he was not rather than who he was. He was not the Robert Smith who was a member of the First Presbyterian Church and who, according to church records, was married to a woman named Dorothea. That may possibly have been a contemporary, Robert Smith the hatter. More likely he was the Robert Smith who became a member of the St. Andrew's Society in 1752, although early 20th-century biographical sketches of members listed that Smith as coming from Glasgow.[7]

Then a vital clue was discovered in the letter book of David, "Edinburgh Davey," Hall, Benjamin Franklin's printing partner. Through Hall's contacts, booksellers Hamilton and Balfour in Edinburgh, Smith, in 1759 and the 1760s, was sending money to his widowed mother, Martha.[8] She still lived in the hamlet of Lugton near Dalkeith on the outskirts of Edinburgh.[9] With this name, and Smith's birth date

Robert Smith may have been born in one of the low, pantiled cottages on the right in this old photograph of Edinburgh Road passing through the hamlet of Lugton, enroute to Dalkeith. Courtesy Dalkeith Historical Society.

established as 1722 from his age at death, it was possible to trace his Scottish background. The future Philadelphia architect-builder was born 14 January 1722, the fourth son of John Smith, a "baxter," or baker, of Lugton and his wife, Martha Lawrie. His baptism was entered in the Dalkeith parish register on January 23rd, with Robert Lawrie (probably the uncle for whom he was named) and James Barrowman as his sponsors.[10] The Smith's eldest son, John, followed his father in the family business. There were, however, several relatives in the vicinity in the building trades, and it was their example that Robert evidently followed.[11]

There is a strong possibility that Robert Smith received an education at the Dalkeith Grammar School. According to a Dalkeith historian:

The Dalkeith Grammar School was for many years the most celebrated in the country, some of Scotland's most illustrious sons of the 18th century having received from it the rudiments of their education. It would not be out of the ordinary for a poor, fatherless boy to sit beside the children of the local gentry for it was intrinsic to the democratic spirit of the Scottish educational system at that time for the offspring of the different social groups to share classrooms and teachers in many parishes. There is no doubt that for a period rich and poor together benefited from Dalkeith's Grammar School. The wealthy, as patrons

of the school, are well-documented; evidence of the craftsman class using the school comes from the *Caledonian Mercury* in an issue during 1736 which reported the Edinburgh Porteous Riot. The report stated that an Archibald Ballantyne, a young gentleman at the school of Dalkeith, was mortally wounded. A significant feature of the report is a further statement that Ballantyne was "to be bound apprentice to a joiner." . . .

Could he [Smith] have attended some other school? Not in Dalkeith. The newspaper report refers to *the* school in Dalkeith; furthermore the church records indicate that there was only one and, for a period, no other school was allowed.[12]

There is no record of how or where Smith received training in his craft. Many men in the area with the surname Smith were in the building trades. The most successful of these was James Smith (c. 1645-1731). This Smith was a mason who transformed Dalkeith Palace, seat of the powerful Dukes of Buccleuch, with the addition of a Palladian front. Robert might have been apprenticed to Richard and Alex Smith, although they were masons. A more likely candidate to take Smith in hand was one of his baptismal sponsors, James Barrowman, who was a wright.[13]

If Smith did attend the Dalkeith Grammar School, he would have been a fellow pupil with John Adam (1721-1792), who was a year older. This was, of course, one of the sons of Scotland's foremost architect of the first half of the eighteenth century, William Adam (1689-1748). This is only one of the possible links between Smith and the Adam family. As a young man, William Adam's father, another John, is believed to have worked for James Smith on Dalkeith Palace. Coming full circle, William Adam was employed at the palace by the Duchess of Buccleuch in the 1740s, and could have hired Smith as a journeyman. It seems telling that Smith's arrival in Philadelphia, probably in 1748, came shortly after Adam's death.

Alternatively, Smith could have learned about William Adam's buildings through the engraved plates that were later issued under the title *Vitruvius Scoticus*, not published until 1812. But Adam had begun making drawings for this project as early as the 1730s, and some of the loose printed plates are on paper made in the Hague in 1746. In presenting the volume to the public in 1812, the publishers, Adam Black and J.J. Robertson, acknowledged this, and that they were able to publish because a "few complete Sets having come into the Publisher's hands," thus implying that individual, unbound prints had been in circulation previously.[14] It undoubtedly was one of the loose plates from this series, the plan and elevation of the Edinburgh Infirmary, that was studied as a prototype for the design of the east wing of the Pennsylvania Hospital (See Catalog #12).

It seems more than likely, however, that Smith had seen the actual buildings, as well as some plates. He probably would not have traveled to Dundee to see the particular form of steeple on the Town House, which was a prototype for his great steeple at Christ Church. But he could have seen the same combination of cupola and spindle on the Orphans' Hospital, built not as shown on the *Vitruvius Scoticus* plate, but topped with a spire. This was a motif that Adam probably had adapted from James Gibbs's Marylebone Chapel. Adam went to London in 1727, where he is known to have visited St. Martin-in-the Fields and St. Mary-le-Strand; he also subscribed to the 1728 edition of Gibbs's *A Book of Architecture,* in which the Marylebone Chapel was depicted.[15] At Dundee Adam combined the lowest stage of the St. Martin's steeple with the upper stages of that of the chapel and the spire of St. Martin's. Smith emulated this design with slight variations at Christ Church, Philadelphia (Catalog #4). The particular variation was the substitution of a triangular motif supported on brackets over the "clock faces" or oculi in the lowest stage of the tower. It came from another Gibbs design, Plate 30 in *A Book of Architecture.* A copy of the 1739 edition would have been available to Smith in the library of the Pennsylvania Assembly, which probably purchased the book around 1750.[16] But the main body of Christ Church also was strongly influenced by St. Martin, so it is likely that the first edition of Gibbs's work also was known in Philadelphia.

Another tantalizing possibility is that Smith spent some time in London, working for an architect named James Horne. Little is known about Horne, but, of the five buildings attributed to him, two bear a striking resemblance to Smith's work. One of these is, or rather was, Christ Church in the Borough of Southwark.[17] It has been recognized that Smith's St. Peter's Church (1758, Catalog #13) bears some resemblance to a plate illustrating Christ Church "Surry" in William Maitland's *History and Survey of London* (1756).[18] While both show a debt to Gibbs's Marylebone Chapel, there are some differences. The window sills resting on brackets, for example, common to both, are absent from the Gibbs building. However, the drawing in Maitland is crude, and does not give a very accurate picture of Christ Church. Perhaps Smith's source were drawings or engravings, possibly obtained from London by a member of the Philadelphia building committee. Certainly the fact that both had a sixty-foot clear-span interior is a coincidence that cannot be explained by the Maitland plate.

The idea that Smith worked for Horne is reinforced by another Smith building, the Almshouse, which shows more than a passing resemblance to another Horne building, the Foundling Hospital, also illustrated in Maitland. Like Watson's Hospital and the Orphans' Hospital in Edinburgh, this was not a hospital, but an orphanage, which would have made it a good model for an almshouse. Children cared for in the Foundling Hospital grew their own vegetables; boys made rope and fishing nets, while girls were responsible for cooking and cleaning. As soon as possible, they were put out to employment.[19] The first wing was begun in 1742 and finished in 1745. The second, although planned earlier, was not completed until 1749. For Smith to understand their relationship before emigrating to Philadelphia would have required knowledge of the plans for the building. The other possibility is that he knew it from the illustration in Maitland, an engraving of far better quality than that of Christ Church. Like the Philadelphia Almshouse the wings of the Foundling Hospital had higher end pavilions with strongly defined horizontals and long rear extensions with open arcades facing a courtyard. The description of the building as "commodious, plain and substantial, without any costly Decorations," defines attributes that would have appealed to Philadelphia sensibilities.[20] The designer of the Foundling Hospital is said to have been its donor, a wealthy business man named Theodore Jacobsen, while Horne supervised the construction.[21] What seems more likely is that the relationship was akin to that between Lord Burlington and William Kent, or for that matter John Kearsley and Robert Smith, where the patron conceived an idea, and the designer gave it architectural form.

Wherever or by whomever he was trained, Smith adopted a motif that was to become something of a signature. This is an octagonal cupola, with arched open-

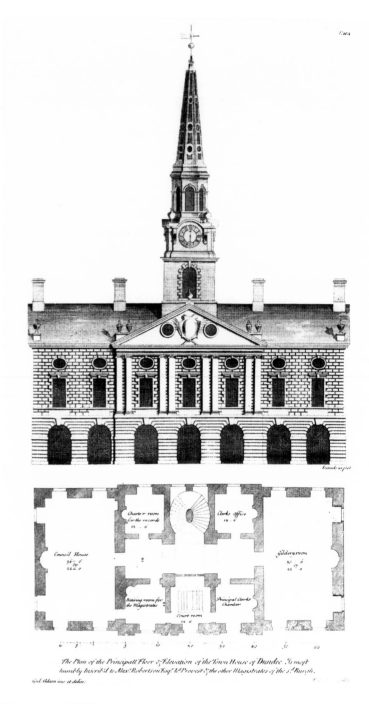

The tower and steeple of Christ Church illustrated as Plate 44 in Owen Biddle's *The Young Carpenter's Assistant*, published in Philadelphia in 1805. Although Smith had been dead for almost thirty years and architectural fashions had changed, Biddle wrote that: "... the justness of its proportions, simplicity and symmetry of its parts is allowed by good judges to be equal if not superior in beauty to any Steeple of the spire kind, either in Europe or America."

Like Smith, William Adam used a number of motifs derived from James Gibbs for the steeple of his Town Hall at Dundee, which appeared as Plate 104 in *Vitruvius Scoticus*. It closely resembles the steeple of Christ Church.

Plate 1 of James Gibbs's *A Book of Architecture*,
first published in London in 1728, depicts his church
of St. Martin-in-the-Fields, built between 1721 and 1726.

Plate 30 of *A Book of Architecture* illustrates three
variants on the steeple of St. Martin.

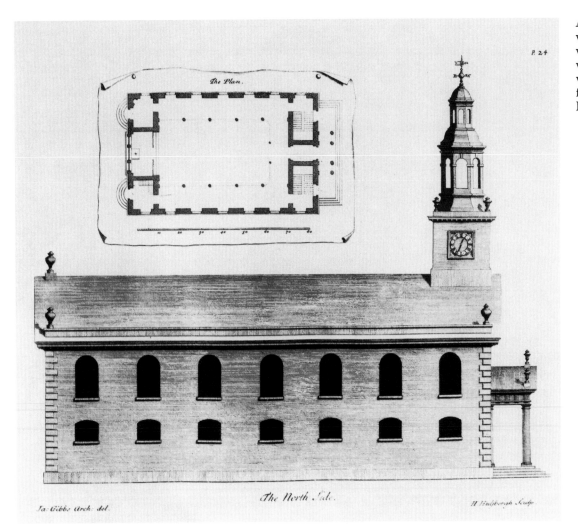

Another influential Gibbs Church was Marylebone Chapel (1721-24), with larger, round-arched upper windows and segmental-arched lower windows, a pattern that would be followed in St. Peter's Church, Philadelphia.

Christ Church, Blackfriars Road Southwark, London (1738-41) by James Horne was one of the churches that showed the influence of the Marylebone Chapel. It is similar to St Peter's in the rusticated corners, and the rusticated window surrounds resting on consoles, with larger windows at the upper level. Much altered in the nineteenth century, it was destroyed by bombing during World War II. King's Maps, xxvii, a-g, British Library.

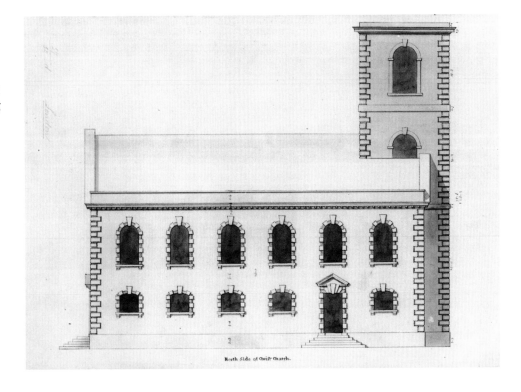

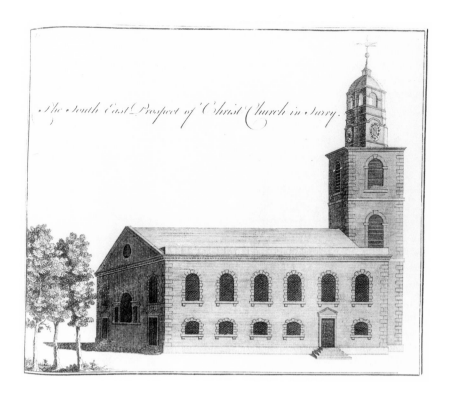

This view of Christ Church, Southwark, is Plate 43 in William Maitland's *History and Survey of London* (1756). Crudely drawn, especially in the depiction of the cupola, it could not have served as a direct model for St. Peter's. Like the more refined engraving from the King's Maps, it shows that the church had a side door, but also indicates that there were doors in the east end.

Christ Church had an octagonal cupola with domed roof, similar in form to that employed by Smith at Nassau Hall, Christ Church in Shrewsbury, and Carpenters' Hall. King's Maps, xxvii, a-g, British Library.

ings, ornamented with a keystone and impost blocks, on each side. It rises from a square base. Unless it carries a spire, the cupola is topped by a hemispherical dome. It appears at Christ Church, Philadelphia, Carpenters' Hall, Christ Church, Shrewsbury, and is illustrated in engravings of Nassau Hall and the Walnut Street Jail. Not all the surviving cupolas were constructed under Smith's direction, and the arrangement of the structural timbers differs from one to another, but the appearance remains the same. Of course, there were other octagonal cupolas in colonial America. John Smibert had put one on Faneuil Hall in Boston in 1740-42. There also was one on the Rhoads-Fox east wing of the Pennsylvania Hospital (Catalog #12), but it had a "pepperpot" roof, rather than Smith's rounded dome. Despite other examples, because of proportion, scale, and the dome, Smith's cupolas remain distinctive. The ultimate source of the design is James Gibbs's Marylebone Chapel. But Smith could have learned it either by actually seeing William Adam's buildings or in plates from *Vitruvius Scoticus*, or, if he indeed was familiar with it, James Horne's Christ Church, Southwark.

Alternatively, he could have taken it directly from Gibbs's *Book of Architecture*. Philadelphia builder-architects had access to books in institutional collections, owned some themselves, and clearly depended on them. Smith himself left "sundrey" architectural books at his death, all purchased in the flush early years of his career. At least three of his books are now in the collection of the Carpenters' Company of Philadelphia: Batty Langley's 1750 publication, *The City and Country Builder's Treasury of Designs*, purchased in 1751; the 1737 London edition of Andrea Palladio's *The Four Books of Architecture*, bought in 1754; and the three volumes of Colen Campbell's *Vitruvius Britannicus*, issued from 1716 to 1725, the last volume signed "Robt Smith His Book 1756." From this, and the lists of volumes owned by other individuals and in institutional collections, it is clear that Philadelphia's builder-architects were interested in classical and Palladian design.[22]

Whether he came directly from Scotland or by way of London, Smith probably emigrated to Philadelphia in late 1748. He arrived at the dawn of the third quarter of the eighteenth century. Mercantile wealth and civic pride were transforming Philadelphia from a colonial outpost to a metropolis. By the outbreak of the Revolutionary War, Philadelphia was one of the largest cities in the English-speaking world. The State House was about to be expanded with the addition of a masonry tower and tall steeple. It was the era of building the greatest of Philadelphia's Georgian town houses and country seats—Mount Pleasant, Cliveden, Port Royal, and Belmont. Smith would play a major role in this transformation of the city as the designer of more public and quasi-public buildings than any of his contemporaries.

Almost immediately, Smith assumed a rank among the premier carpenter-builders of his adopted city. Prestigious commissions came his way from the start, including work, beginning in 1749, on James Hamilton's country seat, Bush Hill (Catalog #1). Early the next year he undertook what probably amounted to the design of the Second Presbyterian Church (Catalog #2). At about the same time, he married Esther Jones, a Quaker.

Smith must have been recognized as a rising star when the Vestry of Christ Church called on him in 1753 for a difficult and, as it turned out, rather daring enterprise—erecting a tall steeple that would dominate the Philadelphia skyline until City Hall was completed in 1881 and several skyscrapers were erected in the twentieth century. Even before the steeple was finished, Smith was tapped for another prestigious job—designing and constructing the main building and president's house at the College of New Jersey, now Princeton University. For a time, he lived in Princeton, buying property, and building at least one, and probably two, houses. During this period, he traveled back and forth between Princeton and Philadelphia, where he was engaged in extensive alterations for the Academy, later the College of Philadelphia, and still later the University of Pennsylvania. Smith undoubtedly was once more living in Philadelphia by 1758, when he signed a contract to design and build St. Peter's Church at the corner of Pine and Third Streets. Commissions for the roof and interior of St. Paul's (1760-1761) and a dormitory for the College of Philadelphia (1762-1763) followed.

Smith continued to be retained as designer and/or builder for important institutional buildings and churches in Philadelphia through the rest of his life: the "Bettering House" or Almshouse (1766-1767), Carpenters' Hall (1770-1774), and the Walnut Street Jail (1773-1774). His churches included Third Presbyterian (Old Pine, 1767-1768) and the mammoth

Zion Lutheran Church (1766). Because less is known about private patrons, few of whose papers survive, it may never be possible to determine how many houses Smith designed or constructed. One was Benjamin Franklin's free-standing house in an interior court between Chestnut and Market Streets. He also carried out extensive renovations for Samuel Powel in one of the greatest of Philadelphia townhouses, still standing at 244 South Third Street. His reputation spread far beyond Philadelphia. It had been established in New Jersey with the building of Nassau Hall, and he was called on in that colony for Christ Church in Shrewsbury (1769) and perhaps other churches as well. The Presbyterian Church in Carlisle (1769) also came from his pen. He provided the design for the "Hospital for Lunatics and Idiots" in Williamsburg, Virginia (1771), and possibly University Hall (1770) at Rhode Island College, now Brown University.

Construction of all these later out-of-town projects was undertaken by others, with Smith solely as designer. Indeed, in the late 1760s and 1770s, Smith increasingly functioned as what is known today as an architect. The documents indicate that he was not involved in construction of the "Bettering House," or the Third Presbyterian Church, or Carpenters' Hall, although he was on the scene at the Walnut Street Jail. He also became engaged in what would now be called structural engineering. In 1769, he presented the Pennsylvania Legislature with a proposal, backed by a model, for a covered, multi-arched truss bridge spanning the Schuylkill River at Market Street. His last work, carried out on behalf of the Revolutionary cause, was to design and supervise the construction of chevaux-de-frise. These were huge log boxes, sunk and filled with stones, with barbed spikes pointing downstream. For a time, they kept the British Navy out of the Delaware River.

Smith evidenced an early interest in structural solutions to design issues. Erecting the steeple for Christ Church posed challenging problems of rigidity and wind resistance. His first attempt was not entirely satisfactory and he had to return to make extensive repairs in 1771. But it is now, and has been for many years, the only surviving pre-Revolutionary steeple in Philadelphia.[23] Smith also introduced to Philadelphia a raised tie beam truss, which made possible the construction of clear spans as wide as sixty or sixty-five feet. These were particularly desirable in large churches, offering the congregation an uninterrupted view of the pulpit. They also allowed for a graceful arched ceiling. The truss Smith is first known to have used at St. Peter's was an adaptation of one pictured in Francis Price's 1733 publication *A Treatise on Carpentry*, reissued in 1735 as *The British Carpenter*, a book available at the Library Company by 1749.[24] The truss illustrated by Price showed the major diagonal braces, which he called "hammer beams" fastened to the raised tie beam by two bolts, and to the king post by an iron strap. Iron straps also reinforced the joints of the tie beam and the principal rafters. Smith modified this and added strength by iron straps connecting the diagonal braces to the foot of the rafter, and a V-shaped iron plate under the king post, forming a Y-shaped yoke. A drawing of a similar truss to Smith's, described as a "60' Roof Truss with 'Arched Ceiling'" appeared over a quarter of a century after the design of St. Peter's as Plate VII in the 1786 rule book of the Carpenters' Company.[25]

Smith may have employed a raised tie beam truss earlier at the Second Presbyterian Church (1749/50-1752). In 1758, when he designed and began construction of St. Peter's, the specifications embodied in the contract called for the roof to be "Truss'd well framed and bound with Iron That the frame of a Circular Ceiling shall be made and fixed under the Roof ready for the Plaisterer . . . ." The adaptation of the Price truss at St. Peter's is much like the one shown in the Carpenters' Company's rule book, except that Smith placed two bolts rather than one to each side of the junction of the king post, tie beam, and diagonal braces. Smith employed the raised tie beam truss in all his Philadelphia churches, except the enormous Zion Lutheran, where the seventy-foot width may have seemed too daunting.[26] He also was aware of how much reinforcement such a truss might need. In 1769, he designed a trussed roof for Christ Church in Shrewsbury, New Jersey. There, always practical, because the span was only thirty-eight feet, he used far less iron.

Although the solutions to structural problems interested Smith and allowed him to introduce innovative building types new to America, such as the clear-span church, it was as a designer that his reputation grew. The progress of his career can to some extent be measured by how others referred to him. In 1749,

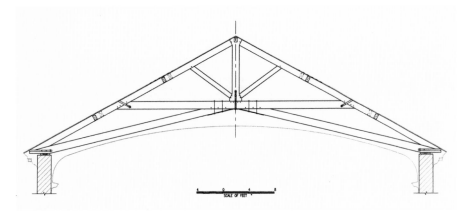

The raised tie beam roof truss at St. Peter's Church, Philadelphia. Robert Smith's truss improved upon the Francis Price model by utilizing additional iron straps at the heel joints and adding an underside yoke strap and extra bolts at the center joint. Measured drawing, 1999, by J.S. Winterle, principal delineator, under the direction of Suzanne Pentz. Courtesy Keast & Hood Co.

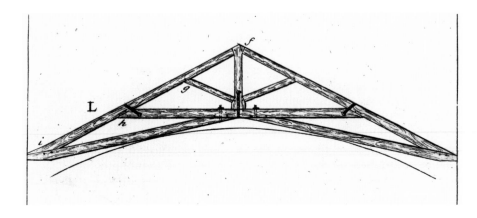

Plate L from Francis Price, *The British Carpenter or, A Treatise on Carpentry* (1733). This roof truss design for a wide-span, arched ceiling featured iron straps and bolts at critical connections. Robert Smith adapted and improved upon the design and utilized it in several of his church commissions. Library Company of Philadelphia.

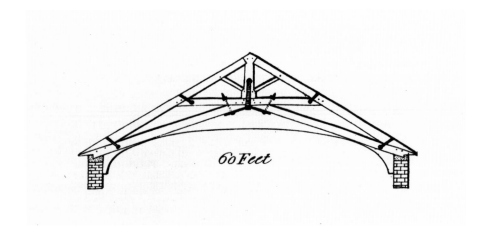

By 1786, when the Carpenters' Company printed its prices in an illustrated book, where this appeared as Plate VII, this type of truss evidently was well known to Philadelphia master carpenters.

James Hamilton, in a rather patronizing manner, called him "my carpenter." He was still a carpenter in 1755, when he was working on alterations to the "New Building" or Academy (Catalog #11), and at St. Paul's in 1760. When he signed a contract with Mary Maddox in 1763 he was a "house carpenter" (Catalog #22) as he also was identified in a 1774 deed. This had a slightly different connotation, suggesting that he was a builder, and "builder" was what his boarder, the plasterer James Clow, called him in 1763. But by 1764, the building committee at St. Michael's Lutheran Church referred to him as the "celebrated architect" (Catalog #26), and the Third Presbyterian Church (Catalog #31) also referred to him as "architect." Finally, in 1768, when the Lutherans, who seemed to have great confidence in Smith, asked him to be an arbitrator at St. Peter's Church, Barren Hill (Catalog #33), they identified him as "Architector." This was a clear distinction between Smith and his fellow arbitrator, a "Master Builder."

As an architect, what did Smith do? Like architects today, he was called on to provide drawings, specifications, and estimates. Most eighteenth-century drawings were rudimentary, or so it seems from the few that have survived.[27] Yet drawings were recognized as a symbol of the master builder's or architect's craft. Charles Willson Peale (1741-1827) painted portraits of two of Smith's contemporaries. Gunning Bedford, his fellow member of the Carpenters' Company, posed late in life, seated before a window, through which an archway under construction can be seen, and holding in his hand a sketchy drawing of an aedicule. The far livelier portrait of London-trained William Buckland also has an architectural background, in this case scaffolding, and a remarkable colossal Corinthian portico with five columns! Buckland holds a pen, while other tools of his craft lie on the table at which he is seated, along with a sophisticated sketch of a plan and elevation.

Certainly Smith made drawings. The earliest projects for which he may have done so were the Second Presbyterian Church (Catalog #2) and Christ Church steeple (Catalog #4). At the latter, it seems unlikely that the workmen could have accomplished the complicated business of fitting together all the pieces of a new kind of design and construction without drawings to guide them. At Nassau Hall (Catalog #7), in 1754, he provided the plan, as well as acting as builder

for all but the masonry. Thereafter, there is a steady stream of references to a plan or plans for various projects. What these consisted of is uncertain, because, although they are documented, they have not survived. In several cases, they were accompanied by highly detailed specifications in the form of a contract, as at St. Peter's (Catalog #13), or a description, as at the Williamsburg hospital (Catalog #43). Carpenters in Philadelphia, who by this time shared a standardized vernacular Palladian vocabulary, could transmute the language of these specifications into a building that would meet Smith's design requirements. Where this was not the case, as at Williamsburg, the result looked quite different from the buildings of Smith's home city. Usually the specifications included estimates of the amounts of material needed and the costs.

Although plans and elevations were the most common types, they were not, as sometimes has been thought, the only drawings made.[28] Benjamin Loxley prepared a site plan for Carpenters' Court (Catalog #35) and the trustees of the College of Philadelphia evidently had a site plan, prepared by Smith, in front of them when they determined the placement of a new dormitory (Catalog #16). There were also some perspectives. One exists for Cliveden, perhaps drawn by its owner, Benjamin Chew.[29]

Probably architects' drawings served as the basis for some engravings. George Heap made the drawing of the famous "East Prospect" of Philadelphia in 1752, advertising it as available for viewing in the *Pennsylvania Gazette* on September 28th. (The engraving by Nicholas Scull was not available until 1754.) Two steeples are depicted: that of the Second Presbyterian Church (Catalog #2), probably by Robert Smith, and that of Christ Church (Catalog #4), certainly from his hand. Yet the Presbyterian Church spire was never built in the form shown, and construction of the Christ Church spire had not begun. But Christ Church certainly is pictured accurately, so that Heap must have had a drawing at hand. Indeed, there is confirmation that such a drawing (or drawings) existed. Writing to his uncle in July 1753, John Penn noted that the steeple "will be a very handsome thing, if executed according to the plan."[30]

Two competing engravings of perspective views of the Pennsylvania Hospital are other examples. They show the building as complete, not as it was eventually built in the early nineteenth century, but as it was conceived in 1754-1755. Although the proportions of the building shown in the engravings differ, the detailing is the same. This suggests that the engravers worked from the same model, possibly the architect's drawing. The same holds true for a c.1767 painting of the Almshouse (Catalog #29), and an engraving made from it in 1769. Again they show the building with the center building complete, which was not the case. The engraving was made in London by James Hulett, to whom a drawing must have been sent.[31]

Some ideas of the types of drawings that might be made come from documents related to one of Smith's peers, Thomas Nevell. Nevell's account book shows that he was providing private tutelage as early as 1766, when he charged John King £2 for instruction in the "Art of Drawing Sundry Proportion in Architecture."[32] King evidently put his lessons to good use. He went on to become a member of the Carpenters' Company.[33] Five years later, in the *Pennsylvania Gazette* of 31 October 1771, Nevell advertised the opening of a drawing school. The curriculum spelled out in some detail the types of drawings an architect might be required to provide.

I will take it upon me to instruct a small number of youth, or others, in the right use and construction of lines for the formation of regular or irregular arches, groins for vaults, or cielings [sic], brackets for plaistered [sic] cornices, and the like; the best method for striking out the ramp, and twist rails for stair cases; the most expeditious and approved method of diminishing columns and pilasters; the readiest rule for laying out the flutes and fillet, the method of forming raking cornices for pediments, &c. The geometrical rules for finding the length, back and bevel of hip or valley rafters, to any constructions, streight [sic] or circular, and to lay down principal roofs in ledgement. Most of the performances aforesaid shall be delineated and put in practice in miniature, after which I propose to teach signs, and generally each branch requisite to form a true and compleat architect; all which, by a person of a common capacity, may be gone through and learnt in two months at most.

Putting this "in practice in miniature" suggests that he was teaching his pupils to draw to scale.

Nevell had a competitor, Christopher Colles (1739-1816). Colles went on to produce what were probably the first pocket guides to travel on the roads of the United States, but in 1771 he opened an "EVENING SCHOOL," in which he proposed to teach all branches of mathematics (except calculus), and a number of

trades or professions and the backgrounds for them, including among others book-keeping, navigation, mensuration, fortification and gunnery, the design of canals and waterworks, and the construction of mills and engines. In addition, he would teach

the most expeditious method of designing and drawing plans, elevations, sections, and perspective views in architecture, and to embellish the same; likewise exact methods of drawing any mill or engine, though the most complex structure, so that another may be made similar thereto by any intelligent workman, ...[34]

Clearly, the skills needed to produce architectural drawings were widely known by the third quarter of the eighteenth century. Robert Smith undoubtedly made plans, elevations, sections, and some detail drawings. Especially in cases where he provided a design, but would not build or supervise construction, detail drawings would be needed, and documents indicate that he provided them. At Christ Church in Shrewsbury (Catalog #39), this included what must have been a section, for it delineated his favored raised tie beam trussed roof. Another drawing was for the cupola, which must have been more than a mere sketch, for the cupola corresponds in every detail to those known to have been designed by him. The carpenters of the Presbyterian Church in Carlisle, Pennsylvania (Catalog #40), were instructed that "there is Rabits to be made in the walls to receive the Window bases Agreeable to the plan Drawn by Mr. Robert Smith of Philad'a." There also was at least one detail drawing of the Second Presbyterian Church. On 7 January 1750/1, Samuel Hazard, a merchant with whom Smith was closely associated at both the church and Nassau Hall (Catalog #7), wrote to William Trotman in London to order window glass for the building. He ordered 745 panes of various sizes, as well as "Glass for the arch part of 19 windows according to the enclosed de[sign]."[35]

There is no doubt that Smith could draw, and that he drew well.[36] Almost twenty years after his death, his drawings still were highly esteemed. In 1795 some were shown in an exhibition in Philosophical Hall held by the "Columbianum, or American Academy of Painting, Sculpture and Architecture, &c.," believed to have been the first show of architectural drawings in America.[37]

Mensuration constituted another branch of Smith's practice. This system of valuation by mensuration, or

Detail from the great "East Prospect of the City of Philadelphia." The view was drawn by George Heap in 1752 and engraved by Nicholas Scull. It shows the steeple of Christ Church to the left and that proposed for the Second Presbyterian Church to the right. Neither of these was standing when Heap pictured them, so he must have worked from an architect's drawings. The Athenæum of Philadelphia.

measuring was found both in Britain and early America. No one has explained the procedure better than Sir Christopher Wren, who, in a letter of 1681 to the Bishop of Oxford, discussed the methods of undertaking a construction project.

There are three ways of working: by the Day, by Measure, by Great; if by the Day it tells me when they are lazy. If by Measure it gives me light on every particular, and tells me what I am to provide. If by the Great I can make a sure bargain neither to be overreached nor to hurt the undertaker: for in things they are not every day used to, they doe often injure themselves, and when they begin to find it, they shuffle and slight the works to save themselves. I think the best way in this business is to worke by measure: according to the prices in the Estimate or lower if you can, and measure the work at 3 or 4 measurements as it rises. But you must have an understanding trusty Measurer . . . .[38]

At various times Smith was paid by each of these methods: by the day, or what would now be termed for time and materials; by the "great," that is, by a fixed contract, and by measurement by one of his peers.

British authorities suggest that the practice of determining value by measuring originated in the mid-sixteenth century, perhaps coming into common use after the Great Fire of London in 1666.[39] Contracts executed by Roger Pratt (1620-1685) and Christopher Wren (1632-1723) were limited to calling for the work to be completed in accordance with the last measure. The building owner purchased materials directly. The contracts contained no reference to drawings. None of these contracts specified a lump sum. To determine the amount of payment due to a tradesman, it was necessary to calculate the amount of work he had carried out.[40] By the eighteenth century, measuring in Britain had become a separate profession, with James Noble noting in 1836 that "the first 'measurer' ever remunerated by a commission in the amount or value of the work was a Mr. Hele, a very able, and, it appears, avaricious individual (about 1760 to 1770) who was solely employed by workmen; and both the architect and measurer soon discovered their mutual advantages . . . ."[41]

The subject of measuring perhaps was introduced to America through a now obscure volume by John Barker (fl. 1692-1718), entitled *The Measurer's Guide; or, the Whole Art of Measuring Made Short Plain and Easie*, first published in London c.1692. (A copy appeared very early in the library of Christ Church,

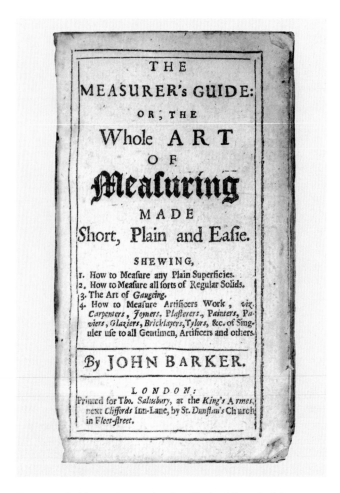

A copy of this work was in the Christ Church Library at an early date. William Andrews Clark Memorial Library, University of California, Los Angeles.

Philadelphia, but is now missing.) Barker, however, devoted comparatively little time to what he called "Artificers Work," the product of "Carpenters, Joyners, Plasterers, Painters, Glaziers, Bricklayers, Tylers [roofers], &c."[42] An extremely popular work on the subject was William Hawney's *The Compleat Measurer*. The third chapter of this is on "measuring the works of the several Artificers relating to Building and what Methods and Customs are observed therein." The following chapter covers measuring board, timber, and stone. The book went through sixteen editions between 1717 and 1789. Revised by Thomas Keith, it was issued four more times in England up to 1824, and at least three times in America.[43]

Matthew Carey issued an edition in Philadelphia in 1801. But the book was available in the city much earlier. Benjamin Franklin first offered it for sale in *The Pennsylvania Gazette* of 12 August 1742. His partner, David Hall, advertised the book in April and May 1748, as part of a new shipment in March 1748/49, and as late as November 1762.

Another substantial contribution to the subject was a booklet printed in 1748 "by B. Franklin and D. Hall at the New-Printing-Office in Market Street," under the title of *The American Instructor: or the Young Man's Best Companion*. This was the ninth edition of a work by George Fisher, accountant, revised and corrected. The publishers claimed it to be "better adapted to the American Colonies than any other book of Like Kind." Thirty-seven pages were devoted to "the Carpenters' Plain and Exact Rules: Shewing how to measure Carpenters, Joyners, Sawyers, Bricklayers, Plaisterers, Plumbers, Masons, Glasiers, and Painters Work. How to undertake each Work, and at what Price: the Rates of each Commodity, and the common Wages of Journeymen...."[44] The details seem to be based on London practice.

Several years before *The American Instructor* appeared, however, the practicing of measuring for value was in use in Philadelphia. By the 1730s, Edward Warner was billing James Logan for measuring at the Richmond Hill estate.[45] In 1740/41, Samuel Rhoads, Joseph Fox, Samuel Powel, and John Nicholas, all members of the Carpenters' Company, were asked to measure the work of a fellow member, Edmund Woolley, on the State House [Independence Hall].[46] A later instance was in 1761, when Benjamin Loxley billed on November 21st for measuring and valuing a large new porch on the Pennsylvania Hospital, built by William Craige. He judged it to be worth £7.4[47]

In the colonies, in contrast to Britain, architect-builders continued to measure the buildings of their peers in the 1760s and 1770s. Thomas Nevell, for example, measured Gunning Bedford's work on Edward Stiles's mansion, Port Royal, built in 1761 on the Delaware River.[48] Nevell in turn had his work at Mount Pleasant measured by Robert Smith and John Thornhill (1711-1783), another member of the Carpenters' Company. They must have done so on at least three occasions. Nevell submitted three bills to the owner, John MacPherson, each covering valuation of a different aspect of the work (Catalog #25).

In 1766, Smith shared with Thornhill the task of measuring another great Philadelphia suburban mansion, Cliveden, in Germantown (Catalog #30). There the two master carpenters evaluated the carpentry of Jacob Knor. In turn, Knor measured the work of stonemason John Hesser and painter Philip Warner.[49]

Smith, Nevell, Bedford, and Thornhill all were members of the Carpenters' Company of the City and County of Philadelphia. The Carpenters' Company is probably the oldest builders' organization in the United States, and perhaps the oldest American organization devoted to any trade. It is not a union, but rather a guild. Undoubtedly it was fashioned after such English organizations as the Worshipful Company of Carpenters of London, which still flourishes and enjoys a friendly intercourse with the Philadelphia company. Originating in medieval times, the English institution provided aid to injured members, "as by falling down of a house or hurting of an eye or other direct sicknesses," and decent burial of the dead.[50] The Philadelphia Carpenters' Company had similar aims, including "obtaining instruction in the science of architecture and assisting such of their members as should by accident be in need of support, or the widows and minor children of members...."[51]

The members of the Carpenters' Company also had a virtual monopoly on the system of measuring

Measurers at work as shown in William Leybourn's *Art of Measuring* (London, 1669).

work after completion to determine its value, which they protected assiduously. Indeed, Carpenters' Hall was built as a place "to meet in as occasion may require, to Transact the business of Sd. Compy. & to Calculate & Settle their private Accots of Measuring & Valueing Carpenters work."[52] As early as 1769, the company established a Committee on Prices of Work. By 1774, a set of recognized prices was recorded by hand in a book, kept at Carpenters' Hall, where members had to come and make copies personally if they wished to have the list. Eventually, in 1786, they expressed the system in printed form in an illustrated rule book, setting down a price for each type of carpenter's work. So secret were their practices that any member showing the book to outsiders was liable to expulsion. When a member died, his fellows immediately called on the widow for return of his copy. Even Thomas Jefferson, writing from Monticello in 1817 to request a copy, could not obtain one.[53] Despite their monopoly, the members of the company thought they were fair to all concerned in setting prices.

... such prices are judged to be the value of the following articles, when they are done in a substantial, neat, workmanlike manner. And if any part is done otherwise, we desire that the price may be lowered, at the discretion of those that are good judges.

The real intent and meaning of what hath been done is, that every gentleman concerned in building may have the value of his money, and that every workman may have the worth of his labour.[54]

When members of a newer association, the Friendship Carpenters' Company, compiled their own rules in 1769, they sought to reconcile them with the more august institution. Robert Smith replied, on behalf of the Carpenters' Company.

As to scandal or Reproach we for ourselves are not sensible of any just cause for either, being conscious that the Methods for measuring and valueing we persue is more Equitable Expressive and satisfactory than any method ever practiced in this City before and many of us are Sensible that it is not Inferior to the best methods practis'd in any City within the King's Dominions.[55]

The Carpenters' Company's and Friendship Carpenters' Company's price lists were not the only such documents available in colonial America. There was a manuscript list in Providence by about 1750, and one

was published in Boston on the eve of the Revolution, in 1774.[56] In addition to establishing the value of work by the measure, such a book of prices also could be used to estimate the cost of proposed work from quantities taken from drawings; that is exactly what is done today by estimators using "unit prices."

The method of establishing the cost of work after construction must have persisted for some time in Philadelphia. The Carpenters' Company printed its last edition of the price book in 1853. An incomplete, and unsigned certificate in the company's records, dated 17 January 1878, refers to measuring "Carpenter Work" executed by Henry Barry for Jacob Simons at Portico Stable. Today the practice of valuing completed work by measurement has died out in the United States, although, in greatly modified form, it survives in Great Britain, carried out by licensed quantity surveyors. Maintaining tradition, the president of the Carpenters' Company still appoints a "Price Committee" annually, but the term has long since lost its meaning.

Robert Smith was a highly respected member of the Carpenters' Company. He probably was sworn in fairly early in his career. In a chronological list of 133 members, living and dead, in the 1786 *Rule Book*, Smith's name appears twenty-second, after such luminaries as the first Samuel Powel, Edmund Woolley, and Samuel Rhoads, but before Thomas Nevell and Gunning Bedford. He was one of three men signing the 1768 deed for purchase of the property on which Carpenters' Hall would be built.[57] In 1769, Smith became a member of the all-important Committee on Prices of Work, established at the same time. Finally, the group, all themselves master builders, chose Smith to design their new hall.

The members of the Carpenters' Company enjoyed a collegial relationship, working together in a variety of ways. As already noted, Smith and John Thornhill measured and valued Thomas Nevell's work at Mount Pleasant. Thomas Nevell, in turn, had measured Gunning Bedford's Port Royal. Among those with whom Smith was most deeply intertwined was Samuel Rhoads. Like Smith, Rhoads sometimes acted as a designer and contractor, although he became wealthy as a developer.[58] Rhoads, along with Joseph Fox, was a manager and designer for the Pennsylvania Hospital, a project for which Smith was a consultant. Rhoads served in the same capacity for the

Almshouse. He handled the finances when Smith built Benjamin Franklin's House, where another Carpenters' Company member, Robert Allison (?-1811) executed the interior woodwork.[59]

Rhoads and Smith served together on a committee of the American Philosophical Society, of which Smith had been elected a member in 1768, overseeing a platform to observe the Transit of Venus in 1769.

There is ample evidence that Smith was respected as an architect by his peers. His professional success did not translate, however, into social or financial success. Even in so highly stratified a society as England, it was possible to rise from the artisan class to gentry as an architect.

Architecture was open to all. A Vanbrugh or an Archer might come to it as gentlemen with a passion for building and under no obligation to find themselves a 'place' . . . On the other hand, many of the most distinguished architects were trained as craftsmen . . . Kent [was] a coach-maker. A writer of 1747 (R. Campbell, *The London Tradesman*), speaking of architects, says 'I scarce know of any in *England* who have had an education regularly designed for the Profession, Bricklayers, carpenters, etc., all commence (i.e. set up as) Architects . . .' One often finds a man described as Mr. So-an-so, Esq., architect . . . .

Speculative building and the architectural profession were the two goals of success for men entering the London building trade. The roles might be, and often were combined. But the man who was temperamentally fitted for the more academic and literary parts of the business usually contrived to find himself a patron, with whose help he advanced along the road of pure professionalism as far as a country estate of his own, a carriage, a coat-of arms, and a fortune of £10,000 or £20,000.[60]

In the New World, there were few peers or patrons of sufficient wealth to sustain an individual's architectural career. Real estate development was the road to wealth and status, a path followed by the first Samuel Powel and Samuel Rhoads. Smith attempted to do the same, but the results were disastrous. He either was unlucky or was a poor business man. His contemporaries may have thought the latter was the case, for he never was chosen to serve as manager of major public projects, as Rhoads and Joseph Fox were.

The role of manager was defined well in 1784, when the congregation of the Presbyterian Church in Princeton, which had been damaged badly during the Revolutionary War, decided to rebuild.

That all the subscriptions should be taken on one paper, payable in two payments, into the hands of Enos Kelsey, who was chosen treasurer for this purpose, and was directed to pay all orders for this service drawn on him by Messrs. Robert Stockton, James Hamilton and John Little, managers chosen to purchase materials, employ workmen and *superintend the whole of the repairs* [emphasis added] and report through an examining committee to the congregation.[61]

From early in his career, Smith, with relatively slender resources, attempted to achieve financial success through speculative ventures. While working on Nassau Hall and the President's House at the College of New Jersey, Smith bought two pieces of property, and probably built houses on both of them (Catalog #9).[62] He undoubtedly believed that the hamlet of Princeton would grow more swiftly than it did after the arrival of the college. He sold at least one of the properties in 1765, perhaps because he wanted money to develop property he had acquired on Second Street in Southwark (Catalog #17) or to build Buck Tavern on a piece of land he owned in Moyamensing (Catalog #27).

Perhaps the venture in real estate that provided the most satisfaction to his family was his 1761 purchase from Samuel Rhoads of a sizeable piece of property. It lay between the west side of Second Street and the east side of George Street at the corner of Cedar [now South] Street in a district of Philadelphia soon to be known as Southwark.[63] Smith obviously was enjoying a period of financial success, having completed, or being in the midst of work on St. Peter's, St. Paul's, and a dormitory for the College of Philadelphia. Tax lists, deeds, and estate records offer ample evidence that Smith was established on this property from about 1761 until he died. Soon after acquiring it, Smith built a three-story house at the corner of Second and Cedar Streets, where Number 606 Second Street now stands. He probably located his lumberyard and shop behind it; later records indicate that his subdivided lot was 151 feet deep. On 29 December 1763, the newly arrived stucco worker, James Clow, advertised his talents in *The Pennsylvania Journal and Weekly Advertiser,* saying he could be contacted "at Mr. Robert Smith's builder, in Second Street on Society Hill."

Smith's name appears in the 1767 and 1769 Southwark tax lists as owning a dwelling, horse, and cow. Besides the Second Street property, he owned three acres of meadowland in Passyunk, and a house and lot in Moyamensing, a part of which had been assigned to John Inglis in 1762.[64] He probably built the brick house and made the improvements to the Moyamensing lot that were mentioned when the property was advertised for sale and sold after his death.[65] In 1770, his Second Street parcel was slightly enlarged as part of the proprietors' settlement of the city's southern boundary, and, sometime before 1772, Smith divided his land into the eleven lots shown in the plat accompanying papers prepared for settlement of his estate.[66]

In addition to the large house on the corner of Second Street where Smith lived, three of the other Second Street lots contained two-story brick kitchens, with the corner lot, number 4, occupied by a frame store and wash house. Smith valued the three kitchens and "shop" at £1400. Lot 8, with twenty-foot frontage on Cedar Street, and abutting lot 1 at the rear, contained a "new stable and chair house [privy]" in 1774, a structure not accounted for in the 1769 tax list.

The Southwark property took on something of the character of a family compound with members of Smith's family living on the west side of Second Street, some probably in the "brick kitchens" already mentioned.[67] After his death his widow Esther and her young sons, James and Henry, occupied the brick house on lot 1. James grew up to be a silversmith and continued to reside in Southwark, presumably on the family property. Henry, went to sea in 1780, when he was about eighteen. Tragically, he was never seen again. Smith's daughter Hester and her husband, master carpenter William Williams (c.1749-1794), also lived in Southwark, with Williams remaining after his wife's death in 1783. Both the 1790 census and city directories of 1785 and 1791 document his occupation and residence.

In 1772, Smith granted use of lot 11, on the south side of Cedar Street and subject to a ground rent, to house carpenter John O'Neal, probably the same man who worked on the cupola at Carpenters' Hall. Smith's wife Esther and eldest son John were witnesses to the recorded transaction.[68] The adjoining lot, number 10, was conveyed to merchant Thomas Lake in two installments, subject to the same conditions.[69] By 1774 only three small lots and one full-length lot were undeveloped.[70]

Smith's most successful venture was the 1768 purchase of a lot on Second Street, probably between Walnut and Spruce, from Samuel Powel for £441.13.

6 1/2. He promptly built a house, which he soon sold for £1500 (Catalog #41). This was evidently the only time that he was able to pursue a speculative project in what was perhaps Philadelphia's most desirable residential area. With limited capital, Smith usually operated on the outer fringes of the city. Certainly his biggest failure, the north side of Spruce Street between Fourth and Fifth Streets, the freehold of which he purchased from Christ Church in 1771, fell into that category. By the time of his death, only five out of seventeen lots had been sold, at least one with a partially finished house on it. A rental "tenement" occupied another of the lots. (See Catalog #47.)

Perhaps Smith's timing was unlucky. Professionally he was busy, and soon he would be caught up in preparations for the Revolutionary War. Smith was an ardent patriot. On 18 June 1774 "a very large and Respectable Meeting of the Freeholders and Freemen of the City and County of Philadelphia" assembled to protest the closing of the port of Boston. They called for a Congress to meet to secure American rights and liberties and a Committee of Correspondence to communicate with like-minded citizens in other counties and states. They also resolved to appoint what became known as the Committee of Forty Three to raise money for the relief of those harmed economically by the port closing. Robert Smith, identified as a carpenter, was chosen as a member.[71]

By early 1776, he was deeply involved in planning the defenses of the Delaware River, traveling to Fort Mifflin to see what additional works were needed there, and designing and supervising the construction of chevaux-de-frise (Catalog #53). Barracks constructed under his supervision at Billingsport, New Jersey, were his last buildings.

On a wintry February morning in 1777, Robert Smith died at his house on Second Street "after a tedious and painful indisposition."[72] The nature of his illness is unknown. Perhaps it was exacerbated or caused by his work along the banks of the icy Delaware, where he was active until late November or early December. Philadelphia diarist Jacob Hiltzheimer was among the "many persons of character," who attended Smith's burial at the Friends' cemetery in Arch Street.[73]

Smith died intestate and in debt, leaving a tangle of financial dealings that would not be resolved until long after the last of his property was auctioned at sheriff's sale in 1790.[74] Appointed executors of his estate in April 1777, his widow Esther and eldest son John relied on a 1774 account from Robert Smith's books to compile an inventory of real estate holdings, available anticipated income, and debts.[75] The latter amounted to £6004, plus a year's interest; his assets were far less. He had borrowed money from James Tilghman, Samuel Rhoads, Thomas Paschall, and others, and given mortgages to Mary Maddox and Dr. John Redman. Sadly, one of the largest amounts owed was £400 to "Workmen and Plasterrers [sic]." This debt indicates that on projects where Robert Smith was the builder, he was responsible for paying his journeymen and at least one related trade. At times, when he was responsible for a large project, such as Zion Lutheran Church or the Walnut Street Jail, he may have employed a number of workmen. His difficulties in meeting their wages may have been due to the inability of some of his clients to reimburse him in a timely fashion. Institutional clients, in particular, sometimes paid slowly or only partially.

Although sometimes Smith was paid on the basis of measuring, he also executed contracts with some clients. Those with Mary Maddox and St. Peter's Church probably were typical. They were not unlike construction contracts today, although payments were scheduled more frequently, while the amounts were relatively smaller. They would start with a small payment when the work began, with an equal sum the following month, another two months later, and yet another five months after that. Thereafter, the payments were tied to the completion of phases of the work. (For a typical contract, see Catalog #13) Problems arose when there were cost overruns or the client simply lacked the funds to pay in full. This was the case, for example at St. Peter's Church. It is difficult to sort out the accounts, because they are part of those of Christ Church, and are entangled with work done there. Still, it is clear that when St. Peter's was finished, the congregation had not raised enough money to pay the entire amount expended. It is not certain that Smith ever was paid in full for construction of the building, but it is clear that he installed a chancel rail and pulpit in 1764, for which he still was billing in 1768. At the College of Philadelphia, he completed a dormitory by early 1762, but was not paid in full until 1764 (Catalog #16). When he built the Provost's House for the same institution in 1774,

he often received only partial payment, for example, £40 when he had billed for £250.

Because no Robert Smith payrolls have been found, it is impossible to judge just how substantial they were and what demands they made on his resources. It also means that the names of only a few of his workmen are known. At Princeton, New Jersey, there were four working at the farm of Esther Burr, the widowed mother of the future vice-president of the United States. Peter Arthur, Thomas Paterson, Albertus Sacklear, and John Biddale [sic], probably were from Philadelphia, because, except possibly for Paterson, theirs were not local names. James Clow, who evidently boarded with the Smiths when he first arrived in America, molded the elaborate plasterwork at the Samuel Powel House. Carpenter John O'Neal lived at the Second Street compound. The identities of two of Smith's apprentices, in addition to his son John, are known. His nephew by marriage, Robert Jones (1758-1802), must have been one. In 1773 and again in 1776, Jones collected payments from Samuel Powel on Smith's behalf, in one instance describing him as "my Uncle" and in the other as "my Master."[76] Another apprentice was John Keen (1747-1832), who served as vice-president of the Carpenters' Company in 1801.[77]

Joseph Rhoads, another member of the Carpenters' Company, also may have worked for Smith, or had other financial dealings with him. In 1787, his widow, Ann, wrote a pathetic letter to Benjamin Franklin, begging his assistance in collecting money due her husband's account. John Smith, she claimed had refused to pay her "one cent;" without receiving the money, she feared that she would be turned out of doors.[78] Others who worked with Smith were, probably happily for them, paid directly rather than by him. At the Franklin House, carpenter Robert Allison received his pay from Samuel Rhoads, whom Franklin had left in charge of disbursements for construction costs.[79] Sometimes, Smith must have retained sub-contractors. When he worked for John Lawrence in 1767, he forwarded a nine-shilling bill from William Warner to the client "for Boering the Collumns of the frontispiece to the front Door" (Catalog #32).

Smith's personal estate, valued at £520.19.9, was inventoried by Joseph Rakestraw and the cabinet maker, Thomas Affleck, who also were named guardians of the minor children, Henry (c. 1762-1780) and James

(c. 1763-before 1804).[80] In addition to household goods, the inventory listed numerous items related to Smith's profession. The most important were "Sundrey Carpenter Tools," valued at £11.0.0, and "Sundrey Books of Architecture and Drawing Instrumts," valued at £23.16.6. Other items included blocks and ropes, glass, paint, and lumber, some in the "Yeard by the house," and some in the "Shop yeard including the Lumber in Shop."

Almost two-and-a half years after Smith's death, the judges of the Orphans' Court sat on 17 June 1780 to partition his real estate.[81] This had been evaluated for distribution by a large committee under the direction of Sheriff James Claypoole. One member was Smith's old collaborator at the Franklin House, Robert Allison. The property was divided into six equal shares, with a portion going to Esther Smith and the remainder to the surviving children: John, James, Henry, Mary (1752-1834) and her husband William Holton[82], and Hester (1753-1783) and her husband William Williams. Esther also retained her one-third dower right and life estate in all the properties.

The properties were those in Moyamensing and Passyunk, and in the city at Second and Cedar and on Spruce Street. In addition, there was a lot on Second Street near Christian Street, bounded by land of the Swedes Church. John Smith received the three-story house at the corner of Second and Cedar, subject to Esther Smith's life estate. He also was granted one of the two-story kitchens, with the other going to James. Another part of his share was Lot 20 on the Spruce Street property, while Hester and William Williams obtained Lots 26 and 27. These three lots were not among the Smith properties offered at sheriff's sale in 1790, so it is probable that the carpenter-builder brothers-in-law had built houses and sold them. Henry's portion included the rental house on Fourth Street north of Spruce. But Henry was lost at sea, and the family petitioned, in June 1782, to have him declared legally dead and his share apportioned among the other heirs.[83] It is not clear who then received the rental property, but it was among the items offered at sheriff's sale in 1790.

The tale of Smith's eldest son John, named for his paternal grandfather, is an unhappy one. He appears to have inherited his father's poor business sense, but not his talent. Born about 1751, he attended the Academy from 1760 to 1765.[84] He may not have been a

good student. His letters exhibit worse grammar and a far less sure grasp of spelling than those of his Scottish-educated father. Undoubtedly after leaving school he apprenticed with his father, with whom he worked on the Provost's House in 1774 (Catalog #51). Three years later, he assisted his father with the construction of chevaux-de-frise at Billingsport, taking over the project after Robert Smith's death (Catalog #53). He continued to serve the patriot cause as a superintendent of carpenters erecting cannon platforms from September through November 1778.[85]

The same year, John Smith took up his duties as administrator of his father's estate, and was elected to membership in the Carpenters' Company, signing the articles in 1779. He later was elected Senior Warden, but was unable to serve by 1784, having "removed into Chester County."[86] Perhaps because of the economic chaos and inflation brought about by the war, he never was able to put his father's estate on a firm financial footing, or, indeed, become successful in his own right. He evidently managed to develop one of the Spruce Street lots he had inherited, but by the late 1780s, after the move to Chester County, he was clearly in difficulties. One reason for his move may have been that, a few months after his father's death, on 12 April 1777, he had married Ann Kerlin, whose family owned property in Chester County.[87] The move was not a success. In 1786 and 1787 he tried to collect money from Benjamin Franklin, claiming it was still owed for Robert Smith's work on the Franklin House. He was being sued for £130, and his property had been seized by the Chester County sheriff. Franklin refused to pay, setting forth in a long letter his reasons for believing his accounts with Robert Smith settled.[88]

John Smith was back in Philadelphia by 1794, working as assistant master carpenter for the President's House on Market Street. His brother-in-law, William Williams, probably had designed the building and was the master carpenter. When Williams died in October, Smith and Robert Allison jointly assumed the role of master carpenter. This probably was John Smith's most important work. In 1795, he had twenty-three men working on the circular stairs, and, on completion of the project, Governor Mifflin referred to him as the "architect." The house, completed in 1797, had been intended as an official residence for the President of the United States, but John

Adams refused to live in it. The College of Philadelphia, soon to become the University of Pennsylvania, then purchased it in anticipation of a move from its cramped quarters at Fourth and Arch Streets. From having supervised its construction, John Smith descended to the position of caretaker, a post in which he served from 1797 to 1801.[89] In a pathetic letter, Smith requested an unspecified payment for acting as caretaker from 15 July 1800 to 11 April 1801.

As the weather permitted I oppened the windows to air the house & shut them when the Occasion required. I had to get the snow frequently carried out that drifted in & to have some of the floors where the storm drove the rain in wip'd up & frequently to mend the fence about the portico & repair the blinds of the ground story which it was out of my power to keep the boys from damaging & doing a great deal of Mischief to the building for which service I hope you will consider me.[90]

Things only got worse. In January 1804, he threw himself on the mercy of the Carpenters' Company.

Gentlemen

Throo the dulness of the times and the scarcity of Circulating Cash &c—I have had no buizeness this three Months past that I have earn'd a farthing by. I have sustain'd several badd debts—likewise Money owing to Me which canott immediately Collectt—I likewise have been at a Considerable expense by My Wife haveing two spells of sickness within this Six Months past—therefore from the Above mention'd circumstances I am nessiated to aply to You for a loan of One hundred Dollars to answer some Imediate demands upon me for which I can give You good security—I expect I shall not want it long as I am dealing with a Gentleman for the sale of some property belonging to Me sittuated in Prince town New Jersey which I expect will be settele'd shortly—Your Complyance with the above request will be Greatfully Acknowled'd—

By Your friend &c
John Smith

N.. Joseph Morris & W^m. Powell purchac'd @ Vendue some of my furniture sett up for sale by ye Sheriff I belive to ye amount of 38 Doll^s Which I look upon Myselfe to be debttor to the Hall in that sum—which I should wish to secure with the Above mention'd Sum if thought proper—

J^o Smith[91]

The Princeton property to which he referred had been purchased by his father in 1757 (Catalog #9).[92] Robert Smith must have retained his copy of the deed, for it was listed in his estate accounts, "a Lot at Prince Town Colledge," although he had sold the land to the

College of New Jersey in 1765. On August 12th, John Smith and his wife, Ann, sold this lot to Josias Ferguson. It was a transaction that would lead to considerable legal embroilment, only settled by arbitration after John Smith's death.

In the meantime, the Carpenters' Company seems to have been supporting the Smiths. On 7 and 21 March 1804, John Smith received a total of $24.00 for "Archatect Books, "undoubtedly the books inherited from his father and now in the company's library. Between 9 May 1804 and 23 January 1805, the company's minutes report a steady drumbeat of payments to Smith for "relief." On 2 February 1805, James Crawford received $12.00 "for a walnut Coffin for our Late Member." Subsequently, William Linnard was paid $4.33 for muslin for a winding sheet.

John and Ann Smith may have traveled to Princeton to sell the lot he claimed he owned there, or Ferguson came to Philadelphia to complete the transaction. In any event, Smith must have loaned Ferguson a book. On 20 February 1805, the Carpenters' Company appointed George Summers as a "Committee to go to Prinstown for the widow Smith and Get the Book they Lent to Mr Furgason and Get such information about the Lot hee Can." Summers reported on the 27th that he had gone and "sene Mr Ferguson and Got the Book that was Lent to him by John Smith and he says he has got a Deed for the Lot." Whether the last "he" in the sentence refers to Summers or Ferguson is not clear. Summers received $15.20 "for expences going to prince town and Including three dollars was Gave to Mrs Smith to pruve the [word missing]."

It was son-in-law William Williams, rather than John, who inherited Robert Smith's mantle as architect-builder. Too little is known about Williams, although he appears to have been one of Philadelphia's most important builder-architects in the waning years of the eighteenth century. He spent some time abroad, returning to Philadelphia in 1772, after receiving architectural training in London. He then advertised that he proposed

carrying on the business of HOUSE CARPENTRY in the most useful and ornamental manner, as is now executed in the city of London and most parts of England . . . in a new, bold, light and elegant taste, which has been lately introduced by the great architect of the Adelphia Buildings [Robert Adam] . . . [93]

Williams died suddenly in 1794, possibly from yellow fever. Letters of administration and associated estate papers attest to his thriving business interests, comfortable furnishings, and completion of a "New House in South Second Street below Ceder [sic] Streets."[94] This was one of the properties he and his first wife Hester had received in the partition of Robert Smith's estate. His drawings, along with his father-in-law's, were exhibited posthumously at the 1795 exhibition arranged by the Columbianum or American Academy of Painting, Sculpture, and Architecture, &c.

Despite the fact that he did not establish an architectural dynasty, Robert Smith left a deep imprint on his adopted city. Because he was versatile, capable of designing a number of different building types, and of finding solutions to what were then difficult engineering problems, Smith received commissions for important public and institutional buildings. He is therefore represented by far more surviving examples (and far more documentation) than his contemporaries. Thomas Nevell is remembered for a single great house, Mount Pleasant, and Gunning Bedford for another, Port Royal (long since demolished, although some of its interiors are at Winterthur). In contrast, the quality of Smith's work is still evident in several prominent Philadelphia landmarks—the spire of Christ Church, St. Peter's Church, and Carpenters' Hall—as well as significant buildings in other places, such as Nassau Hall at Princeton.

Whether at churches, colleges, or other institutions Smith's knowledge of *au courant* British sources was highly visible and could be admired by potential patrons. But his buildings never attempted to emulate British high style; rather he adapted popular classical, Georgian design principles and design motifs in a manner suitable for America. The symmetry, balance, and axial organization he employed already were accepted principles when he arrived in Philadelphia. But Smith's confidence in his design skills, and his superior understanding of building technology, enabled him to take on large projects. Early in his career, prominent designs for Nassau Hall, when built the largest public building in the colonies, and the soaring spire of Christ Church must have made his reputation. In these, and subsequent works, he employed a vernacular Palladian vocabulary that would have been familiar to his contemporaries. Later, therefore, when he functioned as a designer rather than architect-builder, others were able to execute his designs in a characteristic manner. The scope and quality of his work have led to recognition of Smith as among the handful of great American colonial architects.

1. *Pennsylvania Evening Post*, 11 February 1777.

2. James Mease, *The Picture of Philadelphia, giving an account of its origin, increase and improvements in arts, sciences, manufactures, commerce and revenue,* Philadelphia (1811), 180.

3. In chronological order, these are J. Thomas Scharf and Thompson Westcott, *History of Philadelphia, 1609-1884,* 3 vols., Philadelphia (1884), 1:290; and Joseph Jackson, *Early Philadelphia Architects and Engineers,* Philadelphia (1923), 66-69. More substantial, but still relatively slight, biographical sketches appeared in C. P. Stacey, "Robert Smith," in the *Dictionary of American Biography,* New York (1935); and Carl and Jessica Bridenbaugh, *Rebels and Gentlemen: Philadelphia in the Age of Franklin,* Philadelphia (1942).

4. Charles E. Peterson, "Carpenters' Hall," in *Historic Philadelphia,* ed. by Luther P. Eisenhart, Philadelphia (1953), 96-128; Carl Bridenbaugh, *Peter Harrison,* Chapel Hill (1949).

5. The drawing belongs to the Society for the Propagation of the Gospel in London. It is reproduced in H.M.J. Klein and William Diller, *History of St. James Church,* Lancaster, PA (1944), 26.

6. The marriage was reported as "out of unity" with Friends. See Francis James Dallett, "The Family of Mrs. Robert Smith: A Commentary on the Genealogy of Esther Jones," *The Pennsylvania Genealogical Magazine,* 33:4 (1984), 308-309; Charles E. Peterson, "Carpenters' Hall," 119, n3 and 4.

7. *An Historical Catalogue of The St. Andrew's Society of Philadelphia,* [Philadelphia] (1907), 315. The account is based on Scharf and Westcott.

8. D. Hall Letter Book, No II, American Philosophical Society.

9. This discovery was made in the manuscript at the American Philosophical Society by Willman Spawn, then a conservationist at that institution.

10. Register of the Childrens' Names Baptised in the Church of Dalkeith since Martmas 1712, together with an Account of the Dayes of their Birth and Baptism, bound ms., p. 67, Edinburgh General Record Office.

11. Beatrice B Garvan, "Robert Smith," in *Philadelphia: Three Centuries of American Art,* Philadelphia (1976), 31.

12. David R. Smith, *Robert Smith, 1722-1777: Dalkeith to Philadelphia,* [Dalkeith] (1982), 7-8.

13. Ibid.

14. John Gifford, *William Adam, 1689-1748,* Edinburgh (1989), 179. *Vitruvius Scoticus* is discussed at length in Eileen Harris and Nicholas Savage, *British Architectural Books and Writers, 1556-1785,* Cambridge (1990), 94-104. A reduced-size facsimile, with an introduction and notes by James Simpson was published in Edinburgh in 1980.

15. Terry Friedman, *James Gibbs,* New Haven and London (1984), 262.

16. The Assembly's library still exists, and is held in the State Library in Harrisburg.

17. Southwark is now a part of London, but in the eighteenth century the church was referred to as in the County of Surrey, or in the area called Blackfriars because of a monastery once located there. Much altered in the nineteenth century, the church was destroyed by German bombs in World War II.

18. Beatrice B. Garvan, "St. Peter's Church," in *Philadelphia.* For a brief biography of Horne, see Howard Colvin, *Biographical Dictionary of British Architects,* 3rd ed., New Haven (1995), 516-517.

19. William Maitland, *History and Survey of London,* London (1756), 2: 1298-1300. For a discussion of this work, see Harris and Savage, *British Architectural Books,* 188-189.

20. Maitland, *London*, 2:1301.

21. John Summerson, *Georgian London*, revised ed., New York (1970), 120.

22. Charles E. Peterson, *Philadelphia Carpentry According to Palladio*, Philadelphia (1990), 21-30. This small edition, of fifty copies, is an offprint, correcting some errors in the placement of illustrations, of a chapter in Mario di Valmarana, ed., *Building by the Book-3*, Charlottesville, Virginia (1990). The standard work is Helen Park, *A List of Architectural Books Available in America before the Revolution*, Los Angeles (1973). Also useful is Janice G. Schimmelman, *Architectural Treatises and Building Handbooks Available in American Libraries and Bookstores through 1800*, Worcester, MA (1986) and Roger W. Moss, Jr., *Master Builders*, Ann Arbor (1972).

23. Steeples on the Second Presbyterian Church, St. Michael's Church, and the State House all failed and had to be taken down.

24. The book undoubtedly was available in Philadelphia. David Hall advertised Price's "Carpentry" in the *Pennsylvania Gazette* for 7 March 1748/49, as well as in later issues. Another possible place Smith may have seen the book was in the library of Samuel Hazard, with whom Smith was associated at the Second Presbyterian Church and Nassau Hall. Hazard ordered a copy of the second edition (1735) from a London bookseller on 3 May 1751. See Samuel Hazard Letter Book, Gen. Mss. [bound], Manuscripts Division, Dept. of Rare Books and Special Collections, Princeton University Library. This seems late for the Second Presbyterian Church, construction of which was well advanced by this time. But it might have been in time to affect the design of the roof. David T. Yeomans first discussed the raised tie beam trusses at St. Peter's Philadelphia, and Christ Church, Shrewsbury, in "A Preliminary Study of 'English' Roofs in Colonial America," *APT Bulletin*, 13, 4 (1981): 9-18. He subsequently pointed out the similarity of the truss illustrated as Plate K in Francis Price's book to one illustrated in the price book published by the Carpenters' Company of the City and County of Philadelphia in "British and American Roofing Solutions to a Roofing Problem," *Journal of the Society of Architectural Historians*, 50 (September 1991):266-272 and *The Trussed Roof: its history and development*. Aldershot, England and Brookfield, VT (1992). Joseph W. Hammond extended the study of raised tie beam trusses to other Smith churches, and presented his findings in a paper, entitled "Timber Framing Engineering of Robert Smith: Leading Builder/Architect of Colonial America," presented at Robert Smith's Birthday, Philadelphia, 14 January 1995 and annual APT/DVC symposium on Historic Timber Framing, Philadelphia, 2 March 1996.

25. The rule book, originally entitled *Articles of the Carpenters Company of Philadelphia and their Rules for Measuring and Valuing House-Carpenters Work*, Philadelphia (1786) has been reprinted as Charles E. Peterson, FAIA, ed., *The Rules of Work of the Carpenters' Company of the City and County of Philadelphia, 1786*, Princeton (1971) [hereafter CCCCP Rule Book]. It may be clear evidence of Price's influence that the description of this truss on page 5 refers to hammer beams.

26. But by 1795, when William Colladay rebuilt Zion to the same dimensions, there was more confidence in the iron-strapped raised tie beam truss, which he employed.

27. See David Gebhard, "Drawings and Intent in American Architecture," in *200 Years of American Architectural Drawing*, New York (1977), 28-30; James F. O'Gorman, "The Philadelphia Architectural Drawing in Its Historical Context: An Overview," in *Drawing toward Building*, Philadelphia (1986), 2-4; William S. Rasmussen, "Idea, Tool, Evidence," in *The Making of Virginia Architecture*, Richmond (1992), 133-144.

28. Gebhard, p. 30, is mistaken in saying that site plans and perspectives did not exist.

29. The Loxley plan is reproduced in Roger W. Moss, "The Origins of the Carpenters' Company of Philadelphia," in *Building Early America*, ed. by Charles E. Peterson, Radnor, PA (1976), 44. The Cliveden perspective appears in James F. O'Gorman, *The Perspective of Anglo-American Architecture*, Philadelphia (1995), 12; and *Drawing Toward Building*, 2.

30. John Penn to Thomas Penn, 7 July 1753, Penn Papers, private corr., 4:117, Historical Society of Pennsylvania [hereafter HSP].

31. Martin P. Snyder, *City of Independence*, New York (1975), 80-82.

32. Thomas Nevell, Day Book, 1762-1782, Wetherill Papers, Division of Special Collections, Van Pelt Library, University of Pennsylvania; Hannah B. Roach, "Thomas Nevell (1721-1797) Carpenter, Educator, Patriot," *Journal of the Society of Architectural Historians*, 24 (1965): 153-64.

33. See entry for John King in Sandra Tatman and Roger W. Moss, *Biographical Dictionary of Philadelphia Architects*, Philadelphia (1985), 646-647. At the time of his death, King owned "3 books of architecture."

34. *Pennsylvania Gazette*, 26 September 1771.

35. Hazard Letter Book

36. Garvan, "Robert Smith," 32, is mistaken in thinking that the caricatures reproduced in John Frederick Lewis, *The History of an Old Philadelphia Land Title*, Philadelphia (1934), are by Robert Smith, the architect-builder. For one thing, the signature is not his. For another the three men depicted as middle aged—William Rawle (1759-1836), Moses Levy (1756-1826), and William Lewis (1745-1819)—were not Smith's contemporaries, but of a later generation, who would not have reached middle age until after Robert Smith's death.

37. O'Gorman, *The Perspective of Anglo-American Architecture*, 3.

38. Quoted in Frank Jenkins, *Architect and Patron*, London (1961), 128-129.

39. A number of British authors have discussed mensuration. Among them was James Noble. Colvin considers his *The Professional Practice of Architecture and That of Measuring Surveyors and References to Builders, &c &c from the Time of the Celebrated Earl of Burlington*, London (1836), the earliest English book on architectural practice. In addition to mensuration, Noble's book deals with a great variety of miscellany, quoting acts of Parliament, and discussing the cost of chimneys in party walls, the history of architectural style, problems of sewage and water supply, and the cost of wrought and cast iron. More recently, in addition to *Architect and Patron*, cited above, the subject has been discussed in Kaye Barrington, *The Development of the Architectural Profession in Britain*, London (1961); and James Nisbet, *Fair and Reasonable: Building Contracts Since 1550*, London (1993) and *A Proper Price: Quantity Surveying in London, 1650 to 1940*, London (1993).

40. Nisbet, *Fair and Reasonable*, 21 and 32.

41. Noble, *Professional Practice*, 13.

42. Harris and Savage, 118. A second edition appeared in 1718.

43. Ibid., 233-234.

44. These subjects are covered on pages 189-208 in the copy at the American Philosophical Society. An interesting example of an apprenticeship indenture appears on page 279.

45. Logan Papers, 18:100, 16 May 1732, 18:102, 15 July 1732, 18:115, 16 May, 1733, 19:4, 10 May 1735, HSP.

46. Samuel Hazard, ed., *Register of Pennsylvania*, Philadelphia (1828)2:376.

47. Pennsylvania Hospital Archives. Information about the lives and works of the builders and architects cited in this and the following paragraphs can be found in Tatman and Moss, *Biographical Dictionary*. Their dates are: Samuel Rhoads (1711-1784), Joseph Fox (1709-1799), Samuel Powel (1673?-1756), John Nicholas (d. 1756), Benjamin Loxley (1720-1801), Thomas Nevell (1721-1797), Gunning Bedford (1720-1802), John Thornhill (1716-1783), Jacob Knor.

48. John M. Dickey, FAIA, and Sandra Mackenzie Lloyd, "Historic Structures Report: Mount Pleasant," July 1987.

49. Margaret B. Tinkcom, "Cliveden: The Building of a Philadelphia Countryseat, 1763-1767," *Pennsylvania Magazine of History and Biography*, 88, 1 (January 1964): 2-36.

50. Quoted in H. Westbury Preston, *The Worshipful Company of Carpenters*, London (1933), 25-29. Histories of the venerable English association can also be found in B.W.E. Alford and T.C. Barker, *A History of the Carpenters' Company*, London (1969); Ed-

ward B. Jupp, *Historical Account of the Worshipful Company of Carpenters of the City of London*, London (1887); and Jasper Ridley, *A History of the Carpenters' Company*, London (1995).

51. *Charter, By-Laws, Rules and Regulations of the Carpenters' Company of the City and County of Philadelphia*, Philadelphia (1916), 5; Roger W. Moss, "The Origins of the Carpenters' Company of Philadelphia," in *Building Early America*, ed. Charles E. Peterson, Radnor, PA, (1976), 35-53.

52. Warden's Book, 1769-1781, Carpenters' Company Library.

53. CCCCP Rule Book, ix.

54. Ibid., 7.

55. Robert Smith, 20 August 1770, quoted in CCCCP Rule Book, xvi.

56. For a list of similar publications, see Louise Hall, "Artificer to Architect in America," unpublished Ph.D. dissertation, Radcliffe College, 1954.

57. Philadelphia County Deed Book I-4:146, 3 February 1768, Philadelphia City Archives [hereafter PCA].

58. Rhoads oversaw the work of thirteen carpenters in construction of Charles Norris's mansion. His drawing for a 'Venetian Window for a Stair Case' is reproduced in Jeffrey A. Cohen, "Early American Architectural Drawings and Philadelphia, 1730-1860," in *Drawing Toward Building*, 35.

59. Allison was elected to the Carpenters' Company in 1773. He was active in reinforcing the river defenses at Fort Island. After the war he assisted with repairs at the State House, and along with Joseph Rakestraw provided plans for a large brick structure (measuring 45' by 60') for Washington College at Chestertown, Maryland. Tatman and Moss, *Biographical Dictionary*, 9. See also M.P. White, Jr., "An Account of the First College Edifice of Washington College, 1783-1827," M.A. Thesis, University of Delaware, 1966.

60. Summerson, *Georgian London*, 71.

61. John F. Hageman, *History of Princeton and its Institutions*, 2 vols., Philadelphia (1879), 2:87.

62. There are deeds for only one of the Princeton properties. The other is known only by references to it as an adjoinder to an adjacent property.

63. Samuel Rhoads to Robert Smith, 10 March 1761, Deed Book I-8:523, Recorder of Deeds, PCA.

64. 1767 Tax, Southwark, 157; 1769 Tax, Southwark, 150, PCA.

65. Estate of Robert Smith, Orphans' Court Book 11:81, 18 February 1779, PCA.

66. See Catalog #16.

67. The term "kitchen" had a somewhat different meaning in eighteenth-century Philadelphia. It referred to a small building toward the back of the lot, which might contain cooking space and pantries on the first floor, with two or three rooms on the second. Eventually, a house could be built at the front of the lot, connected to the kitchen by a "piazza" or link, which generally contained the main staircase.

68. Robert Smith to John O'Neal, 1 March 1772, Deed Book D-17: 437, Recorder of Deeds, PCA.

69. Robert Smith to Thomas Lake, 1 May 1772, Deed Book D-68:429, 1 January 1773, Deed Book EF-28:100, Ibid.

70. Estate of Robert Smith. A summary of Smith's holdings at that date is attached to his estate papers.

71. *Pennsylvania Gazette*, 22 June 1774.

72. *Pennsylvania Evening Post*, 13 February 1777.

73. Jacob Hiltzheimer, Diary, 12 February 1777, microfilm at the American Philosophical Society.

74. *Federal Gazette and Philadelphia Daily Advertiser*, 2 April 1790.

75. *Pennsylvania Gazette*, 23 April 1777; Estate of Robert Smith, Orphans' Court Records, PCA.

76. Francis James Dallett, "The Family of Mrs. Robert Smith: A Commentary on the Genealogy of Esther Jones," *Pennsylvania Genealogical Magazine*, 33, 4 (1984): 317 and 323, n86 and n87; 16 November and 15 December 1773, Samuel Powel III, Receipt Book, 8 March 1773-29-December 1774, Library Company of Philadelphia (on deposit at HSP).

77. Gregory B. Keen, "The Descendants of Joran Kyn, the Founder of Upland," *Pennsylvania Magazine of History and Biography*, 4 (1880), 349-350.

78. Rhoads to Franklin 15 December 1786, Franklin Papers, 34:10, American Philosophical Society. For a biography of Joseph Rhoads, see Tatman and Moss, *Biographical Dictionary*, 656.

79. Rhoads kept these accounts in the Franklin Receipt Book, 1764-1766, Historical Society of Pennsylvania.

80. Register of Wills, 1777, 52 and Notice of Settlement, Orphans' Court Records, 11:79, 25 July 1777, PCA; *Pennsylvania Gazette*, 9 April 1777. Thomas Affleck (1740-1795) Smith's fellow Scot and member of the St. Andrew's Society, was a Quaker, whose pacifist stance resulted in his designation as a "dangerous person" by the Supreme Executive Council in August 1777. It is doubtful that he was of much use to the Smith boys, for he was among a group of prominent Quakers exiled to Virginia during the war. Joseph Rakestraw was a master builder, active in Carpenters' Company business, assuming the presidency of the company in 1779. He may have previously served with Smith on the Price Committee, and had worked with him on several projects. Biographical information is based on Garvan, "Thomas Affleck" in *Three Centuries of American Art*, 98-99 and "Joseph Rakestraw" in Tatman and Moss, *Biographical Dictionary*, 641-642.

81. Orphans' Court 11:219-227.

82. Mary Smith Holton, subsequently left a widow with several children, of whom two survived to maturity, was married a second time to Solomon Marache. Genealogical information is drawn from Dallett, "The Family of Mrs. Robert Smith," and correspondence with Jane Adams Clarke, Jo Eslinger, and Wanda S. Gunning.

83. Orphans' Court 11:420-422, 7 June 1782.

84. College Tuition Book, 1758-1769, MS 1559, University of Pennsylvania Archives.

85. Tatman and Moss, *Biographical Dictionary*, 739.

86. Minutes of the Carpenters' Company of the City and County of Philadelphia, 18 January 1779, 12 April 1784.

87. Transcript of Records, St. Michael and Zion Church, Historical Society of Pennsylvania, Ph 24:6.

88. Smith to Franklin 20 March 1786, 34:43; 24 August 1787, 35:111; Franklin to Smith, 31 August 1787, 45:211, Franklin Papers, American Philosophical Society.

89. Dennis C. Kurjack, "Who Designed the President's House," *Journal of the Society of Architectural Historians*, 12, 2 (May 1953): 27-28. See also Dennis C. Kurjack, "The 'President's House' in Philadelphia, *Pennsylvania History* 20 (October 1953): 380-394. In 1800, Benjamin Henry Latrobe wrote a report on the difficulties of adapting the house for use by the college, which can be found in University Papers, Vol. 13, University of Pennsylvania Archives. The ill-starred building was demolished in 1829, to make way for the new medical school designed by William Strickland.

90. Smith to the "honorable board of the trusties," University Papers, 4, 1800-1801, item 38, University of Pennsylvania Archives.

91. Smith to "The Gentlemen of the Sitting Committee of the Carpenters Hall Philadelphia," 8 January 1804, Minutes, CCCCP.

92. For documentation of the Princeton transactions, see Catalog #9.

93. *Pennsylvania Packet*, 4 January 1773. On Williams see, Roger W. Moss, *The American Country House* (1990), 84-85.

94. Estate of William Williams, Register of Wills, #227, 1794, PCA.

CATALOG OF THE WORKS OF ROBERT SMITH

Editorial Note

THIS CATALOG is arranged in chronological order, determined by the starting date of each project. Entries are numbered sequentially; for buildings that have been or are now attributed to Smith, the number is followed by the letter "A." Bibliographies for each entry follow the text. Primary sources are listed as "documentation," secondary sources as "references." In the latter, special forms of reference, such as speeches or Historic American Buildings Survey drawings, are separated from published works. The following abbreviations are used for frequently cited sources:

Faris   Faris, John T[homson]. *Old Churches in and About Philadelphia*. Philadelphia (1926).

HABS   Historic American Buildings survey.

HP   *Historic Philadelphia*. Edited by Luther P. Eisenhart. Philadelphia (1953). Issued as *Transactions of the American Philosophical Society*, 43, 1.

HSP   Historical Society of Pennsylvania.

PMHB   *Pennsylvania Magazine of History and Biography*.

S&W   Scharf, J. Thomas and Thompson Westcott. *History of Philadelphia*. Philadelphia (1884).

Tatman and Moss   Tatman, Sandra and Roger W. Moss, Jr., *Biographical Dictionary of Philadelphia Architects*. Boston (1985).

Watson (1830)   Watson, John Fanning. *Annals of Philadelphia*. Philadelphia (1830).

Watson (Hazard)   *Annals of Philadelphia*. Ed. and rev. by Wallis P. Hazard. Philadelphia (1879-80). Editions of 1870 and 1927 are also cited.

The names of the following carpenter-builders and other artisans appear in catalog entries. Rather than interpolating their dates in each instance, they are, where known, given below. Members of the Carpenters' Company of the City and County of Philadelphia are marked by an asterisk. Biographical information can be found in Tatman and Moss.

Robert Allison* (fl. 1770-1790)
Gunning Bedford* (1720-1802)
Abraham Carlile* (1730-1778)
William Colladay* (1738-1823)
Hercules Courtenay (1736-?)
Joseph Fox* (1709-1799)
Jacob Graeff (fl. 1760s)
John Harrison, Jr.* (d. 1801)
John Harrison, Sr.* (d. 1760
Robert Jones (1758-1802)
John Kean* (1747-1832)
Jacob Knor (fl. 1760s)
Benjamin Loxley* (1720-1801)
Matthew M'Glathery* (d. 1800)
Thomas Nevell* (1721-1797)
John Palmer (fl. 1750s-1760s)
Joseph Rakestraw* (c. 1735-1794)
Joseph Rhoads* (fl. 1760s-d. 1784)
Samuel Rhoads* (1711-1784)
John Smith* (c. 1750-1805)
John Thornhill* (1716-1783)
William Williams* (1749?-1794)
Edmund Woolley* (c.1695-1771)
James Worrell* (c. 1731-1797)

1

Alterations and Construction at Bush Hill

Part of Springettsbury Manor, in the vicinity of 12th to 19th
Streets, north of Vine Street, Philadelphia
1749, demolished

By the beginning of the nineteenth century,
Robert Smith's first documented American project had sheltered a Pennsylvania governor, a Vice
President of the United States, victims of the 1793
yellow fever epidemic, and patrons of a popular tavern—in a house on property once part of William
Penn's Springettsbury Manor.

This land had been granted to Andrew Hamilton
(1676-1741), a lawyer and high-ranking government
official, in 1726 and 1729. Hamilton received the
patent in January 1734 and possibly began construction of a house sometime before his death in 1741.
The standard Philadelphia histories uniformly repeat
the supposition "that the Bush Hill house was erected about 1740" (Westcott, 417; Watson, 493; S&W,
2:872), but there are no assurances that the house had
been finished, or, indeed, even begun.

James Hamilton (1710-1783) completed his father's
term as prothonotary of the Court of Common Pleas.
He inherited, in addition to other property, the parcel acquired from the Penns. He shared ownership of
some real estate with his brother, and also individu-
ally owned city lots on Chestnut Street, where he
resided. No doubt the brothers made improvements
to their various buildings. Although Hamilton's cash
book often includes the name of the project for which
payment is due, he just as often records only the recipient's name and amount. Consequently, it is
difficult to definitively allocate many of the expenditures listed in his books.

Hamilton's accounts do, however, document aspects of the construction at Bush Hill. Considerable
building activity occurred between 1742 and 1745,
when Hamilton left for England and halted work on
this project. He was appointed Deputy Governor of
Pennsylvania in 1747, and returned in late 1748, beginning his official duties on St. Andrew's Day, November 30th (*Historical Catalogue*, 196). Shortly
thereafter, Hamilton paid Robert Smith, described in

the cash books as "my Carpenter," £50 for work on
his property, possibly at Bush Hill.

In July 1749, Hamilton wrote of his intent to "alter my house at Bush Hill" and reside there (Letter
Book, 3 July 1749). Already he had determined to employ an Italian stucco worker, presumably to work on
new rooms because he intended to raise the house a
story (Richard Hockley to Thomas Penn, 30 April
1749). The house was expected to be very handsome
"when compleated agreable to yᵉ design" (Hockley to
Penn, 4 August 1749). This suggests that Hockley had
seen drawings, and it is tempting to think that Robert
Smith had made them. Clearly Smith was a key figure
in the transformation of Hamilton's country house;
he was paid £680 for his work and materials between
January 1749 and July 1751.[1] The sums were significant and exceeded those paid to any other craftsman employed during the period.

In addition to possibly providing a design, Smith
was probably responsible for the framing and interi-
or carpentry. In September 1749, he was paid £10
"for raising the house." In October 1749, Hamilton
was planning a greenhouse and gratefully accepted
Thomas Penn's offer to supply some trees for it. The
gift also included a "younge fawn" (Hockley to Penn,
25 October 1749 and 15 February 1749/50).

Engravings published in the *Universal Magazine* in
May 1787 and *The New-York Magazine* for February
1793 show a rather elaborate complex of buildings adjoining a large, three-story house with hip roof, nearly square in plan. Ornament included a pedimented
entry, belt courses, and decorative window treatment.
The house is an interpretation of a modest English
country house design. Adjacent to it probably was a
kitchen garden, surrounded by a board fence, within
which was a rather utilitarian outbuilding, possibly a
kitchen. Beyond this was what appears to have been
an orangerie, probably the "greenhouse" built when
the house was enlarged; there also was a "fish house"
on the Schuylkill (*New York Magazine*).

Hamilton's estate was both a family seat and noteworthy setting for his extensive collection of paint-

---

1. While many entries in Hamilton's Cash Book identify the
Bush Hill project by name ("work on Bush Hill") and describe the
task ("hauling") and materials ("Nails, Brads, plank, Scant[lin]g")
for which he is paying, it is impossible to categorically state that
all payments made to Smith during the period 1749-1751 were for
work on Bush Hill.

This view of Bush Hill appeared in *The New York Magazine* for February 1793. After the alterations were complete, Richard Hockley described it to Thomas Penn as a "double house." So, in addition to raising the building a story, the work may have enlarged a house one-room deep to the two-room deep structure illustrated. Library Company of Philadelphia.

ings and statuary. Outings to Bush Hill were a popular diversion for young Philadelphians, as well as for visitors from further afield. While in residence at Bush Hill, Hamilton not only was busy with public affairs, but also with "entertaining Strangers of which there is a great number at present from all parts and what they call here People of Fashion" (Hockley to Penn, 10 October 1751). New Englander Ezra Stiles (1727-1795), a noted preacher and future president of Yale University, visited Governor Hamilton's country seat in September 1754 and recorded his impressions: "Took a walk in his very elegant garden, in which are

7 statues in fine Italian marble curiously wrot [sic]; invited into his house; viewed the very splendid & grand apartments magnificently decorated & adorned with curious paintings, hangings & statuary & marble tablets, etc." (Stiles, 30 September 1754).

It was to this commodious dwelling that John and Abigail Adams came in Autumn 1790, when, along with the rest of the federal government, they moved to Philadelphia. Mrs. Adams wrote of the beauty of the place in several letters to friends and family. While the building and some marble statues survived the Revolutionary War, "the British troops rob'd

[the] place of its principal glory by cutting down all the Trees in front of the House . . . leaving it wholly Naked," (To Mrs. Smith, 21 November 1790, *Letters* [1848], 348) but "the work within is superior . . ." (To Mrs. Smith, 9 January 1791, *Letters* [1947], 67), and, despite difficulties with the roads in getting to and from the city, Mrs. Adams was generally approving in her remarks.

Her assessment was echoed in a description of Bush Hill published in *The New-York Magazine* for February 1793. The writer touted its "high and beautiful situation . . . not exceeded by any seat in the vicinity of Philadelphia," but lamented that the "once elegant Villa [had] not yet recovered from the state of almost total demolition, which it suffered from the hands of a furious and inveterate enemy." Despite the estate's loss of grandeur, it remained an important icon in the city's collective memory.

During the disastrous summer of 1793, when a yellow fever epidemic swept through Philadelphia, city officials sought properties in the nearby countryside as places of refuge and treatment for those afflicted with the disease. Bush Hill had been vacant since 1791 and its owner, William Hamilton, who was James Hamilton's nephew and heir, was in Europe. His agents leased the house to the city for use as a hospital. Bush Hill, once the site of a sumptuous party given by Governor James Hamilton in 1752 to honor the king's birthday, now sheltered those too ill to care for themselves and deemed a threat to their fellow citizens.

Forty years earlier, work on such a project as Bush Hill, for a prominent individual like Hamilton, had helped launch Robert Smith as a Philadelphia carpenter/architect. While working on Bush Hill, Smith was approached by members of the building committee for the Second Presbyterian Church (Catalog #2) and, when he undertook that project, began an association with "New Light" Presbyterians that would profoundly affect his career.

DOCUMENTATION:

"Account of Bush Hill, the Seat of William Hamilton, Esq., near Philadelphia." *The New York Magazine* (4 February 1793); *Letters of Mrs. Adams, The Wife of John Adams.* 4th ed. Boston (1848); Mitchell, Stewart, ed. *New Letters of Abigail Adams, 1788-1801.* Boston (1947). James Hamilton Papers. Cash Book 1739-1757, Letter Book 1749-1783, Daybook

1759-1783. Collection #1446; HSP. Christopher Marshall Papers. Diaries and Notes 1774-93. Collection #395. Richard Hockley to Thomas Penn. Penn Papers, Official Corr., 4:185-187, 201-203, 215-217, 241, 5:183; Stiles, Ezra. Notebook of Itineraries. Ezra Stiles Papers. Miscellaneous Papers. Beinecke Rare Book and Manuscript Library, Yale University (microfilm at American Philosophical Society).

REFERENCES:

An Historical Catalogue of the St. Andrew's Society of Philadelphia, with Biographical Sketches of Deceased Members, 1747-1907. Philadelphia (1907); S&W; Watson (1879); Westcott (1877).

2

Carpenter/Builder for Second Presbyterian Church

Northwest corner of Third and Arch Streets, Philadelphia 1749/50, alterations 1809, demolished

ROBERT SMITH was recently arrived in Philadelphia and at work on Governor James Hamilton's Bush Hill estate (Catalog #1) when he was approached by the managers of the building committee for a new Presbyterian Church. Smith and Gunning Bedford (1720-1802) were asked "to undertake the Carpenters Work of the said House" to be built on a recently purchased lot at the corner of Third and Arch Streets (Minutes of the Congregation, 19 February 1749[/50]). Although the trustees used an Old Style date, correspondence recorded in the letter book of Samuel Hazard, a trustee of the church, shows that the date actually was 1750 New Style.

Clearly, Smith was recognized as an accomplished craftsman when he settled in the city or he would not have received commissions from prominent, well-connected, knowledgeable individuals; because of his skill, he became part of a network with access to coveted projects. The mason hired by the building committee as bricklayer for the proposed church was John Palmer, with whom Smith was working at Bush Hill and would soon work at Christ Church; other names listed in the minutes dominated the city's building trades. Associations with Philadelphia's finest craftsmen, formed within the first years of Smith's arrival, lasted throughout his career.

The Great Awakening of the 1740s provided the impetus for building a second Presbyterian church in Philadelphia. The evangelical preaching of George Whitefield attracted a substantial following. When he was denied access to local churches, his adherents undertook construction of a large meeting place. This "New Building" on Fourth Street, completed in 1742/3, was destined to become the College of Philadelphia, when altered by Robert Smith in 1755 (See Catalog #11), but it began life as a planned community center with rooms for educating children and space for accommodating crowds. Eventually, although the free school held classes as required by a deed restriction, and Whitefield did preach in the unfinished hall, the building was completed for use as a meeting house by the followers of the Reverend Gilbert Tennent (1703-1764), who had recently separated themselves from the First Presbyterian Church.

In 1747, creditors of the "New Building" decided to sell it, and petitioned the Assembly for permission to do so. Benjamin Franklin thought the "New Building" would provide a suitable site for an academy; but what was a perfect solution for advocates of Franklin's proposal put Tennent and his followers out on the street. Tennent was given liberty to preach elsewhere, but that was only temporarily acceptable, and the group committed themselves to purchasing a lot, building a church, and establishing a burial ground. They moved quickly, and the corner stone was laid on 17 May 1750 (Mackie, 221). The building was under roof that year, and gold letters were mounted in the pediment, forming the inscription, "Templum Presbyterianum, annuente numine, erectum. Anno Dom. MDCCL" (Kalm 1:22-23). The congregation attended the first worship service in the church in June 1752.

Although the building went up swiftly, financing, as was not uncommon, proved difficult. Generally, a building project was funded by subscriptions, or, possibly, a lottery. In the customary way, money also was raised by "letting" pews, the principal source of funding not only for paying off the construction debt, but also for day-to-day operations. Early fund-raising went well, with a "great part of our Gentry [hav-

ing] subscribed handsomely." (Samuel Hazard to Nathaniel Hazard, 16 February 1749/50.) An undated subscription list in Tennent's papers at the Presbyterian Historical Society records commitments from many individuals. However, the eight hundred pounds he professed to have in hand when he wrote to a fellow clergyman, Philip Doddridge, in Massachusetts in 1751, was insufficient because

the lands to build on & bury in have cost no less than 1,161 pounds . . . & the House which is 80 × 60 foot will not cost less than 2,000 . . . The State of our case being so necessitous & distressing, I apply'd to Several Gentlemen of other Persuasions both in Town & Country for their charitable assistance & thro divine Goodness gott some considerable help. But there being a great Stagnation in trade here & Several Bigotts of differing partys being very industrious to obstruct the design, there is a moral certainty our Loosing entirely many hundreds of pds promis'd, which is a great discouragement in carying on of the work.

One of those to whom Tennent appealed was Benjamin Franklin, whose name is on Tennent's subscription list for five pounds. Franklin recalled Tennent's solicitation in his autobiography.

. . . the Revd Gilbert Tennent came to me, with a Request that I would assist him in procuring a Subscription for erecting a new Meeting-house. It was to be for the Use of a Congregation he had gathered among the Presbyterians who were originally Disciples of Mr. Whitefield. Unwilling to make myself disagreeable to my fellow Citizens, by too frequently soliciting their Contributions, I absolutely refus'd. He then desir'd I would furnish him with a List of the Names of Persons I knew by Experience to be generous and public-spirited. I thought it would be unbecoming in me, after their kind Compliance with my Solicitations, to mark them out to be worried by other Beggars, and therefore refus'd also to give such a List. He then desir'd I would at least give him my Advice. That I will readily do, said I; and, in the first Place, I advise you to apply to all those whom you know will give something; next to those whom you are uncertain whether they will give any thing or not; and show them the List of those who have given; and lastly, do not neglect those who you are sure will give nothing; for in some of them you may be mistaken. He laugh'd, thank'd me, and said that he would take my Advice. He did so, for he ask'd every body; and he obtain'd a much larger Sum than he expected, with which he erected the capacious and very elegant Meeting-house that stands in Arch Street (Franklin, 166).

Robert Smith has been credited with design of the church and he may have prepared the drawings, but as was generally the case, the trustees and building committee played an important role in devising the plan. On 8 February 1749/50, trustees were named and committee members appointed. They were charged with meeting "together, & consult[ing] about, the General Form, & Plan of the said Presbyterian Church, or Meeting House ... & may also agree, who shall be the Head Workmen to build the Same" (Minutes of the Congregation). Eleven days later, they met again and agreed that

...the New Presbyterian Church aforesaid shall be built in the following Form, that is to say the Front upon Arch Street shall be eighty Feet Long & the Front, or End upon Third Street, shall [be] Sixty Feet long, & shall be placed eight Feet back from the Arch Street, & six Feet back from Third Street, & that the Stone Work for the Foundatn [sic] shall be carried six Inches higher than the Regulation of the pavement at the North East Corner, & from thence levell'd towards Arch Street. That The Elevation of the Brick Work from the Top of the Foundation, to the Eves, shall be about Thirty three, or thirty four Feet: That the South Front shall have two Doors mad[e] Pediment wise, & two arched Windows, equally disposed, between the Doors in the first Story; & four Windows in the Upper Story. That the East Front shall have an Arch'd door in the middle, & one Window on each Side the Door, & the North, or back Front have two Windows in each Story; & the same in the West End of the House. That the Roof of the said House shall be made with strait Rafters not Hipt (Minutes of the Congregation, 19 February 1749[/50]).

That same day, the managers agreed to arrange with Smith and Bedford for the carpenters' work and to employ Palmer "to do the Masons & Bricklayers Work of the House." It is probable that the managers had consulted with the craftsmen about the design, and then memorialized their acceptance of the plan in the minutes. Unfortunately, the written record does not credit anyone with the design, nor are there building accounts documenting who did what. There also is no known image of the church as described in the Minutes of the Congregation, but changes recorded in the minutes sixty years later indicate that the church was built as planned. Although written descriptions suggest a workmanlike building, Gilbert Tennent considered it a "very elegant Meetinghouse" (Tennent to Doddridge).

Some in the congregation may have thought the building too elaborate. Tennent defended its design and decor in his 1751 letter, and in a dedicatory sermon on the first day of worship in June 1752, justifying ornamentation of "Structures of a religious kind." After acknowledging the financial support of the Governor, Chief Justice and other notables, he began to build his case. Buildings in cities, "where there is a greater Resort of Persons of Honour, Distinction, and polite Taste," could be more decorated than those in "obscurer Places." Nevertheless, the deciding factor was the judgement of the trustees to

William L. Breton's 1830 lithograph shows the Second Presbyterian Church as enlarged in 1809. By that time the spire erected in 1762 to the design of Thomas Nevell had already failed and been taken down. Historical Society of Pennsylvania.

whom funds were entrusted "not for Themselves, but the Honour and Worship of the most high God." If every donor felt entitled to an opinion and demanded approval of each ornament "then it wou'd be like weaving Penelope's Web, never finished, for what one wou'd approve, the other wou'd condemn, and demolish!" Delivering his final salvo, Tennent disclosed that most of the grumbling came from "a few of our own Society who have hitherto given little (or nothing) towards this Structure." He went on to declare,

that in my Opinion there is not one Ornament more than is proper in this Structure; the Building is manly and plain, its chief Beauty is the Simplicity of the whole, and the just Proportion of its several Parts, which are enlivened by the exactness of the Workmanship, and a few Ornaments interspersed, which are well devised, well executed, and well placed; without which so large an Edifice, wou'd appear flat, dead, and disagreeable, being destitute of its proper Decency and Dignity" (Tennent, 55-67).

Although the documents are silent about who designed the church, there are a number of features that point to Robert Smith. Its general form, and the dimensions of sixty by eighty feet, are similar to other churches he designed, such as St. Peter's (Catalog #13). The pedimented door surrounds and arched windows of the written description were part of the architectural vocabulary of the day, but practices of the period gave considerable license to the carpenters to fashion the structural elements, moldings, and decorative appointments in forms they generally used, unless otherwise specified in a contract. The oculus in the gable, and urns on the roof also are part of Smith's vocabulary. From what can be judged from the lithograph by William. L. Breton, showing the building after it was altered in 1809, the earlier detailing appears to be Smith's work.

Although the Palladian windows were not described in the trustees' minutes, they undoubtedly were original. Samuel Hazard ordered the window glass from England. It was to be:

... good common glass tho the panes are somewhat larger than the common size that come for sale. You have enclose [sic] a draft which will show the quantity and sizes of the glass for the arches....

Glass for the arch part of 19 windows according to the enclosed de[/sign]
175 panes of 16 by 10 1/2 [inches]
260 do   14 1/4 by 10

225	do	13 by 10 1/2
65	do	14 by 10
20	do	12 by 12
745		(Hazard to William Trotman, 7 January 1750/51)

Because of Robert Smith's introduction of the raised tie beam truss, the written record seems to point to him as designer of the roof "to be made with strait Rafters not Hipt." Other large meeting houses, like St. Michael's Lutheran Church, had gambrel or hip roofs, which made the specification of straight rafters an innovation. Smith may have suggested an arched, clear-span ceiling, which usually relied upon a raised tie beam roof truss, rather than a conventional truss, for support. He is known to have used such a roof system at St. Peter's in 1758 (Catalog #13), and in his later churches as well. He may have used it earlier at the Second Presbyterian Church.

At least two accounts of later alterations hint at an original clear-span ceiling. The church was so popular, that by the time it was finished in 1752, installation of galleries was required to supply all those who wanted seating. (Hazard to Richard Cary, 1 July 1752). In 1753, the committee charged with fixing pew rental fees decided that "a fifth shall be allow'd out of the yearly Rent of any Pew that have two Columns in it & a Sixth of the Rent out of any that [have] one Column" (Minutes of the Congregation, 17 April 1753). The arrangement of the columns was never discussed, but this entry strongly suggests that they only supported the galleries, in which case the building would have had a clear-span ceiling. It could be argued, however, that these columns could have been full height, helping to support the ceiling, as they did, for example, in Christ Church. However, further evidence for a clear-span ceiling comes from a description of alterations in 1809. One change lowered the ceiling "making it partly flat, & somewhat ornamental" (Minutes of the Congregation, 18 March 1809). Unfortunately, the building was demolished in the 1830s, so there is no physical evidence of the original ceiling configuration.

The Second Presbyterian Church was a work in progress. Galleries were not, as noted, installed until 1753; the marble steps did not appear until 1769; and the steeple was not raised until 1761. (Minutes of the Congregation, 8 June 1753, 25 June 1754; Early Notes, 6 December 1768). It is not clear whether the urns ornamenting the roof were original; they were puttied and painted in 1765 (Minutes of the Congregation, 10 September 1765).

It was the steeple that proved most difficult. In 1750, when Thomas Penn expressed a desire for a perspective view of Philadelphia, his agent, Richard Peters, told him that "the City of Philadelphia will make a most miserable Perspective for want of Steeples." But a race to put up tall steeples had begun already. The Pennsylvania Assembly ordered construction of a tower and steeple at the State House in January 1749/50. The Presbyterians were not far behind. In March Samuel Hazard wrote to his brother, then in London, asking him to

bring us 2 or 3 handsome branches [chandeliers] & if you could add a very good bell to it we should like it the better, for you must know that we intend to have a steeple and a handsome one too, built from the ground & not on the House. Little matters won't satisfy us we are in a country of dissenters & we can see no reason why Presbyterians mayn't have as good a Church and Steeple here as the English church who are no more established here than we are & han't got half so good a minister—in short if you don't get something handsome for us you must expect to be severely reproved when we see you if we proceed to no higher censure (Letter Book 1 March 1749/50).

Edmund Woolley was in charge of construction at the State House, completing the work by April 1753, just as the Second Presbyterian Church and Christ Church (Catalog #4) were setting up competing subscriptions. Hazard complained that

...the Church of England here have been mean enough to set up a second lottery for their steeple in opposition to ours. (For they knew our intention a long time before.) Though we scorned to interfere with theirs yet they with the utmost secrecy published a second scheme and have appointed the first day of June for drawing it—we are however determined to be beforehand with them & therefore we have fixed the drawing of ours to the 16th of May...some of the most considerable gentlemen of this city...much resent the conduct of the Church of England in acting so mean & selfish a part (Hazard to Richard Cary, Letter Book, 27 February 1753).

The fund-raising was not as successful as that of Christ Church. The masonry tower on which the steeple would rest was up to the eaves by November 1753. It was assumed that it would be completed as shown in the Scull and Heap view (Hockly to Penn). In 1754 John Palmer, the mason who had construct-

This detail of the "East Prospect of Philadelphia" reflects Robert Smith's design for the steeple of the Second Presbyterian Church, which must have been designed, but was never executed.
Courtesy The Athenæum of Philadelphia.

ed the body of the building, was authorized "to carry the Steeple up to its full height," (Minutes of the Congregation, 19 July 1754). (This probably meant not the full steeple, but completion of the masonry tower.) But there it stopped, probably capped with a temporary roof, until a steeple finally was erected to Thomas Nevell's design in 1761 (Catalog #15).

It is virtually certain that the Second Presbyterian Church had a design by Smith on hand when they began their lottery. As noted in the introduction, a steeple identified as that of the Presbyterian Church appears on the Scull and Heap "East Prospect," the drawing for which was made in 1752. The Scull and Heap view shows a steeple similar to that of Christ Church, although more slender and not quite as well integrated. It employed motifs derived from James Gibbs, possibly by way of William Adam. (For a discussion of the sources of the Christ Church design, see Catalog #4.)

The 1830 Breton lithograph shows the church after 1809, when alterations were made and the building enlarged one bay to the west. On the interior, the ceiling, as noted, was altered, the pulpit was moved to the west wall and the interior arrangement of the pews was changed (Minutes of the Congregation, March-April 1809, 84-95).

When all is said and done, what was Smith's role at Second Presbyterian? The record is not clear. He was asked to participate as a carpenter-builder, and may have been consulted on the design. The normal practice for a skilled master carpenter also implied considerable "on the job" design input. This project for the Second Presbyterian Church, early in his career, involves almost all the questions posed at other Smith jobs, such as: the role of the carpenter-builder; the nature of ultimate design responsibility; and Smith's interaction both with other trades and with a building committee. Certainly he was chosen to participate—he was on the list—and as a relative newcomer to the city that in itself is a testament to his capability, as evaluated by his peers and those in a position to hire the best craftsmen.

DOCUMENTATION:

Presbyterian Historical Society. "An Account of the origin, progress & present state of the Second Presbyterian Church in the City of Philadelphia." 2 May 1792; "Early Notes of the Building"; Elders of the Second Presbyterian Church (1745-1790); Gilbert Tennent to Philip Doddridge. 20 July 1751; Minutes of the Congregation, Second Presbyterian Church (January 1749-August 1772, 1792-1803, 1805-1811); Subscription List. Gilbert Tennent. n.d.; Franklin, Benjamin. *The Autobiography of Benjamin Franklin.* New York (1951), 166; Hazard, Samuel. Letter Book. Gen. mss. [bound]. Manuscripts Division, Dept. of Rare Books and Special Collections, Princeton University Library; HSP. Hockley, Richard to Thomas Penn. Penn Papers, official correspondence, 6:147. Insurance Survey, 7 June 1763. Philadelphia Contributionship; Hogan, Edmund. *The Prospect of Philadelphia.* Philadelphia (1795); Kalm, Peter. *America in 1750: Peter Kalm's Travels in North America.* Ed. by Adolph B. Benson. New York (1937). *Pennsylvania Gazette.* 21 June 1770; Tennent, Gilbert. *The Divine Government over all considered, and, The necessity of Gratitude, or Benefits conferred, (by it,) Represented, in two SERMONS, Preach'd June the 7th 1752, in the Presbyterian Church lately erected in Arch-Street, in the City of Philadelphia, on the occasion Of the first Celebration of religious Worship there.* Philadelphia (1752).

REFERENCES:

Faris, 42-51; Mackie, Alexander. "The Presbyterian Churches of Old Philadelphia." In *HP*, 217-229; O'Gorman, James F. "A New York Architect Visits Philadelphia in 1822." *PMHB*, 117, 3 (July 1993): 153-176; S&W, 2:1263-1280; Tatman and Moss, 54-55; Watson (1870), 391-392; Watson (1927), 3:445.

3 A

Pine Street Meeting [Hill Meeting]

Pine Street between Front and Second Streets, Philadelphia 1752, demolished

A TANTALIZING BIT of evidence connects Robert Smith with Pine Street Meeting. In early June 1752, William Logan of Stenton wrote to Smith chastising him for not communicating with the committee overseeing the building of the new meeting house. Smith was to supply the boards, but nothing had been heard from him. "Thou art to Consider as I told thee at first the Care is different from that of a private man. In this the whole body of Friends are concerned, & in case of a disappointment which I hope will not happen thou will be much blamed." (Logan to Smith, 6 March 1752).

Between 1700 and 1776 only one new Quaker meeting house was built in Philadelphia.[1] Located on the south side of Pine Street near the New Market, the brick meeting house stood on ground willed to the Society of Friends in 1747 by Samuel Powel (Bronner, 212). Also known as "Hill Meeting," because of its location on Society Hill, the building served two groups of Friends until Orange Street Meeting built its own house on Washington Square in 1832. Four years later the Pine Street Meeting House was sold (*Society*, 94).

Given Logan's letter Smith must have had a role in construction of the meeting house, but what this was cannot be documented. Evidently Smith was to supply boards for the project, but, the nature of the building, and the people associated with it, strongly suggest the possibility of Smith's involvement as a carpenter-builder. Meeting minutes record many activities related to construction, but shed no light on Smith's participation. William Logan, John Smith, Samuel Rhoads, and Samuel Wetherill were the committeemen authorized to execute title to the ground and devise a plan. Rhoads, with whom Smith would be associated on many projects, was a member of the Carpenters' Company, and Wetherill served an apprenticeship as a carpenter. (For Rhoads, see Tatman and Moss, 656-658). They certainly were equal to the task of superintending construction of the meeting house. In late 1752, monthly minutes report progress, giving the dimensions of the "house [as] 60 feet long and 43 feet broad," and noting a projected cost of £800 (Minutes, 27 October month 1752). The following year, the house was "near finished," and deemed suitable for meetings "during our late Annual Solemnity." (Minutes, 28 September 1753). Afterwards, the building often was the site of Quarterly as well as Annual Meetings.

Derelict and abandoned, the Pine Street Meeting was photographed in 1859, two years before it was demolished. Free Library of Philadelphia.

REFERENCES:

Bronner, Edwin B. "Quaker Landmarks in Early Philadelphia." In *HP*, 211-212; "The Pine Street Meeting." In *Society of Friends in Pennsylvania*. Philadelphia (1941); S&W, 2; Tatman and Moss.

DOCUMENTATION:

William Logan to Robert Smith. William Logan Letter Book. HSP; Minutes. Philadelphia Monthly Meeting, Southern District, (1750-1753). Quaker Collection. Haverford College.

---

1. Two other meeting houses were erected before the Revolution. The 1755 Greater Meeting House replaced an earlier building, and the Fourth Street Meeting, built in 1763, provided a site for Quarterly Meeting and housing for students at the nearby Friends' School. Neither housed a newly organized meeting for worship.

Design and Build the Steeple for Christ Church

West side Second Street between Market and Arch Streets,
  Philadelphia
1751-1753, Steeple Repair (Catalog #44), 1771

WHEN the tall brick walls of Christ Church rose above the modest streets of Quaker Philadelphia, the building must have been the architectural sensation of its time. The early Swedes and Dutch had hacked the town site out of a forest with only scattered clearings fewer than fifty years earlier. But, already in 1727, the parish fathers were emulating the great works of Sir Christopher Wren and Nicholas Hawksmoor in faraway London. There is no eyewitness description of this monumental project, and only a fragmentary knowledge of its progress. But what is known is interesting.

A great parchment in the Christ Church records attests to the fact that the building site, which fronted one hundred feet on Second Street, was bought in 1695. The first church was begun the following year, completed soon afterwards, and by the summer of 1700 needed enlarging (Perry, 2:16). The Vestry Minutes, which begin only in the year 1717, document the need for a larger church "to Accommodate divers New Settlers and other well wishers to the Church who are forced either to stay at home or frequent dissenting Congregations for want of Seats." A steeple with a set of bells was envisioned. Thereupon, an additional twenty-foot strip of land was acquired to the north and a subscription book opened. By 1727 the vestry resolved to build the first thirty-three feet of a wholly new structure (Perry, 2:37). This took the extraordinary form of a monumental addition to the west end of the small existing church, the latter continuing in use for some years.

Work seems to have continued all through the 1730s, and for some time the church must have presented a most ungainly sight; the grand, tall new west end, executed with elaborate brickwork, joined to the little old wooden church still abutting Second Street. But to the eyes of those lately come from the old country, and accustomed to the incongruities of an-cient churches built in installments at different periods and in different styles, this would not have seemed unusual.

Within a few years, the original church fell into a ruinous state and a fund drive to replace it was started (Minutes, 16 March and 20 June 1732). In the spring of 1735 the vestry agreed to complete the exterior of the new building as soon as work on the western galleries was paid for and the scaffolding taken down (Minutes, 25 May 1735). A new subscription book, begun in May 1739, noted that "the Body of the new church on the outside was almost finished" and that the foundation of a steeple had been laid.

The latter was probably a small structure riding the ridge line and carrying a clock as noted by traveller Peter Kalm in 1748: "The English established church stands in the northern part of the town . . . and is the finest of all. It has a small insignificant steeple, in which a bell is rung when it is time to go to church, and at burials. It has likewise a clock which strikes the hours. This building, which is called Christ Church, was founded towards the end of the last century, but has lately been rebuilt and more adorned" (Benson, 20-21). There is no image of the "insignificant steeple" reported by Kalm. Possibly it was removed and stored for re-use elsewhere by architect-builder Robert Smith, who erected the present steeple in 1753.

In eighteenth-century Philadelphia a distinction was often made between the tower of a building, generally of masonry, and the steeple or spire—a lighter wood frame construction which topped it. In the case of Christ Church the distinction is important because the tower and steeple were designed by different parties at different times.

Hope for a steeple on Christ Church went back at least to 1717, (Minutes, 11 June 1717)—well before the present edifice was begun—and the foundations of a tower were laid as early as 1727 (Minutes, 2 May 1727). When the body of the church was complete, the vestry was reminded "that it is the zealous inclination of very many inhabitants of this City to Contribute Handsome Sums of Money toward building a tower or Steeple for Holding a ring of Bells" (Minutes, 3 April 1744). Two years later, the church wardens were directed "to consult with Skillful Artichets[1]

---

1. The misspelling of the word architect here says something about its unfamiliarity in early Philadelphia.

This view of Christ Church is believed to have been drawn by Charles Willson Peale and engraved by James Trenchard. It appeared in the *Columbian Magazine* for August 1787. The south facade clearly owes a debt to James Gibbs's St. Martin-in-the-Fields. Courtesy The Athenæum of Philadelphia.

[sic] and Workmen and endeavor to get a plan or Draft thereof" together with an estimate (Minutes, 24 April 1746). By June of 1746, a plan drawn by a "Mr. Harrison" was adopted and a committee delegated to show it to the Governor (Minutes, 2 June 1746).[2] But nothing came of it, and as late as 28 October 1750, Richard Peters of Philadelphia advised the Proprietor in England that the view of the city the latter requested was hardly worth painting "for want of steeples" on the skyline. (Wainwright, 18). By this time, however, the tower/stairhall/steeple of the State House was already six months into construction and a Philadelphia artist, George Heap, finally accepted the challenge, undertaking a view as seen from the Jersey shore of the Delaware River, and completing it by September 1752. It was May 11th of the next year before a copy of this view was made and shipped off to England (Wainwright, 19), and it seems likely that Peters had been waiting for the new design for Christ Church steeple.

Construction had started just two weeks before Heap's drawing was sent off to London, as signalled by a cash payment for scaffolding, spars, and poles to carry the carpenters and their work high up into the sky. And so the design as executed could and did appear on the new engraving, the printing of which began in June 1754. The engraving, though crudely drawn in detail, corresponds well enough with the building as it stands. Furthermore, there is confirmation that there was such a drawing. As noted in the Introduction, John Penn had viewed a "plan," indicating that he had seen one or more drawings.

In the race to put up Philadelphia's first steeple, Christ Church had begun its subscription list three weeks before construction started at the State House, but not until a year later were the managers of the building program asked to proceed (Minutes, 11 March 1750[/51] and 29 April 1751). By this time they probably had in hand the design John Penn had seen. It came from the pen of a new star, the Scottish immigrant Robert Smith, whose career would bridge the gap between the trade of carpenter or builder and the profession of architect. Smith already had worked at Bush Hill (Catalog #1) and the Second Presbyterian

Church (Catalog #2) with master mason John Palmer, who was to build the tower. By the time Christ Church steeple was designed, Smith was well on his way to success.

Beginning in the spring of 1751, there is a more or less connected and comprehensive building record in the form of a little paperbound manuscript, neatly copied out in a professional hand. The Steeple Account—for that is how it is labeled on the cover—begins on 10 May 1751, with an entry in favor of William Pyewell for "Bords and Halling" (£9.4.3). The second entry records rum bought for boat crews bringing in stone. Those "flattmen" were to consume a lot of the stuff; such treats were customary in the eighteenth century. Lime and sand for mortar and poles for scaffolding were assembled at the site in quantity. It is not generally realized that the foundation of the tower and a large part of the walls above grade are of stone hidden under a veneer of brick.[3] John Grant and John Armstrong cut the stone on the site; it was laid up by Thomas Ward, stonemason. John Coats, the well-known brickmaker of Northern Liberties, got £140.19.1 for his product.

John Palmer, bricklayer, was first paid on 17 July 1751, and payments for the tower continued until 29 May 1752, when Isaac Roberts got 4s 8 1/2d "for Measuring ye wall" to value Palmer's work (Steeple Accounts). Then it was discovered that there was not enough money on hand to pay the tradesmen (Minutes, 6 August 1752). In this crisis the vestry decided to hold a lottery, and Benjamin Franklin, reliable champion of civic progress, was enlisted as one of the committeeman (Minutes, 27 and 30 October 1752; *Pennsylvania Gazette*, 2 November 1752). The lottery did not bring in the whole sum needed, so a "supplement" was mounted with emphasis on acquiring a set of bells (Minutes, 22 February 1753). By the end of 1753 a set had been ordered from London (Minutes, 3 December 1753).

Smith would have been on the site by the spring of 1753, when poles and spars were bought to erect the steeple or spire. A large order for cedar lumber went to Job Lippincott, and George Fudge recapped the brickwork on which the frame would be seated. Progress was fast. Carpenters had finished the major

---

2. This was either John Harrison, Jr., or his brother Joseph, who were among the earliest members of the Carpenters' Company (Tatman and Moss, 338-340). Gough, 48, believes that John Harrison designed the tower.

---

3. The same thing happened on the tower of Independence Hall. Stone was a basically stronger material, less porous and more waterproof.

framing members, fabricated on the ground, by July 11th when they received a cash distribution of 15 shillings. On September 5th, "the Coppersmith Boys" got a pourboire of 7s.6d, and, on October 2nd, there were two big payments for a collation "at raising" indicating a really outstanding celebration (£17.2.2 1/2)! There was yet another by October 30th for "raising the Spindle" (£3.18.3 1/2). Rigger John Coburn as steeplejack would have been the hero on that occasion. On 6 November 1753, Richard Hockley wrote to Thomas Penn that the "Church Steeple is quite up but not yet covered in, it is the compleatest thing in all America and but few such ever in London." By the following year, the "compleatest thing" undoubtedly was complete. The last of eighteen payments was made to Robert Smith on 19 December 1754, his total coming to the large amount of £396.4.6.

To finish off the job, carpenter John Thornhill did the necessary woodwork, which probably included laying floors, partitions, and staircases in the tower. (Minutes, 23 August 1756 and 14 April 1759) Probably the tower had been left hollow until this time, so it could be used as a conduit to haul up scaffolding and timbers for construction of the steeple (Suzanne M. Pentz to Constance M. Greiff, 21 July 1999).

The design of the tower and spire of Christ Church is of considerable interest as related to other roughly contemporary colonial churches, such as Christ Church (Old North), Boston (1723) and Trinity Church, Newport (1726). Although the towers of these were built in the 1720s, the spires were not erected until 1740 in the case of Boston, and 1741 in the case of the Newport, although the latter spire was designed in 1726. Both the New England churches bear a resemblance to a number of Christopher Wren's London churches. In the 1720s, there were few English "pattern books" offering church designs and few prints to send across the Atlantic. One theory has been that there may have been available in Boston an engraving of Wren's Church of St. James, which delineates an elevation and two floor plans. This copperplate print, engraved by Henry Hulsbergh[4] from drawings made by Anthony Griffen,

___
4. Hulsbergh also engraved the plates for James Gibbs's *A Book of Architecture*, the first edition of which was published in London in 1728. The second edition, the one known to have been available in Philadelphia, appeared in 1739.

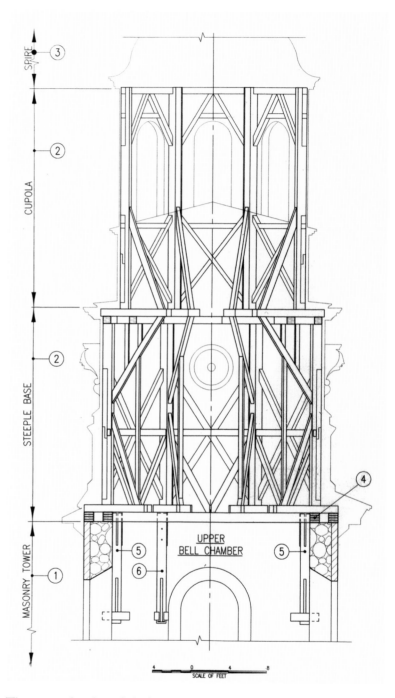

The extant framing of the lower stages of Robert Smith's spire is diagrammed in this section. How much of this dates from the original construction and how much to repairs Smith made in 1771 is unknown. The laminated sill plates are certainly replacements for the originals, which had deteriorated because of fungal decay. J.S. Winterle, principal delineator under Suzanne Pentz. Courtesy Keast & Hood Co.

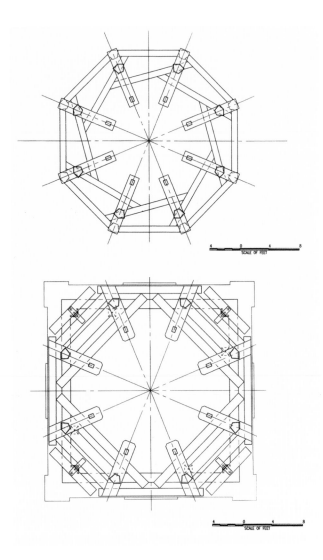

The timber framing at the base of the cupola has a "pinwheel" arrangement, which facilitated a vertical offset of the eight pentagonal columns at the transition between the cupola and steeple base. The placement of the short timbers served to brace the structure against wind and permit an open area in the center. J.S. Winterle, principal delineator under Suzanne Pentz. Courtesy Keast & Hood Co.

As it had been for Smith's roof trusses, Francis Price's *The British Carpenter* seems to have been the guide for the framing of the Christ Church steeple. This method of framing a steeple appears in the volume as Plate P*Q***. Library Company of Philadelphia.

shows an arrangement of four superimposed masonry openings in the tower on the entrance side (Foley, 71). It may have influenced the New England builders. The Boston church has been much altered, but the Newport Church, far more intact, reflects elements of several Wren churches, including details of its interior. Rather than depending on a single print, the resemblance to Wren's churches may have come from design assistance offered to the colonial builders by the Society for the Propagation of the Gospel in Foreign Parts (Downing, 54-55; Tucci, 3-4).

Philadelphia also looked to London. When the body of Christ Chuch was begun, its concept may have owed a debt to Christopher Wren's churches. But by the time the walls began to rise, a more *au courant*, and classical adaptation of the Palladian style was used, based on the work of James Gibbs. His 1728 publication, *A Book of Architecture*, was widely disseminated, and a copy must have been available in Philadelphia. It is obvious that the north and south elevation, as well as the interior, are derived from Gibbs's St. Martin-in-the-Fields, the exterior of which was illustrated as Plate 1. Smith also used the St. Martin's design for the lowest stage of the steeple. Above it, however, he placed a cupola and spindle based on Gibbs's Marylebone Chapel [St Peter's, Vere Street]. This was a combination that had already

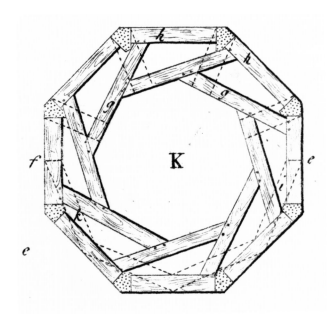

Detail of one of eight sculpted consoles at the top of the first stage of the steeple. They were carved by Samuel Harding, who also provided wood embellishments for the interior and exterior of the Pennsylvania State House [Independence Hall]. Photograph by Nicholas Gianopulos, PE, 1986. Courtesy Keast and Hood Co.

been used by William Adam at the Town House in Dundee. Whether Smith knew this building from personal experience or only through the engraving made for *Vitruvius Scoticus* is irrelevant. The debt to Gibbs, via Adam is obvious. The only differences appear to be the omission of the corner columns and the substitution of triangular forms over the oculi for the segmental arches used by Gibbs and Adam. This variation appears in a trio of steeples shown in Gibbs's Plate 30. The urns also moved from above to below the first stage of the tower.

Structurally, the Christ Church steeple differs from other surviving pre-Revolutionary steeples.[5] Those were generally framed in telescoping fashion,

with vertical timber columns rising through two stages for greater rigidity. At Christ Church, each stage is framed separately with a horizontal level of framing as support for the columns above and link to the columns below (Suzanne M. Pentz to Constance M. Greiff, 14 July 1999). The horizontal framing seems to be based on an illustration in Francis Price's *The British Carpenter*, first published in 1733; the second edition of 1735, was at the Library Company by 1739.[6] Smith thus drew on his knowledge of British sources to create something novel on this side of the Atlantic, well adapted to the demands of a sophisticated, but still colonial city. The steeple remains as one of his greatest monuments.

DOCUMENTATION:

Christ Church Archives. Vestry, Building and Steeple Fund (1739-1754). Loose Documents (1760). Minutes (1717-1761), 1761-1773). The Steeple Account (1751); Hockley, Richard to Thomas Penn. Penn Papers, official corr., 6:147. HSP; Kalm, Peter. *America in 1750: Peter Kalm's Travels in North America*. Edited by Adolph B. Benson. New York (1937); Penn, John to Thomas Penn. Penn Papers, private corr., 4:117. HSP. *Pennsylvania Gazette*, 2 November 1752.

REFERENCES:

Dorr, Benjamin. *A Historical Account of Christ Church, Philadelphia: from its Foundation, A.D.1695, to A.D.1841*. New York (1841); Downing, Antoinette F. and Vincent J. Scully, Jr., *The Architectural Heritage of Newport, Rhode Island*. 2nd rev. ed. New York (1967); Foley, Suzanne. "Christ Church, Boston." *Old Time New England* 51, 3 (January-March, 1961):67-83; Gough, Deborah Mathias. *Christ Church, Philadelphia*. Philadelphia (1995); Perry, William S. *The History of the American Episcopal Church, 1587-1883*. 2 vols. Boston (1885); *Historical Collections Relating to the American Colonial Church*. Vol 2. Edited by William S. Perry. Reprint edition. New York (1969); Shoemaker, Robert. "Christ Church, St. Peter's, and St. Paul's." In *HP*, 187-198; Tucci, Douglass Shand, *Built in Boston*, Boston (1978); Wainwright, Nicholas B. "Scull and Heap's East Prospect of Philadelphia." *PMHB*, 73, 1 (January 1949):16-25; Washburn, Louis C. *Christ Church, Philadelphia: A Symposium*. Philadelphia (1925).

5. The steeple of Old North in Boston has been rebuilt more than once. The other survivors are the Newport Church, St Michael's in Charleston (c. 1760-1764), and the First Baptist Meeting House in Providence, Rhode Island, (1775).

6. When the book first was published in London, its title was *A Treatise on Carpentry*. The second and subsequent editions bore the title by which the publication is generally known, *The British Carpenter*.

5 A

Freemasons' Lodge

Norris Alley [Lodge Alley] above Second Street,
  Philadelphia
1754, demolished 1801

THE FREEMASON'S LODGE, described by contemporaries as "a noble and spacious building... somewhere behind Billy Logan's new house" (Shippen in Balch, 32) is attributed to Robert Smith on the basis of time, place and patronage, as well as the more elusive and subjective assessment of style. The full-Georgian plan brick building, with its paired end chimneys and pedimented entry, was "the first Masonic Hall in the Western World" (Sachse, 56) and supplanted an earlier meeting site at Tun Tavern. Smith's name does not appear in the "Book of Proceedings" as either a member or guest; however, in February 1750, when the Masons met at the Royal Standard Tavern, "Smith and Kiddie [were paid] ten Pounds 12.2 for the Pedestal" ordered in October (Book of Proceedings, 25 October 1749 and 8 February 1749/50). It is possible Robert Smith was the carpenter named in the record. At the time, Smith was at work on Bush Hill (Catalog #1) for Governor James Hamilton, an important figure in Masonic circles. Hamilton may have recommended Smith to his fellow Masons.

By 1752, there were repeated objections to utilizing taverns for meetings and a committee was appointed "to look out for a suitable Lot whereon to erect a Building" (*PBF*, 235-237). Two years later the committee agreed to buy a lot and Robert Smith was among those subscribing toward its purchase and the "erection of Freemason's Hall" (Sachse, 46). The building was completed quickly, at a cost of £730, and dedicated on St. John's Day in June 1755. Philadelphians were entertained by a grand procession from the Lodge to Christ Church, where the Rev. Mr. William Smith preached on brotherhood (S&W, 3:2063).

Routine expenses were offset by income from rentals, and the St. Andrew's Society was one of the early tenants. That organization, founded in 1749, listed both Smith's patron, James Hamilton, and a Robert Smith as members, and offers another layer of association with the Freemasons' Lodge. Coupled with Smith's financial support, these connections suggest that he was a likely participant in some aspect of the building project.

DOCUMENTATION:

Book of proceedings of the Mason's Lodge held at the Tun Tavern, 1749-1755, Manuscript Collection, HSP; *The Papers of Benjamin Franklin* [*PBF*]. Vol. 5. Ed. by Leonard W. Labaree. New Haven (1962); Joseph Shippen to James Burd, 6 April 1754. *Letters and Papers relating chiefly to the Provincial History of Pennsylvania.* Edited by Thomas Willing Balch. Philadelphia (1855).

REFERENCES:

Barratt, Norris S. and Julius F. Sachse, *Freemasonry in Pennsylvania, 1727-1907.* Philadelphia (1908); Beath, Robert B., comp. *Historical Catalogue of the St. Andrew's Society of Philadelphia.* Vol. 2. Philadelphia (1913); Huss, Wayne A. *The Master Builders: A History of the Grand Lodge of Free and Accepted Masons of Pennsylvania.* Vol. 1. Philadelphia (1962); Sachse, Julius F. *Old Masonic Lodges of Pennsylvania "Moderns" and "Ancients" 1730-1800.* Vol. 1. Philadelphia (1912). S&W, 3.

6

Alterations to House for Thomas Penn

Second Street south of Dock Creek Bridge
1754, demolished

IN 1736, Thomas Penn had rented a house in Second street from the second Samuel Powel. In 1751, planning to return to America, he deliberated about building a new house (Penn to Richard Peters, 20 September 1751, Letter Book). He finally decided to occupy the rented property, but ordered extensive work, including painting and papering, adding cornices, and altering the stairs (Penn to Richard Hockley, 24 September 1751, Letter Book).

Work on this project by a number of Philadelphia craftsmen may be documented by bills in the Penn-Physick Papers. Carpenter William Henderson had done some work for the widow of Samuel Powel in 1750, and billed Penn for a coach house door and garden boxes in 1753. But this work could have been done elsewhere, at Springettsbury or at Penn Point.

Like James Hamilton, Thomas Penn did not indicate where the work had been done when he made payments. The largest sums for carpentry in this period went to Ebenezer Tomlinson, Edmund Woolley's collaborator on the State House.

By October 1754, the proprietarial secretary could report that, "The house is entirely finish'd and furnish'd . . . it looks better than ever I saw it as the new painting with stone color sets it off much to advantage" (Hockley to Penn, 4 October 1754, Family Corr.). Robert Smith put on a few of the finishing touches. In September 1754, he billed £5.12.8 1/2 for two doors upstairs and a new garden door, including hardware and "hangen yᵉ bell" (Penn-Physick Papers). Isaac Janvier was the painter, and followed Penn's instructions to paint the brick exterior and the hall stone color, with a dark chocolate door (Penn to Hockley, 11 July 1752, Letter Book).

After all his detailed and lengthy correspondence about making the house ready for his occupancy, Thomas Penn never moved in. Instead he sent Richard Hunter Morris to serve as Governor, and arranged for John Penn to board with him (Penn to John Penn, Richard Peters, and Richard Hockley, 15 May 1754, and to John Penn, 12 June 1754, Letter Book).

DOCUMENTATION:

HSP. Penn Papers, Thomas Penn Letter Books. Official Corr., Vol. 5 and 6. Private Corr., Vol 4. Correspondence of the Penn Family, 1732-1767; Penn-Physick Papers, Vol. 10.

7

Assist with Design, Provide the Plan and Build Nassau Hall for the College of New Jersey (Princeton University)

Nassau Street, Princeton, NJ
1754, severely damaged and altered after Revolutionary War and fires in 1802 and 1855

EDUCATION for the ministry was one of the major purposes of eighteenth-century schools and colleges. New England had Harvard and Yale for Con-gregationalists (and later Brown for Baptists), and Virginia William and Mary for Anglicans, but there was no comparable institutions for Presbyterians. Stirred by the oratory of George Whitefield and other evangelists, and spurred by the inability of the New England colleges or European universities to supply enough ministers for the growing Scotch-Irish population of the Middle Atlantic colonies, New York and East New Jersey Presbyterians, along with some Philadelphians, were determined to remedy the situation. Their cause was strengthened by the knowledge that no ministers other than those trained by Harvard or Yale, or in Europe, would be ordained by the conservative Philadelphia Synod.

Members of the New York Synod and New Brunswick Presbytery, together with supporters in Philadelphia, received a charter for a college from New Jersey's governor in 1746, and a small school opened in 1747 in Elizabeth under Rev. Jonathan Dickinson. A few months later, Dickinson died. When Rev. Aaron Burr (1715-1757) was named the second president, the infant college moved to Newark where he was pastor. Still, there was opposition to the college from Anglicans and Quakers. In 1748, a new charter, granted by Governor Jonathan Belcher, declared that the institution would be non-sectarian; a new group of trustees reappointed Burr as president. Despite the non-sectarian status of the college, most of its trustees were Presbyterians, and, until the third quarter of the twentieth century, its presidents were Presbyterian ministers or Presbyterian ministers' sons.

Within a few years of the move to Newark, it became clear that the situation there was not tenable. The college needed a place of its own, with its president able to spend full time on teaching and administration. The trustees debated about a suitable site, setting space requirements and financial conditions, which would determine their selection. Princeton eventually was chosen, partly because of its central location, but largely because a few of its prominent citizens made the best offer of land and money. This was gladly accepted by the trustees at their meeting on 24 January 1753 (PUA, 1:29).

Part of the offer was Nathaniel FitzRandolph's donation of four-and-a-half acres of land along the town's main street. Ideas about a building to house the college must already have been considered, for at the same meeting the trustees reviewed a plan shown

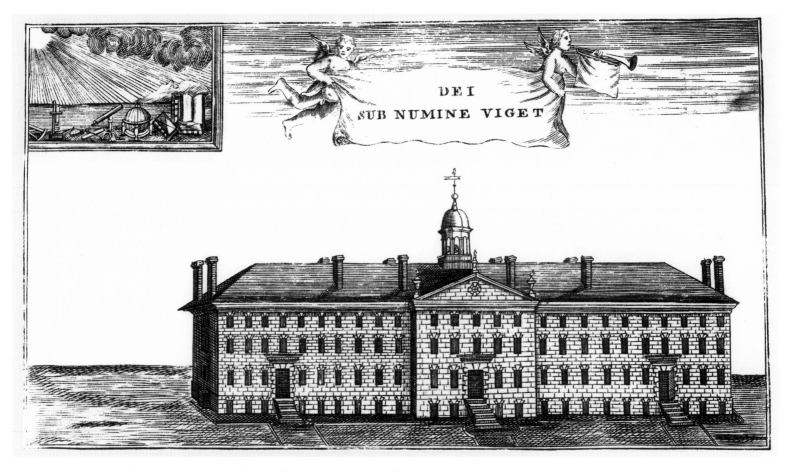

DEI
SUB NUMINE VIGET

The earliest known view of Nassau Hall appeared in the *New American Magazine*,
27 (March 1760), published in Woodbridge, New Jersey, by James Parker. The artist and
engraver are unknown. The copperplate engraving flatters the building, portraying the front
as laid in regular ashlar. But it clearly depicts the high basement already fitted up as
the kitchen and buttery, and soon to be turned into more dormitory space as the
student body expanded. Courtesy Dept. of Rare Books and Special Collections,
Princeton University Library. Published with permission of Princeton University Library.

them by Philadelphia trustee Edward Shippen. On January 27th, Edward wrote to his son, a student at the college in Newark, that he attended the meeting and "brought with him a plan for a structure 190 feet long and 50 feet deep" (PUA, 1:40). Inasmuch as the length of the existing building is 177 feet, it is assumed that the plan of January 1753 was the first of two (Norton, 10).

Various fund-raising activities had been launched before ground was broken in summer 1754. These included a complicated lottery, and, in spring 1754, Gilbert Tennent, pastor of the Second Presbyterian Church in Philadelphia, and the Rev. Mr. Samuel Davies, a Virginian, were in Great Britain raising money. On May 27th, acting as "Agents for the Trustees of the College lately established in the Province of New Jersey in America," they presented a petition to the Assembly in Edinburgh, "setting forth the End and Design of [the] Institution, and praying a general Collection through all the Churches of this Kingdom for erecting the publick Buildings..." (*The Caledonian Mercury*, 28 May 1754). Their efforts were successful, and financing for the building project was off to a strong start. The trustees met in Princeton on 22 July 1754 to finalize plans for the building and appoint a committee to oversee its construction. At this meeting, the trustees "Voted: That laying the Foundation of the College be proceeded upon immediately. That the Plan drawn by Doctr. Shippen[1] & Mr. Robert Smith be in general the Plan of the College. That the College be built of Brick if good Brick can be made at Princeton & if Sand can be got reasonably cheap—That it be three Story high & without any Cellar." On the same day, they authorized Samuel Hazard, a trustee from Philadelphia, and Robert Smith to place the building and "mark out the Ground."

The choice of Smith may relate to satisfaction with his work on the Second Presbyterian Church. Three of its members were Dr. William Shippen, brother of a college trustee, and John Redman and Samuel Hazard, who were trustees. It is tempting, however, to speculate that Smith's familiarity with the Orphans' Hospital and Watson's Hospital, by William Adam, may have played a role. Contrary to what has been generally believed in the United States, these were not institutions for the care of the sick, but rather charity boarding schools for boys. Their requirements were much the same as those of a college, although the plan of Nassau Hall is far simpler than either of these possible precedents.

—————
1. This was William Shippen, brother of Trustee Edward Shippen.

Construction began a week later; Nathaniel FitzRandolph noted the fact in his *Book of Records* on 29 July 1754. He was also on the scene when the cornerstone was laid on September 17th. Before this event, the trustees had made some changes to the building as described in January. Stone would be used not only for the foundation, but also for the walls. This undoubtedly had been recommended by William Worth, a local mason accustomed to working the native stone, but not brick. In August Burr wrote to the Rev. David Cowell, a member of the building committee, that he liked "Mr. Worth's Proposals very well on first View" and requested a meeting of the committee (Quoted in Norton, 11). As a Scot, Smith also would have been familiar with stone construction, but not with exposed rubble. In his native country, such construction would have been stuccoed, or dressed stone would have been employed. It was familiarity with the regular surfaces thus achieved, plus the extensive use of brick in Philadelphia, that probably led to Smith's use of brick in all his major buildings.[2]

—————
2. The original stonework would have seemed far rougher than it does today. Its appearance was greatly altered and became more formal after it was pointed to simulate ashlar in the mid-nineteenth century.

The precise inspiration for Nassau Hall has never been identified but its central pavilion with long flanking wings containing double-loaded corridors was common in British institutional buildings of the period, such as William Adam's Orphans' Hospital in Edinburgh, illustrated in *Vitruvius Scoticus*.

Ezra Stiles (1727-1795), a New England clergyman, stopped in Princeton soon after the cornerstone was laid, and "viewed the foundation & plan of the college." He noted the dimensions, "177f. long & 53 2/3f. wide," and carefully drew a floor plan in his diary. Unfortunately, the handwritten record is not among Stiles's papers, although a version was printed in 1892 (*Massachusetts Historical Society*, 6). Despite this loss, Stiles's account documents the dimensions, footprint and arrangement of interior spaces—information gained, no doubt, from the plan.

In September 1754, Belcher and Burr considered an embellishment that would have given Smith an opportunity to show off his skills. They met in Elizabeth, and discussed adding a "handsome Portico." But nothing came of this, either because of expense, or because it did not suit the sober tastes of some of the dissenters on the Board of Trustees (Belcher to Samuel Hazard, 9 September 1754). They also were concerned about lack of daily supervision as the walls went up. Belcher thought that one reliable man should oversee construction, so that the workmen would be kept honest, and the workmanship be of high quality (Belcher to Burr, 19 September 1754). Burr agreed. He wrote to Rev. Cowell on October 28th that "we ought to have had a man to oversee the work *de die in diem*, though I put great confidence in Mr. Worth" (Quoted in Norton, 14).

Nevertheless, there is no indication that anyone ever was appointed to supervise Worth. He and his men probably proceeded on the walls until winter weather intervened. Meanwhile, Smith had other jobs in Philadelphia, notably the steeple for Christ Church (Catalog #4). By spring 1755, however, Smith would have been on the job laying the joists and doing the framing. Probably aware that this large project would require his personal attention on a steady basis, he bought land, built a house and moved his family to Princeton. (See Catalog #9). At the end of May, he received the first payment of £55.16.0 from President Burr "on acct. of ye building the College." The college president or treasurer made three additional payments to Smith in 1755, the largest of which was over £483. Smith clearly was managing the job, requesting payment for others, like the order in favor of Charles Read for scantling "for Window Cases to the College." Progress was being made; in November, the carpenters were ready to erect the roof, at which time Smith was described by FitzRandolph as "the Carpenter who built the timberwork of ye College."

With the building under roof, some interior finishing could take place, weather permitting. Smith received a payment from Burr in February 1756, after work probably had stopped for the season, picking up again as the temperatures rose. By July 1756 the college was "almost finished and look[ed] exceedingly well," and in November the students and tutors moved into Nassau Hall (Wertenbaker, 38, 40). A 1760 engraving of the building appeared in the *New American Magazine*. It is competently drawn, portraying a large, rather plain rectangular structure, twenty-six bays long, with three entries, a central pediment, and cupola. The lack of ornament was in keeping with President Burr's claim "that we do everything in the plainest and cheapest manner, as far as is consistent with Decency & Convenience, having no superfluous Ornaments" (Quoted in Peterson, 295). Obviously, the once-discussed central portico had not been executed.

Various precedents have been cited for Nassau Hall. Wertenbaker (38) fancied a resemblance to Gibbs's King's College, Cambridge; a twentieth-century scholar, coincidentally named Robert Smith, suggested the rear wings of Trinity College, Dublin. One could also, perhaps with more justification, cite William Adam's charity schools in Edinburgh, which would have been familiar to Smith and some of those involved in founding the college. Their roofs carried the signature Smith cupola, which as pointed out in the Introduction, appears to be derived from Adam's vocabulary.

In truth, Nassau Hall was simply a generic eighteenth-century public building, with a hipped roof, projecting, pedimented central pavilion, and long flanking wings. It did, however, have the distinction of size. Nassau Hall was described by Esther Burr, wife of the president, as "the most commodious of any of the Colleges as well as much the largest of any upon the Continent. There is something very striking in it and a grandure and yet a simpliscity [sic] that cant be well expressed" (Esther Burr, 3 August 1756, 215). She was not the only person impressed by the building. Its form became the model for other collegiate structures, especially the "edifice" at the College of Rhode Island which was "to be the same plan as that of Princeton" (Catalog #42A). And when the trustees of the College of Philadelphia decided to build a dormitory (Catalog #16), they visited Nassau Hall to observe the "appointments."

The only exterior ornaments to be seen were stylistic details popular in pattern books of the period. The three urns at the gable of the slightly projecting center bay were almost visually consumed by the sheer size of the building, as was the cupola. Other architectural details, like the rusticated door surrounds and oculus, did little to relieve a formidable, symmetrical Georgian facade. One mystery is the existence and location of a balcony that was described by two eighteenth-century visitors. John Adams stopped by in August 1774 on his way to the First Continental Congress. He went through the whole building, and was taken to "the Balcony of the Colledge [sic], where we have a Prospect of an Horizon of about 80 Miles Diameter" (Adams, 2:112). Nine years later, James Kent, of New York, visited, and wrote that there was "a small Balcony in the middle" (Shelley, 306). No such feature appears in eighteenth-century depictions of the front of the building, and the prayer hall roof would have interfered with a balcony at the rear. An earlier visitor, a Miss Alexander, who came through Princeton in 1762, hints at another possibility. She viewed "many beautiful & rich prospects, especially from the top of the college" ("Notes and Queries"). Perhaps there was a railed walkway around the base of the cupola at the rear. Such a feature may be hinted at in the version of Charles Willson Peale's *Washington at the Battle of Princeton* that now hangs in Nassau Hall. The building is depicted in the background, but the scale is too small for certainty about the accuracy of details. Yet no such feature appears in the two eighteenth-century engravings of the building, so what these visitors saw remains a question.

The interior plan is well known from a number of sources. Ezra Stiles, by then president of Yale, paid a return visit to Princeton in 1784, and made two more sketches, of which the originals fortunately survive. His sketch of the first floor shows the central entrance between two large rooms, which are known, from other sources to have been classrooms. This vestibule led to a long cross-hall, flanked on either side by students' rooms. In a projection at the rear was the prayer hall. There was a pulpit on the east side of the prayer hall and a handsome organ on the

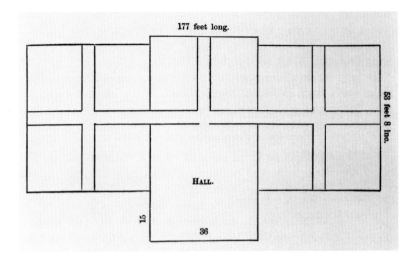

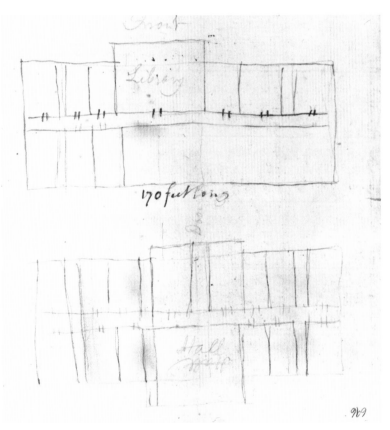

Nassau Hall evidently fascinated Ezra Stiles, for he drew its plans more than once. His first attempt in 1754 was published in the *Proceedings of the Massachusetts Historical Society*. It is a plan of the first floor, although only the foundation was in when he viewed the building. Evidently he also saw a drawing of the plan. On a return visit in 1784, he sketched both the first and second floors. The plan of the second floor is of particular interest because it shows that the prayer hall was not a full two stories in height. Beinecke Library, Yale University.

49

west (Green, 470). The prayer hall also had a gallery, probably on the west side. On the second floor, the library occupied the central position at the front, and the double-loaded corridors were repeated. The projecting hall at the rear is not shown on Stiles's second floor plan, indicating that it did not rise the full height of the building. Adams described the rooms flanking the corridors as suites consisting of two studies and a chamber. James Kent put the number of student rooms at forty-two. While the central entry terminated at the entrance to the prayer hall, the other two ran through the building, so that there were stairways and doors on the south side as well as the north (Green, 470). These openings have been converted to windows. But the south side was even plainer in design than the front in every respect. While the windows on the front are capped by flat arches with keystones, the openings on the back have simple segmental arches, and it is doubtful that the doors had rusticated surrounds.

The severe simplicity of Nassau Hall, warmed only by the golden color of its stone, conveyed the seriousness of its educational mission and was in keeping with its Presbyterian sponsorship. Gilbert Tennent had to defend the ornamentation of Second Presbyterian Church in Philadelphia, so the same mistake would not be made in Princeton. Yet, despite, or perhaps because of, its simplicity, the building was dignified and impressive. It also demonstrated that Smith was capable of managing a large commission. The project utilized his carpentry skills, tapped into his repertoire of stylistic details, demonstrated successful management of a large crew, and brought his work to the attention of those outside the city of Philadelphia. He also was paid promptly.

Unfortunately, his work would not survive. The building was severely damaged during the Revolution when it was occupied by both British and American troops.

The College is in a very ruinous situation, but has suffered more from the Licentiousness of our own Troops than from the ravages of the Enemy. The latter knocked down a Study in each Room, but the former destroyed the Library, damaged the Orrery, broke down the Pews and Rostrum in the Hall, cut the Pillars, which supported the Gallery, stole all the Pipes of the Organ, . . . All the Windows of the College are broken, & every room in it looks like a stable (Hazard, in Shelley, 172).

It is unlikely that any of Smith's interior woodwork survived this onslaught. Two fires in 1802 and 1855 destroyed the cupola and roof structure, and all evidence of his craftsmanship. Subsequent alterations and additions obscured any remaining details, but William Worth's walls remain; they and surviving cellar partitions suggest the general plan devised by William Shippen and Robert Smith in 1754.

DOCUMENTATION:

Adams, John. *Diary 1771-1781*. Vol. 2 of *Diary and Autobiography of John Adams*. Ed. by Lyman H. Butterfield. Cambridge, MA (1961); Belcher Papers, Massachusetts Historical Society; *The Caledonian Mercury* (Edinburgh), 29 May 1754; Gen Mss. [Misc.]. Manuscripts Division, Dept. of Rare Books and Special Collections, Princeton University Library. Published with permission of PUL.[3] Green, Ashbel."Dr. Witherspoon's Administration at Princeton College." *The Presbyterian Magazine* 4 (1854):467-472; Trustees' Minutes, Princeton University Archives [hereafter PUA]; "Notes and Queries." *PMHB 10 (1886): 115;* Shelley, Fred. "Ebenezer Hazard's Diary: New Jersey During the Revolution." *Proceedings of the New Jersey Historical Society*, 90, 3 (Autumn 1972): 169-179; ———. "Travel Contrasts: Chancellor Kent's Impressions of New Jersey." *Proceedings of the New Jersey Historical Society,* 73 (October 1955):300-305; Stiles, Ezra. Notebook of Itineraries, 20 September 1754. Printed as "Diary of Ezra Stiles." *Proceedings of the Massachusetts Historical Society.* 2nd series, 7 (March 1892): 338-345; Notebook of Itineraries, Ezra Stiles Papers, 3:696, Miscellaneous Papers. Beinecke Rare Book and Manuscript Library. Yale University (microfilm at American Philosophical Society).

REFERENCES:

Balch, Elise Willing. "Edward Shippen." In Keith, Charles P. *The Provincial Councillors of Pennsylvania, who held office between 1733 and 1776 . . . .* Philadelphia (1883); Greiff, Constance M., Mary W. Gibbons and Elizabeth G.C. Menzies. *Princeton Architecture: A Pictorial History of Town and Campus.* Princeton (1967); Norton, Paul. "Robert Smith's Nassau Hall and the President's House" and Robert Smith. "John Notman's Nassau Hall." In *Nassau Hall, 1756-1956.* Edited by Henry Lyttleton Savage. Princeton (1956); Peterson, Charles E. "Robert Smith, Philadelphia Builder-Architect: From Dalkeith to Princeton." In *Scotland and America In the Age of the Enlightenment.* Edited by Richard B. Sher and Jeffrey R. Smitten, Princeton (1990), 275-299; Schuyler, Montgomery. "Architecture of American Colleges, III-Princeton." *Architectural Record*, 27 (1910): 129-160; Wertenbaker, Thomas Jefferson. *Princeton 1746-1896.* Princeton (1946).
HABS, NJ-249

---

3. Unless otherwise indicated, all quotations and references to documents are from this source.

Nassau Hall appears again in this 1764 copperplate engraving drawn by W. Tennent and engraved by H. Dawkins. It was published following the title page of Samuel Blair's *Account of the College of New Jersey*, also printed in Woodbridge by James Parker. This rendition also shows the President's House, with its prominent keystones and fanlit doorway, as well as the fence Smith erected around its dooryard. Courtesy Dept. of Rare Books and Special Collections, Princeton University Library. Published with permission of Princeton University Library.

8

Design and Build President's House
for the College of New Jersey
(Now Known as Maclean House)

Nassau Street, Princeton, NJ
1754 [?]-1757, altered 1868 and afterward

ON THE SAME DAY that the trustees of the College of New Jersey approved the plan for Nassau Hall (Catalog #7), they decided to "also proceed in building a Presidents House & Kitchen..." (Minutes, 22 July 1754). The building was to be frame, but in this instance Robert Smith, who was to design and build the house, was able to utilize his preferred material, brick. The change may have been made in deference to his suggestion.

The house for the president was situated near the main road, forward of the college building, rather like a dependency. Its five-bay, full Georgian plan facade is shown in the Tennent-Dawkins engraving of 1764, which also shows the "pale fence" around its dooryard, valued by Smith at £38 in July 1760.[1] The house

_____

1. Although today a pale fence means one made of boards, in the eighteenth century it could mean a picket fence, as shown in the *Articles of the Carpenters Company of Philadelphia...*, issued in 1786.

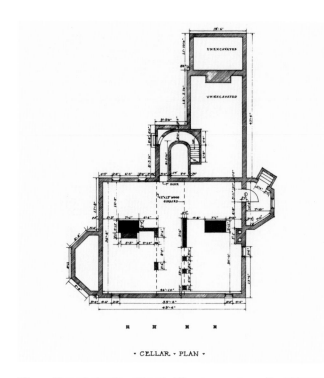

· CELLAR · PLAN ·

The cellar of the President's House preserves Smith's original plan, with chimneys centered on the inner walls of the rooms flanking the central passage. This is an unusual feature in the area, where gable end chimneys, often with back-to-back corner fireplaces, are common. The plan also shows the foundations of the protruding stair hall. The bays and rear service wing are later additions. Historic American Buildings Survey, NJ-88.

was more ornamented than Nassau Hall with a fan-light, pedimented entry, and prominent dentil or modillion cornice. The interior also was elaborated with simple, but well executed, Middle Georgian motifs: an arch in the hallway, a staircase with turned vasiform balusters, and paneling in the main rooms. Altogether, the design demonstrated a flair for the pattern book stylistic details expected in such a structure.

The plan was unusual for central New Jersey, with chimneys rising between the front and back rooms, which were located on either side of the central passage. (Most local buildings had gable-end chimneys, frequently with back-to-back corner fireplaces.) An ingenious feature of the plan is a rear projection, into which the stair extends, thus providing for a more

ample central passage than would be possible in a conventional, rectangular Georgian plan. There also is a door at the south end of the east facade, leading to what was the president's study. Students could enter for a tutorial, or to confer with the president, without disturbing the rest of the household.

Smith's bills to President Burr and the college treasurer for "Building New Jersey College" probably include charges for the house; however, only one bill, paid in December 1758 after Burr's death, mentions the "President's House" specifically. Evidently Aaron Burr paid for some amenities himself. Smith billed him for "Shelves in your Study," as well as for "bringing a marble hearth from Philadelphia."

It is unknown just when the house was finished. Burr is supposed to have moved in around December, dying of malaria in September 1757. His early death was only the beginning of his family's tragedy. In February 1758, his father-in-law, the Rev. Jonathan Edwards (1703-1758) reluctantly succeeded him as president of the College of New Jersey and was installed as its third president. Days later he died from the effects of a smallpox vaccination. His daughter, Burr's widow Esther, died suddenly in April at the age of twenty-six, leaving two small children, Sally and Aaron. While her mother was en route to Princeton to get the children, she, too, died, making the precariousness of life in the eighteenth century all too apparent.

The house built by Smith remained the home of the presidents of the college until 1879, when it became known as the Dean's House. An observer in 1910 deemed it "quite without architectural interest, but happily, also, without architectural pretension or offensiveness, being quite the kind of thing the unambitious builder would naturally adjoin to Nassau Hall, to which it conforms apparently in material, and certainly in color" (Schuyler, 144). Schuyler's judgment was harsh, and his description incorrect; both the materials and color of the two buildings have always differed.

Altered several times, the brick two-and-a-half story house with a rear ell still stands on Nassau Street. In September 1791, the trustees noted that "the kitchen of the President's house is in a ruinous condition," and appropriated $200 for a new one. On the exterior some of Smith's workmanship is obscured by its raised roof, porch, bay windows, and other nineteenth-century additions. But because there were leaks

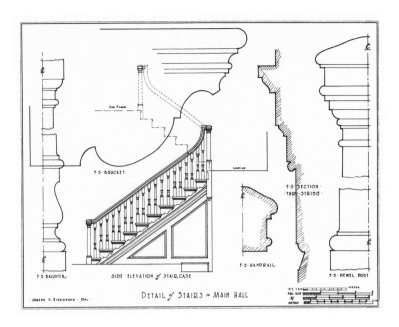

·JOSEPH C. EISENBACH · DEL·   DETAIL of STAIRS ~ MAIN HALL

With the exception of the elaborate woodwork of the Samuel Powel House, the stair, and some paneling in the study and on the second floor are the only remaining examples of the interior trim of one of Smith's domestic commissions. Historic American Buildings Survey, NJ-88.

in the east wall, it was furred and clapboarded at an early date. When the boards were replaced in the late 1960s, their removal revealed pristine Flemish bond brickwork of the highest quality, and an oculus in the gable. And, despite alterations, the interior provides a rare example of the type of woodwork Smith employed for a residential commission.

DOCUMENTATION:

Burr, Esther. *The Journal of Esther Edwards Burr, 1754-1757.* Edited by Carol F. Karlsen and Laurie Crumpacker. New Haven (1984); Gen. Mss. [Misc.]. Manuscripts Division, Dept. of Rare Books and Special Collections, Princeton University Library. Published with permission of PUL; Trustees' Minutes, Princeton University Archives.

REFERENCES:

Norton, Paul. "The President's House." In *Nassau Hall 1756-1956.* Edited by Henry Lyttleton Savage. Princeton (1956), 20-26; Schuyler, Montgomery. "Architecture of American Colleges, III-Princeton," *Architectural Record,* 27 (February 1910): 129-160; Wertenbaker, Thomas Jefferson. *Princeton 1746-1896.* Princeton (1946).

HABS, NJ-88

9

Construct Houses

Princeton, New Jersey
c. 1755-1757, demolished

I T HAS BEEN suggested previously that Robert Smith intended to build on property he owned in Princeton and to move there (Norton 9, n11). Indeed, there can be no doubt that for a time he lived in the town. On 3 January 1757, Esther Burr recorded in her diary that she had visited at the Smiths, where Esther Smith "lays in" (Burr, 237). The child born in Princeton may have been a daughter, Martha. Probably named for Smith's mother, she died shortly after the Smiths returned to Philadelphia (Philadelphia Monthly Meeting Minutes).

Unrecorded and lost deeds make it impossible to fully document Smith's property transactions in Princeton. In 1757, he purchased a lot from Samuel Hazard on the town's main street (now known as Nassau Street). This land lay to the east of the college property, between it and what then was known as Norris's Lane (East Jersey Deeds, A-L:345-351, recorded 2 August 1757). The approximate route of the lane is still marked by a driveway leading south from Nassau Street next to Princeton University's Firestone Library. The property's western boundary may be indicated by the fence at the far left of the Dawkins engraving.

Smith sold the western half of this lot in 1765 to Dr. John Redman, who was acting on behalf of the college. He provided Redman with a sketch map of the property, noting that the eastern portion had been sold to Samuel Hornor, who in turn had conveyed it to Mr. [George] Campbell, who intended to build a tavern (Smith to Redman, 2 January 1764). Either Redman did not turn the deed over to the college or it was lost. Although the deed was dated 1 June 1765, it was not recorded until 29 September 1799 (East Jersey Deeds Liber A-T:395-397). The recording seems to have been part of a concerted effort to document the college's ownership. A few years later, John Redman appeared before the mayor of Philadelphia and affirmed the 1765 transaction. He stated that the property was "near the House built by the said Robert Smith at the corner of the Lane" (Maclean Papers).

It is uncertain, however, whether this was the location of the house the Smiths lived in, for they owned at least one other Princeton property with a house on it. Located on the east side of Norris's Lane, the property is referred to several times in deeds for an adjoining parcel, although no deeds for the conveyance to Smith or for his sale of the property exist (Samuel Hazard to George Campbell, 1 October 1762; Thomas Norris to Richard Paterson, 20 March 1759). The most revealing of these is the Norris to Paterson deed, which mentions "Robert Smith buildings" and "Robert Smith brickhouse."

Throughout his career, Smith attempted to emulate the examples of other Philadelphia master builders—like Samuel Powel I and Samuel Rhoads—who had made their fortunes in real estate. Along with Hazard and others, Smith undoubtedly was convinced that, with the arrival of the college, the hamlet of Princeton would grow, and the value of real estate, improved and unimproved, would increase. The town did not live up to his expectations. Smith turned his attention to Philadelphia, where he bought property on Second Street (Catalog #17). Probably by the 1760s, he had sold both Princeton properties.

The 1757 deed from Samuel Hazard must have been among Smith's papers when he died. His eldest son, John, deeply in debt, either did not know the property had been sold, or chose to ignore it. It must be the property referred to in his letter to "The Gentlemen of the Sitting Committee of the Carpenters Hall Philadelphia," in which he requested a loan because of "the dullness of the times and the scarcity of Circulating Cash." Smith justified his petition by assuring the committee members he would not be in need for long. "I am dealing with a Gentleman for the sale of some property belonging to Me situated in Prince town New Jersey which I expect will be settele'd shortly" (Minutes, CCCCP, 8 January 1804).

On 12 August 1804, John, "carpenter of Philadelphia," and his wife Ann sold this "lot of ground with buildings and improvements" to Josias Ferguson (Middlesex County Deeds 5:824-826). The only problem with this transaction was that the college believed it owned the land (having purchased the western half previously) and that on it was the house occupied by the vice-president of the college, John Maclean, Sr., and his wife. A protracted dispute ensued, finally settled by arbitration in 1807. The Macleans retained their premises, subject to a mortgage held by Ferguson (University Land Transactions).

DOCUMENTATION:

Burr, Esther. *The Journal of Esther Edwards Burr.* Edited by Carol F. Karlsen and Laurie Crumpacker. New Haven (1984); Minutes of the Carpenters' Company of the City and County of Philadelphia [CCCCP], on deposit at the American Philosophical Society; New Jersey Division of Archives and Records Management, Trenton. East Jersey Deeds. Middlesex County Deeds (on microfilm); Papers and Letters of John Maclean. Princeton University Archives; Robert Smith to Dr. John Redman, 2 January 1764. New-York Historical Society; University Land Records (1752-1976) AC-28, Princeton University Archives.

REFERENCES:

Dallett, Francis James. "The Family of Mrs. Robert Smith." *Pennsylvania Genealogical Magazine*, 33, 4 (1964: 307-323; Norton, Paul. "Robert Smith's Nassau Hall and the President's House." In *Nassau Hall, 1756-1956.* Ed. by Henry Lyttleton Savage. Princeton (1956).

10

Construction and Additions at the Burr Farm

Princeton Township, New Jersey
1757-1758

IN 1756, Aaron Burr and his wife bought a farm at public vendue. It was along the King's Highway in what is now Princeton Township, a mile to the east of what then constituted the village of Princeton. Rented to a tenant, it would supplement Burr's salary as president of the college.

Nothing is known of any building activity at the farm before Burr's death in September 1757, but the month afterward Smith began keeping an account of work for Esther Burr, continuing until March 1758, a month before her death. It seems likely that she intended to move to the farm during her widowhood. Among the last items on the account is a charge for two days work by one man, "puting up Bedsteads & Sund." Smith also built a small frame house and kitchen. Possibly this was a tenant house, because when the farm was advertised for sale in 1789 and 1790, the main house was described as stone.

An interesting feature of this invoice is that it gives the names of some of Smith's workmen, which no other document does. They probably came with him from Philadelphia, because only one, Thomas Paterson, bore a local name. The others were: Peter Arthur (a Philadelphia carpenter), Thomas Paterson, Albertus Sacklear, and John Biddale [sic]. During Esther Burr's lifetime, Smith was partially reimbursed in farm products—beef, veal, hay, and timber—again indicating that he probably was living in Princeton. But the Burrs' debts also were paid in cash, £17.0.8 on 28 July 1757 and £46.1.11 on 2 December 1758 (Inventory of estates).

DOCUMENTATION:

Gen Mss. [Misc.]. Manuscripts Division, Dept. of Rare Books and Special Collections, Princeton University Library. Published with permission of PUL; The Rev^d. Mr. Aaron Burr to Robt Smith D^r, [Nd] 1757-March 1758; Aaron and Esther Burr to Jonathan Sergeant. Inventory of estates. Indenture, Abraham Vandorn to Aaron Burr, 1 December 1756.

The Revd. Mr. Aaron Burr.
to Robt. Smith, Dr.

To A Slaw Bank, Stuff, Nails, hinges and work	£2 : 9 : 0
To An Ironeng Board .	7 : 6
To Shelves in your Study - Stuff, Nails, work &c.	1 : 12 : 0
To A Chest of Drawers .	2 : 17 : 6
To A Large Pewter Rack .	1 : 5 : 0
To Crown paper .	11 : 0
To A Looking Glass and packing Case .	4 : 0 : 0
To Cash paid for Bringeng the Glass and a Marble hearth from Philadelphia	8 : 6
To Cash paid for Cleaneng your Watch .	3 : 6
To takeng off the Locks from your Room Doors And putteng on Better .	9 : 0
To A Straineng frame And Black Do. And pasteng several sheets of A Large Map .	1 : 5 : 0
To A Gilded Chain for your Watch .	9 : 0
To Cash paid for Bringeng Bedsteds & hands from Philadelphia .	9
To Cash paid Wm Griffen for pullies for your Jack .	1 : 8
To 13 Square Glass and putting in .	13 : 0

Octr. 1757   Mrs. Esther Burr to Robt. Smith, Dr.

To A floor and Doors over the Waggon House at your farm, Boards 502 feet .	2 : 0 : 2
Novr. 11th To 6½ lb. Nails at 10s. 5/8. Work 16/ .	19 : 8
To 900 feet of Cedar Boards sent to y farm to weather Board the House and Kitchin .	3 : 12 : 0
To Planeng jointeng the Boards. and Beadeng of Do.	12 : 0
To 88 feet of pine Board sent to the farm .	6 : 11
To Nails for weather Boardeng and Shingleng the House and Kitchin 132 lb ad 10½ .	5 : 15 : 0
To 3180 Shingles jointed and Sheaved ad 9 : 10/q pm .	14 : 6 : 3
To 9½ Days work of Peter Arthur ad 5/ .	2 : 7 : 6
To 11½ Days of Thos Paterson ad 5/ .	2 : 17 : 6
To 5½ Days of Albartus Sacklear ad 5/ .	1 : 7 : 6
To 12½ Days of John Biddale ad 5/ .	3 : 2 : 6
To Corner Boseat .	2 : 18 : 0
To Laths to Shingle on. for y House and Kitchin 2900 feet ad 3/9 C .	5 : 8 : 9
Carried over	£62 : 14 : 5

Bro. from the other side £62:14:5

To Cash paid for ½ lb Green tea . . . . . . — — — — — 6:0

March 1758 To 60 feet of Boards Delivered to George Crookshanks 5:0

To 4 Sashes for the farm House at 5/6 Each — 1:2:0

To 6 Small Squares of Glass and puting in at the farm. 4:6

To 2 Tables with Drawers — — — — — — 1:0:0

To Jobs done at the House, puting up Bedsteads & sund.
2 Days work of one man 10:0

£66:1:0

To Cash paid for Geting   pales and Rales
for ye Garden at the farm & they was sold to them   1:5:0

67:6:11

4 4 4

63:2:7

Contra Cr

To one Quarter Beef   16 8
To a Load hay   2 10:
To a Quarter Veal   3
To Pasture part of Last summer
for two Cows
To timber for 1100 pales — — — — — — 14:8

4:4:4

Mr Burr has Charged
to 80 ℔ of Beef at 2d   0=16 8
Load of Hay —   2=10=0

17 = 0 = 8
60 = 0 = 0
77 = 0 = 8
63 = 2 = 7
13 = 18 = 1

This long, running account with Aaron and Esther Burr is evidence of an intimate relationship, or at least a close acquaintanceship. Smith was not only working on various carpentry and building projects for the Burrs. He also was executing commissions or them in Philadelphia, where he may have been charged with obtaining objects he believed they would approve of. Courtesy Division of Manuscripts, Dept. of Rare Books and Special Collections, Princeton University Library. Published with permission of Princeton University Library.

II

Alterations to the New Building,[1]
College of Philadelphia

West side Fourth Street, between Market (High) and Arch
  Streets, Philadelphia
1755; demolished

(See also Catalog #16, Dormitory, and Catalog #51,
House for the Provost)

As previously noted, in the entries for the Second Presbyterian Church (Catalog #2) and Nassau Hall (Catalog #7), the Great Awakening of the 1740s was a starting point for a new view of religion and education. Old beliefs and customs did not vanish, but institutions and affiliations grew up to accommodate those espousing transformed beliefs. English preacher George Whitefield's visit to Philadelphia in November 1739 provoked considerable controversy among clergy and laymen alike. Crowds of several thousand assembled to hear him, and many responded to the religious fervor of his plea for individual communion with God. This threatened the established clergy, and Whitefield was denied access to most pulpits.

Franklin was among those listening to Whitefield's sermon requesting support for an orphanage to be built in Georgia. "I silently resolved he should get nothing from me ... As he proceeded I began to soften ... Another Stroke of his Oratory made me ... give the Silver, and he finish'd so admirably that I empty'd my Pocket wholly into the Collector's Dish, Gold and all" (*Autobiography*, 177).

That was not all Franklin would do to advance Whitefield's causes. He published the evangelist's sermons (S&W, 1:238) and, with others, determined to build a meeting house open to itinerant preachers. By the time Whitefield returned to Philadelphia in April 1740, he was aware of these plans. Progress was

speedy, and on Sunday, November 9th, he "Preached in the morning to several thousand, in a house built since my last departure from Philadelphia. It was never preached in before. The roof is not yet up; but the people raised a convenient pulpit, and boarded the bottom" (Quoted in Montgomery, 26). After the initial support, funding was sporadic and construction lagged. The Rev. Gilbert Tennent and his "New Light" Presbyterian followers were among those using the building, and credit for its completion goes to them (Cheyney, 35).

The New Building was not intended only for religious services. A restriction in the deed specified that the building erected on the property must be used for maintaining a charity school as well as a room for itinerant preachers. When the building's creditors demanded settlement of the accumulated debts in 1747, the trustees petitioned the Assembly for the right to sell the building (Turner, 180). This need meshed with Franklin's vision of establishing an academy for the education of Pennsylvania's young men, an idea he formalized in 1749. With the New Building available, he determined that "Providence threw into our way a large house ready built, which, with a few alterations, might well serve our purpose" (Turner, 179). Franklin was, perhaps, too optimistic, because a later assessment viewed the purchase as acquisition of an "encumbered and incomplete building from an insolvent association, which had also failed in its free schooling project, obligating [the Trustees] in part consideration to carry forth its free preaching and educational features" (Montgomery, 113).

Whatever the complexities of differing missions accompanying the purchase of the New Building, Franklin and his fellow trustees were up to them. They borrowed £800, recorded the deed, and engaged Edmund Woolley and other carpenters to undertake alterations to the building, transforming it into the Academy (Minutes, Vol. 1, 6 February 1750). The New Building itself was probably the work of master-carpenter Woolley, builder of the Pennsylvania State House, another large-scale undertaking. His forty-foot spans in the State House compared with those he probably employed in the New Building. Its dimensions of one hundred feet by seventy feet made it the largest building in the colonies, although Nassau Hall would soon surpass it in size, and it is a loss to architectural historians that there is no record of

---

1. The words "New Building" are used in the Trustees' Minutes of the college and academy to connote two different structures. One is the original academy, which was known colloquially in the 1740s as both the "New Building" and Whitefield Hall, and the other is the dormitory, which was later built to Robert Smith's design. For the sake of clarity, "New Building" is used here only for the earlier structure.

its structural details. Assuming Woolley installed galleries, they would have been relatively narrow, probably fifteen feet, or possibly twenty feet, deep; this left a span of thirty to forty feet which, although large, Woolley was capable of engineering.

Franklin initially thought the building lent itself to division into three floors (*Writings*, 2), but subsequently modified his position and agreed to two floors. It was surveyed as such after alterations, and described as "two stories high...the lower story divided into five Rooms and large passage," with the second story comprising "2 school Rooms in South end [the] floors much worn and plaistering broken...one large Room in the North End with pulpit and seats and Arched Ceiling" (Survey, n.d.). This must be the space Franklin was thinking of when he wrote to the president of King's College [now Columbia] in August 1750, describing "a large hall [reserved] for occasional preaching, public lectures, etc., it is 70 feet by 60, furnished with a handsome pulpit, seats, etc...."

A dated survey (1761) includes mention of the belfry added in 1751, which is visible on the Scull and Heap Prospect of 1754. This feature's existence was noted by New Englander Ezra Stiles in the fall of the same year when he "went up" and remarked on "the rods & wires which defend the Academy House from lightning" ("Diary of Ezra Stiles," 20 September 1754). No doubt Franklin's hand can be seen in the installation of this equipment.

Despite claims of limited resources in the trustees' minutes, they allocated funds from the diminished treasury to complete two important projects—the "Bellfrey (being ready for raising) and the plaistering of the Rooms (some materials being already provided)"—requesting they "that be finished as soon as may be..." (Minutes, Vol. 1, 9 April 1751).

These steps to complete the New Building were undertaken by a team probably familiar with its initial construction. Payments to Woolley, Benjamin Loxley, John Coates, and Nathan Bowley appear in the trustees' Day Books from 1750 through 1755. Even John Thornhill was paid for altering the tables and seats, and sundry payments were made for assorted building materials during the same period. The work of constructing the New Building had been begun before Robert Smith had executed any major commissions. By the time significant alterations to the

The Academy, as it looked before the addition of a new dormitory, was illustrated in Scharf and Westcott's 1884 *History of Philadelphia*. This engraving probably was based on a c. 1770 drawing attributed to Pierre Eugène Du Simitière.

building were required, Smith had established his reputation, and the trustees turned to him.

The academy had grown, and was reorganized into the College of Philadelphia, receiving a charter in 1755. The new status required additional modifications to the building to accommodate differing needs of the students, while still maintaining the charity school and public assembly/preaching space required by the initial deed. Robert Smith was called upon to effect these changes, and the trustees made an agreement with him, detailing the nature of the "proposed work" (Minutes, Vol.1, 11 July 1755). Payments to Smith had already begun, and continued through December 1756, when minutes described the work as finished (Day Book, 3 July 1755-27 December 1756).

How much did Smith do? A memorandum of proposed changes, with an estimate of cost, was recorded in the minutes of 30 June 1755. At that meeting, the trustees authorized an expenditure of £443, "concerning the Alterations necessary to be made in the

Hall." The expenditures for the changes, charged to the "Acct of the Buildings &c to Robert Smith Carpenter," appear in the Day Book, and equal the proposed sum. Smith made "Galleries along three sides of the Hall supported with Columns," constructed a "Platform at the Upper Eve with Rails & Ballustrade," installed "8 large Circular Windows & 6 Square ditto," and plastered the "partition Wall." The galleries were to be "finished like those of Mr. Tenent's [sic] Building [the Second Presbyterian Church], the Fronts painted, and under Side of the Joice [joists] plaistered" (Minutes, Vol. 1, 30 June 1755). This "Gallery round three sides with turned Columns & Ionick Caps [and] Dentile Triglips" is noted in the 1761 insurance survey, and its mention in an otherwise terse document attests to its importance in valuing the building.

Smith also undertook more mundane tasks in upgrading the college; described as "Sundry Jobs" in the Day Book, they included making a new floor, pews and fronts, seats for the galleries, and furnishing a table, chairs, and a desk. For this he was paid £51.17 (Day Book, September 1756). While Smith was fulfilling the terms of his agreements with the Trustees, carpenters Edmund Woolley and John Thornhill also were working on various jobs for the college. The fences and walkways were repaired in 1760, the latter probably by bricklayer Joseph Redman, who, in 1761, was paid to pave a large area around the "Academy" (Day Book, 1760-1761). A student described "this front campus [as] devoted solely to the solemn entrance or joyful exit of the pupils, and no play or pranks were here permitted" (Quoted in Montgomery, 124).

Smith's alterations to the New Building began a working relationship with the college and its trustees that lasted twenty years. Smith produced a "master plan" for the institution and oversaw construction of two additional buildings (Catalog #16 and Catalog #51).

DOCUMENTATION:

Archives of the University of Pennsylvania. Account Book [Ledger], January 16 1749/50-2-December 1779; Day Book Belonging to the Trustees of the Academy, 1749-1779; Insurance Survey [resurvey], n.d. Insurance Survey for Policies 697 and 698, 1 December 1761, Philadelphia Contributionship, HSP; Journal A Belonging to the Trustees of the Academy of Philadelphia Anno 1749, [1749-1764]; Minutes of the

Trustees of the College, Academy and Charitable Schools. Vol. 1, 1749-1768; Franklin, Benjamin. *The Autobiography of Benjamin Franklin.* Ed. by Leonard Labaree et al. New Haven (1964); ———. *The Writings of Benjamin Franklin.* Ed. by Albert H. Smith. Vol. 3. New York (1905); Stiles, Ezra. Notebook of Itineraries. Printed as "Diary of Ezra Stiles." *Proceedings of the Massachusetts Historical Society.* 2nd series, 7 (March 1892): 338-345.

REFERENCES:

Cheyney, Edward Potts. *History of the University of Pennsylvania.* Philadelphia (1940); Montgomery, Thomas Harrison. *A History of the University of Pennsylvania from Its Foundation to AD 1770 . . . .* Philadelphia (1900); Nitzsche, George E. *University of Pennsylvania: Its History, Traditions, Buildings and Memorials.* 6th edition. Philadelphia (1916); S&W, 1 and 2; Turner, William L. "The Charity School, the Academy, and the College." In *HP,* 179-186; Westcott, Thompson. "Old Academy, Fourth Street." In *The Historic Mansions and Buildings of Philadelphia.* Philadelphia (1877), 155-170.

12

Consultation on Construction of Additional Building at Pennsylvania Hospital

Eighth and Pine Streets, Philadelphia
1755

WHILE ROBERT SMITH was busy with Nassau Hall at Princeton, construction of the Pennsylvania Hospital began, under the supervision of Samuel Rhoads, described as the "Undertaker" to whom materials should be delivered (*Pennsylvania Gazette,* 10 July 1755). Late in 1753, Rhoads and Joseph Fox were "desired to prepare plans & to consult with all of the Contributors as are skilled in building, that we may proceed to agreeing upon such manner of contriving the hospital." At the same meeting of the managers, Rhoads laid before them a "plan and elevation of the ground-plot and Elevation of a Hospital" (MBM, 30 November 1754). These may have been some of the designs for Bethlehem Hospital [Bedlam] in London, which had been built to house that city's mentally ill, and which are known to have been consulted in Philadelphia (*Pennsylvania Gazette,* 4 January 1759). Rhoads and Fox also were

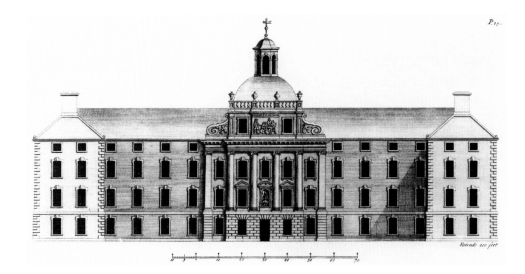

What the managers probably had before them when they were considering a design for the Pennsylvania Hospital was this as yet unbound plate of the Royal Infirmary from William Adam's *Vitruvius Scoticus*.

charged to consult with physicians, and with "all of the contributors who are skilled in building." A month later they showed the board "the several plans and elevation of the Edinburgh Infirmary some parts of which they have taken into their further consideration." (*Pennsylvania Gazette* 22 December 1761). What they undoubtedly saw, given the description of a single elevation but more than one plan, was the engraved plate of Adam's building that later appeared in *Vitruvius Scoticus*. This building also had accommodation for the mentally ill, and it was probably those arrangements that most interested the managers. Study of Bethlehem and the Royal Infirmary constitutes one of the rare occasions when European architectural plans are specifically known to have been consulted for the program of an American building.

Robert Smith was among those "skilled in building," who had contributed funds to the project, along with several other members of the Carpenters' Company, with a gift of £10 (MBM, 33, 165-164). Thus it seems likely that he was among those consulted as the Board of Managers had suggested. As at Nassau Hall, it is tempting to speculate that, based on experience, he suggested study of the Edinburgh Infirmary. On the other hand, many Philadelphians

were familiar with Edinburgh in the eighteenth century; some had studied there. What is certain, however, is that, during the summer of 1755, while construction was well advanced, Smith and William Coleman (a close friend of Benjamin Franklin and member of his "Junto") were asked to comment on a proposal to add "a projection on the South [Pine Street] Side of the Ward" (MBM, 25 August 1755). The managers rejected the proposal when Smith and Coleman reported that "the extension would be no ornament" (MBM 25 September 1755).

Smith already had been associated with Rhoads at the Second Presbyterian Church. Their careers would remain entwined for many years, with both men playing a role at Franklin's House (Catalog #21) and the Walnut Street Jail (Catalog #49).

DOCUMENTATION:

Minutes of the Board of Trustees. Pennsylvania Hospital. Vol. 1 [MBM]; *Pennsylvania Gazette*. 29 May 1755, 4 January 1759, 22 October 1761.

REFERENCES:

Williams, William H. *America's First Hospital: The Pennsylvania Hospital, 1751-1841*. Wayne, PA (1976), 21-25, 157-158.

13

Design and Build Saint Peter's Church

Third and Pine Streets, Philadelphia
1758, tower and spire added 1842

BECAUSE the records of the Second Presbyterian Church (Catalog #2) are not entirely clear about who was responsible for the design of that building, or even what its original appearance was, St. Peter's ranks as the first church documented as entirely Smith's responsibility.

Long before Robert Smith arrived in Philadelphia, some members of Christ Church were commenting unfavorably about overcrowded conditions and the building's remote location north of High [Market] Street. In 1749, the Rev. Richard Peters, Secretary to Governor James Hamilton, wrote to the proprietaries of the need for a new church, assuring them it would be "a chapel of ease to the present church" (Jeffreys, 340). Some time later, this would be a critical point in convincing the rector, the Rev. Robert Jenney, to support the idea. Jenney was not in favor of a new church; he feared the possibility that Christ Church would lose a portion of its congregation to an entirely different parish.

When a group of concerned laymen living in the south end, as Society Hill was known, approached Jenney in March 1753 to request that the issue be brought before the vestry, he made his lack of interest known. Nevertheless, the topic was discussed at the vestry meeting of March 19th, and, despite a lukewarm response, the "Gentlemen from the south end" proceeded (Vestry Minutes; Jeffreys, 342). They pursued acquisition of a parcel of land, and succeeded in convincing Thomas and Richard Penn, who had rejected their Quaker heritage for the Anglican faith, to grant them a plot on the west side of Third Street between Pine and Lombard Streets (Petition, Penn Papers). Subsequently, the vestry added to their holdings by purchasing contiguous parcels (United Congregations, Committee Records, Land Registry).

As soon as the committee received title to the Penn grant in 1757, they began plans for the church building. Robert Smith had designed and built the distinctive steeple for Christ Church in 1753 (Catalog #4). Although he had moved to Princeton for a peri-od to oversee construction of Nassau Hall for the College of New Jersey (Catalog #7), he managed to remain a presence in Philadelphia, making several trips back and forth. (See Catalog #8.) Listed as "absent" from spring and summer meetings of the St. Andrew's Society in 1754, his name appeared on contributors' lists for the Pennsylvania Hospital (Catalog #12) and the Freemason's Lodge (Catalog #5A) the same year. While involved at Princeton, Smith secured the job of altering the New Building belonging to the newly organized College of Philadelphia (Catalog #11), for which he received payments between July 1755 and December 1756. That he may have moved back to the city before the St. Peter's commission is suggested by a directory of Philadelphia Friends, listing Esther Smith, Robert's wife, as a resident of Lombard Street in 1757. So Smith, known to the Christ Church vestry because of the steeple project, probably was living in the south end of town when the decision to build was made.

There is no reason to doubt that he was living in Philadelphia by 5 August 1758, when he signed a lengthy agreement [text below] to build "a Church or House for the Worship of Almighty God." The church was to be located on the east end of the vestry's lot at Third and Pine. It is clear from the contract that Smith was the designer of the building, having submitted "a plan hereunto attached." The contract serves as a detailed description of his design. Unfortunately, no drawings, either for his original design, or for subsequent alterations, survive in the Christ Church Archives.

Construction was to begin immediately and the payment schedule was specified. The projected completion date was November 1759 and, after Smith received the final payment when the building was "finished and painted," he was to be paid a total of £2,310.[1] The start was promising. On 21 September 1758, the *Pennsylvania Gazette* reported that "Last Week . . . the first Stone was laid in the South-east Corner by one of the Wardens of Christ Church," and added the names of those appointed by the vestry to receive subscriptions for the building project. Vestry minutes on 7 February 1759 note alterations

---

1. Smith is sometimes described as "master builder" in the records of the Accounting Warden (25 November 1762). John Palmer, with whom Smith had worked on the Christ Church tower and steeple, was the principal mason (27 June 1760).

to the plan of August 5th, reversing the position of the windows to place the larger ones at the gallery, or second story, level. The building was not finished in November 1759; however, by the following April the building was under roof and a cupola erected, where bells from Christ Church could be installed (Jeffreys, 350). But it was not until a year later, in August 1761, that "the Building Committee reported to the Vestry that the new church was then ready to be opened." At this same vestry meeting, the church received its name (Jeffreys, 351).

The Rev. William Smith, Provost of the College of Philadelphia, delivered the sermon at the formal opening of St. Peter's on 4 September 1761. The event was described in the *Pennsylvania Gazette* six days later and Governor James Hamilton was among the notables present. What sort of building did they see? Two significant interior features, the chancel and reading desk/pulpit, were not completed until 1764, but the church must have been appointed for worship by the opening day. The spacious brick building in which Governor Hamilton, the clergy, vestrymen, parishioners, and guests assembled was remarkably like that described in the contract of August 1758. A rectangle of sixty by ninety feet, the interior was organized around a basic three-aisle plan, with gallery seating along the north and south walls and possibly on the west wall on either side of the base of the tower. The cupola at the west end was supported by a brick base within the building; by 1764 this was paneled on three sides and housed the reading desk/pulpit.

As at Christ Church in Southwark, London, a large Palladian window over the altar was a dominant feature both inside and out. (See the Introduction for possible sources of St. Peter's). Other similarities in the east wall were the oculus punctuating the gable, and the two round-headed windows in the upper story. However, the London church had doors in the east wall, a feature replaced by windows in the Philadelphia building. Smith's design placed pedimented doors on the ends of the north and south walls. But both churches had larger arched windows in the upper story, with smaller ones below; windows at both levels ornamented with moldings, keystones and brackets; and bold "Rustick work" or quoins at the corners.

The five urns called for in the contract were never installed, but another detail of the agreement is worth noting: "That the Roof of the said Building shall be Truss'd well framed and bound with Iron." This is the first proven instance in which Smith utilized a variation of the truss with raised tie beam illustrated in Francis Price's *The British Carpenter*.

Smith may have relied on a pattern book for interior details. St. Peter's distinctive reading desk and pulpit were built between 1763 and 1764, when vestry minutes recorded their completion and receipt of Smith's bill. The pulpit resembles models illustrated in Batty Langley's *Treasury of Designs*, a book Smith owned in 1751 (Richards, 126). But it is the pulpit's placement, rather than its design, that has prompted much discussion. It is situated at the west end of the church, opposite the chancel, requiring the minister to walk the length of the aisle to deliver the sermon. Many reasons for this have been advanced: the political (favoring public rhetoric), the liturgical (note the popularity of Morning Prayer rather than Communion in the eighteenth century); and the architectural design, including Smith's method, new to Philadelphia, of concealing the base of the tower, which stood squarely against the west wall. Perhaps, the rationale for this pulpit placement at St. Peter's will never be known. It does, however, conform to a type of plan which existed in the eighteenth century. (Six distinctive plans are described by James F. White in his 1964 book *Protestant Worship and Church Architecture: Theological and Historical Considerations*. This east/west placement was the sixth and least popular type; nevertheless it was a type.)

When Smith presented his bill for building the pulpit in April 1764, there was no money to pay him, nor had there been sufficient funds to cover some of his prior bills; he also requested payment of money already owed. Church financial records and vestry minutes do not contain a comprehensive building account, which makes it difficult to assign specific charges. What is apparent is that the cost of the church exceeded the £3500 raised by subscription (Jeffreys, 42). By March 1763, a total of £4765.19.6 1/2 had been spent, but this amount included costs associated with purchase of the land. It was noted that the building committee "expended out of their own pockets" the £1200 difference, which was recorded as a debt.

Smith resubmitted his bill of £285.13 for the reading desk/pulpit and chancel rails in June 1764, but it

William L. Breton produced this lithograph of St. Peter's in 1828, before the west tower was added. There are many resemblances between it and Christ Church, Southwark, including the design and placement of the windows. Like Christ Church, St. Peter's could be entered from the side, although it has two doors rather than one. Historical Society of Pennsylvania.

was not until October that a partial payment of £100 was authorized (Vestry Minutes, 13 June and 30 October 1764). Three months later, St. Peter's debt was calculated at £1500. The increase was attributed to a rise in the costs of materials and labor. A lottery was proposed.

On 4 February 1765, "An Act for raising [funds] by way of lottery" was read to the Provincial Council; the bill had been "sent up by the House last week" and was returned to the House for action ("Minutes of the Provincial Council"). The lottery was authorized, but larger political and financial con-

cerns, such as the Stamp Act and Non-Importation Agreement, doomed it to failure.

In June 1768, Smith was still requesting payment, but the accounts were not settled until 1771, thirteen years after the cornerstone was laid[2] (Vestry Minutes, 21 June 1768; Jeffreys, 47). This pattern of drawn-out financial settlements plagued Smith throughout his building career and, because most of his under-

___

2. In 1771 Smith was called upon to make repairs to Christ Church Steeple. Records of the Accounting Warden do not specify the project for which Smith was being paid. Periodic payments of £50 continue into 1772.

Christ Church, Southwark, London, as illustrated opposite page 156 in Thomas H. Shepherd, *London and Environs in the Nineteenth Century*, published in 1829. St. Peter's bears a strong resemblance to this church, designed by James Horne and built between 1738 and 1741. Both owe the essentials of their design to James Gibbs's Marylebone Chapel.

The elevation of the east end of Christ Church indicates that St. Peter's was not an exact copy. The design of the American building omitted the doors in the east facade, but added one at the east end of the building's sides, and made the Palladian window even more prominent. This engraving of the east end of the interior of Christ Church, Southwark is somewhat deceptive. The building did not have a three-aisle plan, but rather *faux* vaulting supported by consoles. Like St. Peter's, it had a sixty-foot clear-span ceiling, but in this case flat and supported by an iron-reinforced king post truss. By this time iron-reinforced trusses were common in England. King's Maps, xxvii, a-g, British Library.

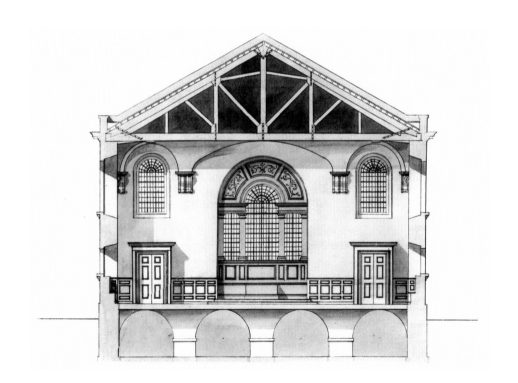

takings were large scale projects, made settlement of his estate an equally prolonged ordeal.

As a "chapel of ease" for the great Christ Church, St. Peter's was not intended as an architectural rival, but had to possess a measure of stylistic clout. Ornamental details derived from newly available pattern books provided the necessary ingredients, and were combined by Smith in a pleasing manner. The result was a simple, but beautiful church, intensely pleasing in its proportions and the quality of the interior light.

ARTICLES of Agreement Indented and made Concluded and fully agreed upon by and between John Kearsley Evan Morgan Jacob Duchee [sic, Sr.] James Child Redmond Conyngham Alexander Stedman Attwood Shute Samuel McCall junr John Willcocks Jospeh Sims and William Plumsted of the City of Philadelphia Gentlemen a Committee of the Vestry of Christ Church in the said City of the one part and Robert Smith of the same city House Carpenter of the other part in manner and form following that is to say, First the said Robert Smith in Consideration of the Covenants promises payments and agreements herein after mentioned on· the part of the said Robert Smith to be performed made fulfill'd and kept for himself his Heirs Executors and Administrators doth Covenant promise and Agree to and with the said John Kearsley Evan Morgan Jacob Duchee James Child Redmond Conyngham Alexander Stedman Attwood Shute Samuel McCall junr John Willcocks Joseph Sims and William Plumsted and each of them their and each of the Heirs Execurs & Adminrs That he the said Robert Smith shall and will with all Convenient Speed Erect Build and in a Workman like manner Substantially Build or Cause to be built on the East End of a Certain Lott of Land lately given for that purpose by the Honble the Proprietories in the said City bounded on Pine Street and third street of said City, a Church or House for the Worship of Almighty God according to the Rites and Ceremonies of the Church of England of the Dimensions and form following, that is to say, of the Length of Ninety feet above the Base or Water Table and of the Breadth of Sixty feet above the Base also that the Foundation of the same Building shall be Stone and Mortar four feet below the present Surface of the Earth That the Bottom or lower part of the said Stone Foundation shall be three feet in Thickness and at the top thereof two feet three Inches thick That the walls above the said Foundation shall be Thirty Seven feet high and composed of good Merchantable Brick and Mortar and to be two Bricks & a half or twenty one Inches thick in the sides of the said Building and Gable Ends or Walls in the pediments above the Square to be one Brick and a half or fourteen Inches thick and to be Carryed up or raised as high as the top of the Roof, That there shall be Rustick Work on each Corner of the said Building to be made of Stock Bricks properly Moulded for that purpose That a Margin shall be made of the said Stock Bricks round each Window of the said Building To Project before the face of the Walls That there shall be in the South and North sides of the said Building two Doors Twelve feet high and five feet wide opposite to each other with Frontispieces That there shall be in the South and North Sides aforesaid large Circular headed Windows below or in the first Story and five Smaller Circular headed Windows above so in the Second Story That the Window Cases and Sashes are to be made are to be made [sic] by the said Smith Independent of the Brick Work That the Sash lights shall be made of Sound two Inch heart of pine plank, and the said Smith shall find and provide good English Glass for the same Sash of Ten by fourteen Inches each pane That in the East End of the Said Building there shall be two large Circular headed windows below or in the first Story with One large Venetian Window neatly finished on the outside that in the same East End there shall be two Smaller Circular headed Windows above or in the Second Story with one Round Window in the Pedement [sic], That in the West End of the said Building there shall be Three large Circular headed Windows below or in the first story and three smaller Circular headed Windows above in the Second Story That there shall be a Cupola Erected and Compleately [sic] finished on the West End of the said Building of Ten feet Diameter and at least Thirty two feet high from the Top of the Roof to the Top of the Vane, that the said Smith shall provide and fix thereon a large ball & vane composed of Copper and to be neatly Gilt That there shall be a large Modillion Cornice to the Eves and round the said Building and five large Urns properly placed & fixed at the Corners & tops of one Pedement at the Ends of the sd Building That the Roof of the said Building shall be Truss'd well framed and bound with Iron That the frame of a Circular Ceiling shall be made and fixed under the Roof ready for the Plaisterer to lath and plaister on together with a large Cornice under the Spring of the Arch for the Circular Ceiling, That there shall be two Stone steps to each of the four doors or more Stone Steps if Necessary That there shall be a Stone Window Stool to each of the Windows to Set the Frames upon with a Moulding on the outer side to project over the Walls to Carry the Water off, That there shall be Key Stones & imposts or Blocks of Stone to the Arch of each Window and the said Robert Smith doth Covenant for himself his Heirs Execurs & Admnrs to and with the sd John Kearsley Evan Morgan Jacob Duchee James Child Redmond Conyngham Alexander Stedman Attwood Shute Samuel McCall junr John Willcocks Joseph Sims and Wm Plumsted and each of them their and each of their Heirs Executors and Admrs by these presents That he the said Robert Smith his Heirs Exrs & Admrs or some or one of them shall and will at his and their own proper Costs and Charges, purchase find & provide all and every the Materials, to wit, Stones Bricks Lime Sand Timber Scantling plank boards, Iron and Smith Work Lead, Copper Nails Shingles and Glass and every Material Necessary for the Erecting Building and in Manner aforesaid Compleatly finishing the Building or House together with all Workmen Artificers and Labourers for doing and performing the same agreeable to the plan thereof hereunto annexed and shall and will at his own proper Costs and Charges paint or cause the whole outside work aforesd to be painted and well finished with three different Coats of paint of a good stone Colour well laid on And if That the said Robert Smith his Executors or Admnrs shall Cause or procure the sd Building to be Erected and finished in manner aforesd and as near agreeable to the hereto annexed plan asmay [sic] be on or before the first day of November which will be in the Year of our Lord One Thousand and Seven Hundred & fifty nine And the sd John Kearsley Evan Morgan Jacob Duchee James Child Redmond Conyngham Alexr Stedman Attwood Shute Saml McCall junr John Willcocks Joseph Sims and William Plumsted for themselves their Heirs Execurs & Admrs in Consideration of the premises do hereby Covenant promise and agree to and with the said Robert Smith his Heirs Exrs & Admrs in manner following That is to say That they the said John Kearsley Evan Morgan Jacob Duchee James Child Redmond Conyngham Alexander Stedman Attwood Shute Saml McCall junr John Willcocks Joseph Sims and William Plumsted their Heirs Exrs & Admrs or some or one of them shall & will well and truly pay or Cause to be paid to the said Robert Smith his Heirs Exrs & Admrs the Just & full Sum of Two Thousand three Hundred and Ten pounds lawful money of Pennsylvania at the days and times and in the proportions hereinafter mentioned for payment thereof, that is to say the Sum of one Hundred pounds Money aforesd on the first day of September next or when the said Robert Smith shall begin to lay the Foundation for the Building aforesd And the Sum of One Hundred Pounds of the first day of October next, the further sum of One Hundred Pounds on the first day of December next and the further Sum of One Hundred Pounds on the first day of May next and the Sum of One Hundred and Seventy Pounds when and so soon as the Masons begin to lay Bricks, the further Sum of One Hundred and Seventy Pounds when so soon as the Brick Work of the said Building all around shall be Six feet high, the further Sum of One Hundred and Seventy Pounds when and so soon as the Brick work aforesd all around shall be Twelve feet high the further Sum of One Hundred and Seventy Pounds when & so Soon as the Brick work afod [sic] all around shall be Eighteen feet high the further Sum of One Hundred and Seventy Pounds when so soon as the Brick Work aforesd all around shall be Twenty four feet high, The further Sum of One Hundred and Seventy Pounds when and so soon as the Brick Work aforesd all around shall be thirty feet high the further Sum of One Hundred & Seventy Pounds when and so soon as the Brick Work afsd all around shall be Thirty Seven feet high the further Sum of One Hundred Pounds when the Roof & Cupola are raised. The further Sum of One Hundred Pounds when the Roof is Shingled inn & the Cupola finished, The further Sum of Two Hundred pounds when the Windows are all Glazed

Fixed and put in and the Residue thereof, to wit the Sum of Three Hundred and Twenty Pounds when the Building aforesaid and [sheet torn] agreement herein before Mentioned and as near as may be to the plan hereunto annexed is Compleatly finished & painted and Lastly the said Robert Smith for himself his Exrs & Admrs doth promise to and with the sd Committee from time to time hereafter to be under the Direction and Instruction of the said Committee touching & Concerning the sd Premises, for the true performance whereof the said parties do Bind themselves their Heirs Execurs and Admrs each to the other in the penal Sum of Four Thousand Pounds money aforesaid. IN TESTIMONY whereof the partys [sic] to these presents have interchangeably set their Hands & Seals the fifth day of August In the Year of Our Lord One Thousand Seven Hundred & fifty Eight. It is agreed that the scaffolds be keept [sic] up for the use of the Plaisterer.

Robt Smith

DOCUMENTATION:

Christ Church Archives. Vestry of Christ Church. Accounting Warden's Journals. Minutes, 1717-1761; Vestry of United Congregations. Minutes, Committee Records and Correspondence, 1761-1834; Penn Papers. Petition, Philadelphia Land Grants, 7:109. HSP; "Minutes of the Provincial Council." *Pennsylvania Archives.* First Series, 9. Harrisburg (1852); *Pennsylvania Gazette.* 21 September 1758, 10 September 1761.

REFERENCES:

"Bankside (The Parishes of St. Saviour and Christ Church, Southwark)." Vol. 22 in *Survey of London.* London (1950); Bowers, Robert Woodger. *Sketches of Southwark Old and New.* London (1905); Dorr, Benjamin. *An Historical Account of Christ Church, Philadelphia: from its Foundation, A.D.1695, to A.D.1841.* New York (1841); Faris; Friedman, Terry. Chapter XI in *James Gibbs.* New Haven (1984); Garvan, Beatrice B. "St. Peter's Church." In *Philadelphia: Three Centuries of American Art.* Philadelphia (1976); Gough, Deborah Mathias. *Christ Church, Philadelphia.* Philadelphia (1995), 43-109; Jackson, Joseph. "Robert Smith." In *Early Philadelphia Architects and Engineers,* Part 2. Philadelphia (1923); Jeffreys, C.P.B. "The Provincial and Revolutionary History of St. Peter's Church, Philadelphia, 1753-1783." *PMHB,* 47 (1923): 328-356 and 48 (1924):39-65, 181-192, 251-269, 354-371; *The Rules of Work of the Carpenters' Company of the City and County of Philadelphia, 1786.* Ed. by Charles E. Peterson. Princeton, NJ (1971); Shoemaker, Robert W. "Christ Church, St. Peter's, and St. Paul's." In *HP,* 187-198; S&W, 2: 134; Yeomans, David T. "British and American Solutions to a Roofing Problem," *Journal of the Society of Architectural Historians.* 50 (September 1991): 266-272; ———. *The Trussed Roof: its history and development.* Aldershot, England, and Brookfield, VT (1992).

"A Celebration: St. Peter's Church Restoration, National Historic Landmark Designation, St. Peter's House Renovation." 20 October 1996; Hammond, Joseph W. "Timber Framing Engineering of Robert Smith: Leading Builder/Architect of Colonial America." Paper presented at Robert Smith's Birthday, Philadelphia, 14 January 1995 and annual APT/DVC symposium on Historic Timber Framing, Philadelphia, 2 March 1996; Richards, Frederick Lee, Jr. "Old St. Peter's Protestant Episcopal Church, Philadelphia: An Architectural History and Inventory (1758-1991)." Unpublished Masters Thesis, University of Pennsylvania, 1991.

Richards, Frederick L., Jr. "St. Peter's Church." National Historic Landmark Nomination, July 1994; HABS, PA-1118.

14

Build St. Paul's Church and Design Roof, Exterior Woodwork and Interior

225 South Third Street, Philadelphia
1760, altered 1823, 1830, 1842 and 1904, renovated 1983-1986

WHILE WORKING on St. Peter's, Robert Smith was given the opportunity of building and designing the roof and interior of a second Anglican church. Remnants of the evangelical enthusiasm engendered by the Great Awakening were evident in the preaching of the Rev. William McClenachan, a Church of England convert from Presbyterianism. McClenachan was sent to the colonies in the late 1750s as a missionary from the Venerable Society for the Propagation of the Gospel in Foreign Parts, and briefly served as an assistant to the Rev. Dr. Jenney, rector of Philadelphia's Christ Church (S&W, 2:1348). There he attracted a loyal following, causing some dissension among parishioners not keen on his style, and earning the disapproval of the rector for his "railings and revilings in the Pulpit" (Shoemaker, 191).

At the same time, the Christ Church vestry was accommodating the needs of church members by finishing construction of St. Peter's as a "chapel of ease" at Third and Pine Streets. Building was underway when McClenachan stormed out of a convocation of clergy held in Philadelphia in April 1760. The rift among parishioners at Christ Church could no longer be ignored. On 22 June 1760, McClenachan conducted a worship service on the steps of the State House, where attendance was estimated at three thousand; this show of interest and support was enough for his followers, who, a few days later, decided to build their own church and make it the same dimensions as St. Peter's (Barratt, 45; Vestry Minutes, 7 July 1760).

Master mason John Palmer—with whom Robert Smith had worked at Bush Hill (Catalog #1), Second Presbyterian Church (Catalog #2), and the Christ Church tower (Catalog #4)—was a trustee of the proposed church, and on July 7th was appointed to the "Committee to purchase the Necessary Materials for building the Church and agreeing with the Workmen." He was also charged with preparing "a Plan of the Church" (Vestry Minutes). Two weeks later, the building was extended to "sixty five Feet Wide," and Palmer produced a plan, presumably to the revised specifications, which was agreed upon (Vestry Minutes, 1, 21 July 1760). Predictably, discussion about the roof followed. On August 4th, "Mr. Robt Smith, Carpenter [was present and] it was mutually agreed betwixt him and the Trustees that he should finish the Roof Doors and Windows of the Church and that he should be paid for the same according to the Estimation of two indifferent Carpenters the one to be chosen by him and the other by the Trustees when the Work was finished" (Vestry Minutes, 4 August 1760).

It is probable that St. Paul's trustees had looked at the roof of St. Peter's, and were convinced of the soundness of the trusses. By the spring of 1760, construction there had proceeded to such a point that bells from Christ Church were installed; therefore, the roof was in place. Smith's adaptation of the raised tie beam truss design published in Francis Price's *The British Carpenter* spanned sixty feet at St. Peter's, and the additional five feet at St. Paul's probably required only slight modifications. Surviving physical evidence shows a center joint almost identical to that at St. Peter's, and the metal work, including iron straps, is of the type used in the eighteenth century (Keast & Hood Co., 1985; Pentz, January 1999). One of the benefits of this particular type of truss was that it permitted installation of an arched ceiling, like that at St. Peter's, and the presence of the raised tie beam truss suggests a similar ceiling for St. Paul's. Indeed, an old photograph of the interior shows an arched ceiling (Barratt, op. 157).

At the end of February 1761, the trustees appointed a committee "to wait on Mr. Smith [and] request him to assist them in Planing [sic] the inside Work of the Church" (Vestry Minutes, 21 February 1761). Exactly what Smith did is unknown because there are no surviving documents, beyond notations in the vestry minutes describing the appearance of the building in the eighteenth century. It is most probable he was responsible for constructing the galleries, pews, chancel rails, and all interior moldings, with the exception of the pulpit, which was to be "made of Mahoggany" by Mr. Claypoole (Vestry Minutes, 13 September 1761). Claypoole was not the only other master carpenter on the job. William Dilworth, a member of the Carpenters' Company, kept detailed work records, which document his service as supervising master at St. Paul's (Moss, 152).

That the church was to be a three-aisle plan was recorded in the minutes in August 1760, but there is no general description of the architectural scheme to be gleaned from the written record. However, the minutes of August 1761 contain two interesting tidbits: "last month the Roof of our Church was raised and we hope by November next it will be so far finished as to admit Divine Service to be performed therein," and it was "Order'd that Mr. Smith prepare a Bill of Scantling for to erect a hansome [sic] Cupola to St. Paul's Church to be carried on Early in the Spring" (Vestry Minutes, 15 and 31 August 1761). The cupola was never mentioned again, but the building was "so far finished" by the Sunday before Christmas that services were held. The interior must have been somewhat crude because plastering and painting had not begun; however, a Palladian window was a focal point on the east wall and five round-arched windows on the north and south walls admitted light to the gallery level. Five other window openings on each of these walls marked the main story, and it is assumed they, too, had "circular heads," because that is how all the windows were described in the 1823 insurance survey.

The enthusiasm that accompanied the founding of St. Paul's generated a substantial initial subscription toward the building. These funds financed the raising of the walls, but little more. Two lotteries, one in 1760, and the other a year later, were authorized to help defray expenses and pay for additional work, but financial woes continued to affect progress (Watson, 2:443-444). There are no surviving account books documenting what or when Smith or other craftsmen were paid for their work.

The brick building of the 1760s has been significantly altered. Minutes of 1762 boasted of its "seat-

St. Paul's Church maintains its original form, mass, and fenestration, but was redone in Greek Revival style and later was gutted to serve an adaptive use. Episcopal Community Services.

ings for near 1000," making St. Paul's "the largest [church] in the province," and the source of much pride for its parishioners (Vestry Minutes, 21 June 1762; S&W, 2:1348). The congregation maintained its revivalist tone and continued to expand in the nineteenth century, becoming a leader in church sponsored outreach ministries. The first Episcopal Sunday School in the United States began at St. Paul's in 1816, and it was activities such as this that demanded alterations to the building. Modifications in the 1830s were made by William Strickland and Thomas U. Walter, and provided not only a completely revamped interior but also a new facade. Alterations continued until the parish began to lose members after the Civil War, as changes in residential patterns reconfigured the neighborhood. In 1904, St. Paul's became the home of Episcopal Community Services. Although the building today does not appear to show the hand of Robert Smith, his signature roof design, agreed to in 1760, and strengthened fifty years later to support slate, has survived.

DOCUMENTATION:

Insurance Survey, 4 October 1823. Philadelphia Contributionship. HSP; Thomas Nevell. Day Book (1762-1782). Wetherill Papers, Division of Special Collections, Van Pelt Library, University of Pennsylvania; *Pennsylvania Gazette*, 30 April 1767; Record Book of St. Paul's Church. Vestry Minutes Vol. 1, July 5, 1760-April 23, 1864. Transcription at the Genealogical Society of Pennsylvania, Philadelphia; Thomas Ustick Walter Papers, The Athenæum of Philadelphia.

REFERENCES:

Barratt, Norris S. *Outline of the History of Old St. Paul's Church*. Philadelphia (1917); Faris; Jeffreys, C.P.B. "The Provincial and Revolutionary History of St. Peter's Church, Philadelphia, 1753-1783," *PMHB*, 48 (1924): 61; Mease, James. *The Picture of Philadelphia....* Philadelphia (1811), 218; Moss, Roger W. *Master Builders: A History of the Colonial Philadelphia Building Trades*. Ann Arbor (1972); S&W, 1:255 and 1761, 2:1348; Shoemaker, Robert W. "Christ Church, St. Peter's and St. Paul's." In *HP*; Watson, (1927).

HABS, PA-1475; Keast & Hood Co. "St. Paul's Field Survey 7/26/85." Peterson Files; John Milner Associates. "A Preliminary Historic Structure Report for Old St. Paul's Church and The Bishop Stevens House," February 1981, Peterson Files; Pentz, Suzanne. Conversation with Maria Thompson. 19 January 1999.

15

Design (not executed) for Steeple for Second Presbyterian Church

Northwest corner Third and Arch Streets, Philadelphia
1761, taken down 1802

WHEN THE COMMITTEE appointed in 1749/50 to purchase a lot and oversee construction of a church envisioned their meeting house at the corner of Third and Arch Streets, they thought of it with a steeple. A plan must have been in the works because the 1754 Scull and Heap "East Prospect" of Philadelphia depicts the steeple marked with the number "4" and identified as "Presbyterian Church," but the profile bears only passing resemblance to the one shown in the 1799 Birch view, "Arch Street with the Second Presbyterian Church." What happened? Minutes of the Congregation and other documentary evidence indicate that the steeple was not built as planned in the 1750s.

After principal financial support for the church was secured, and the main block of the church completed, the committee regulating pews and management of the "Affairs of the Steeple" convened in April 1753. They made the decision to proceed, and, in January 1754, committee members were requested to collect outstanding subscription commitments for the steeple account. Based on the response, the mason, John Palmer, was asked to finish the brick and stone work of the tower "this summer," and, in July 1754, the committee borrowed one hundred pounds "to carry on the design of the Steeple," authorizing Palmer to "carry the Steeple up to its full Heights" (Minutes of the Congregation, 25 June and 2 July 1754). The tower, along with the wooden steeple that was not built, probably were part of the original design for the building. The record implies that Palmer finished the masonry tower, and there it sat. If so, it must have been roofed over, although there is no record of this.

In 1761, the steeple project was revitalized. The congregation wished to acquire a bell, which required construction of a wooden belfry atop the tower. Thomas Nevell, an elder of the church, who eventually built the steeple, was appointed to evaluate conditions of the steeples of the State House and Christ Church and make recommendations to the trustees (Minutes of the Congregation, 3 February 1761). A committee was appointed "to wait on Robert Smith Carpenter for a plan for the Steeple & to know upon what terms he will undertake & finish the Same" (Minutes of the Congregation, 17 September 1761). Builder Gunning Bedford and Doctor John Redman (1722-1808) were members of the committee. Both men had been involved with Second Church and Robert Smith from the beginning, with Bedford and Smith doing the carpentry. Redman was a trustee of the church, and by 1761 also had become a trustee of the College of New Jersey (Catalog #7 and #9). Smith probably had designed an earlier version of the steeple; calling him back suggests satisfaction with his work.

The congregation began acquiring construction materials for the steeple even before Smith was asked for the plan in September. The March minutes noted an outstanding balance due "for scantling for ye use of the Steeple" and the following month a lottery was drawn "in Masters' store, on Market-street wharf" (Minutes of the Congregation, 30 March 1761); Watson (1927), 2:445. There is no record of the lottery's outcome, but it must have succeeded because the project went forward. A new committee was chosen November 9th, with Redman and Bedford joined by five others. It is unclear whether or not Smith ever furnished a plan. He received no payments and presented no bills.

Furthermore, documentation shows that the steeple job went to someone else. Thomas Nevell (1721-1797) received a cash payment of forty pounds from the Committee of the New Presbyterian Church Steeple on 21 August 1762 and payments to him continued through November 1763 (Thomas Nevell Day Book).[1] The project evidently was not completed until 1769, when Nevell received payment for three thousand bricks, and spandrels and molding for a clock (Watson [1830], 392; Nevell Day Book, 5 May and 29 August 1769). Nevell's steeple was old-fashioned compared to the one Smith had designed a decade earlier. Rather than drawing inspiration from Gibbs and Adam, Nevell seem to have turned back to Sir Christopher Wren (1632-1723). The "wedding cake" layering of the Second Presbyterian Church resembled Wren's 1702 spire for St. Bride, Fleet Street.

Sometime during the prolonged period of the steeple's construction, a wag popularized a satirical couplet:

> The Presbyterians built a church,
> And fain would have a steeple;
> We think it may become the church,
> But not become the people.

Perhaps Smith would have been a more fortunate choice than Nevell. Of Philadelphia's three pre-Revolutionary steeples (the others being at the State House and Christ Church), only Smith's Christ Church steeple has survived. The Second Presbyterian Church steeple failed and was taken down in 1802.

DOCUMENTATION:

Presbyterian Historical Society. Second Presbyterian Church. Minutes of the Congregation, 1 (1749-1772). Typescript; Hazard, Samuel. "Notes Respecting Second Church" Minutes of the Congregation, 9 April 1753-6 November 1763; Hazard, Samuel. Letter Book, ca. 1749. Mss. [bound] Collections, Princeton University Library; Thomas Nevell Day

Book, 1762-1782. Wetherill Papers. Division of Special Collections, Van Pelt Library, University of Pennsylvania.

REFERENCES:

Watson (1830); Watson (1927).

16

Design and Build a Dormitory for the College of Philadelphia

West side Fourth Street, between Market (High) and Arch Streets, Philadelphia
1761

(See also Alterations to the New Building, Catalog #11, and House for the Provost, Catalog #51)

So SUCCESSFUL was the College of Philadelphia, that by 1761 it was obvious that there was a need for additional student housing. Enrollees were coming from the city, the surrounding countryside, and neighboring colonies. A few even hailed from more distant colonies and the Caribbean islands (Montgomery, 354).

The college, its academic pursuits, and related student housing requirements, were not the only activities on campus. Deed restrictions accompanying the original property transfer had stipulated provisions for a charity school, as well as space for itinerant preachers. The success of the college combined with these needs to create overcrowded conditions, propelling the trustees into action.

It was perhaps natural that the trustees would turn to Robert Smith, with his experience at Nassau Hall, for the design of a dormitory. In March 1761, the trustees "considered whether it might not be better to have some additional Buildings erected...that might hold a number of the Scholars...and put them upon a Collegiate way of living, as is done in the Jersey and New York Colleges [Kings College, later Columbia]" (Minutes, 10 March 1761). The mention of Jersey suggests that they may already have decided to call on Smith.

Various schemes for funding the building project, ranging from lotteries to a direct appeal to the pub-

---

1. The existence of this document has made it possible to attribute other jobs, such as Mount Pleasant, to Nevell. Unfortunately, no comparable account books or papers survive for Robert Smith, making it very likely that he has been denied credit for projects in Philadelphia and elsewhere.

lic, were discussed and in November the trustees decided "to engage some proper person to go over to England . . . in order to sollicit [sic] the Benevolence of the Good People of Great Britain" in furthering their plans for "Lodging and Superintending the Morals of the Students" (Minutes, 28 November 1761). They agreed "that Dr. [William] Smith was the properest Person" to undertake the fund raising mission and the provost left Philadelphia in January 1762 (Montgomery, 358). When he returned in June 1764, the dormitory was finished, built according to the plan of Robert Smith.[1]

Exactly when Smith was called upon to submit a plan is not recorded in the Trustees' Minutes. However, it is apparent he was asked to devise a master plan for the institution early in 1761, possibly after the March 10th meeting. When the Trustees met the following month, they referred to "a Sett of Buildings for the Lodging and Dieting [of] a Number of Students," and, after their deliberations about financing, agreed in November "to go on in the ensuing Summer with one half of the Buildings contained in the Plan formerly given to us by Mr. Robert Smith" (Minutes, 14 April and 28 November 1761). Smith had proposed two rectangular buildings flanking the New Building or Academy, then housing the college, to form a courtyard facing Fourth Street. The trustees, however, decided to build only one, thus eliminating the classical symmetry Smith had sought in his original plan for the campus.

Having committed themselves to the project, but to a single building, the trustees debated the relative merits of positioning the dormitory to the north or south of the original building. On 12 April 1762, they resolved the issue, deciding "on Account of the South Exposure" to keep "clear the South Door" and place the buildings "at the North End of the Square" (Minutes). Although only one large building was constructed, it is continuously referred to in college records as the "buildings." Perhaps this is because the structure served both the college and the charity school, or because their deliberations always included the old New Building.

Built of brick and three stories high, the dormitory's most conspicuous ornament was its array of evenly spaced multi-paned rectangular windows, which marched along the facade and offered a contrast to the round-headed windows of the earlier building. It was divided into three sections by some means, either a slight projection, or perhaps plain brick pilasters. There were two entries toward the ends of the building with rather unadorned doorways. The end facing the street was somewhat more elaborate than the longer facade. The interior levels were marked by belt courses and the return of the strong cornice created a pedimental gable with a bull's-eye window at its center. Three prominent chimneys punctuated the roof line. The dormitory and college are shown in a contemporary drawing, in which the relative massing of the two buildings reveals the dominance of the earlier structure, although this would not have been the case if both the buildings suggested by Smith had been constructed.

When an estimate was made of the cost of the building in 1761, it was specified that it would be "70 feet long by 30 feet wide and will have on the Ground Floor two Charity Schools, with a Kitchen and a Dining Room, and in the upper stories Sixteen Lodging Rooms, with a cellar beneath the whole" (Minutes, 28 November 1761). This was more or less the arrangement of the building as built, as Samuel Wetherill, Jr., recorded it when he surveyed the dormitory in 1765.

The Lower Story [is] Divided In four parts by 9 Inch Brick partitions A Kitchen at one End A School [classroom] at the Other & two Dining Rooms Between with a pantry to Each partition'd of[f] with plan'd bord, the Second & third Storys, Eight Rooms on a floor, 9 Inch Brick partition Cross ways of the Building & plaistered Bord partition Length way Two Dogleg Stair-Cases and All the Rooms sirbace and Washbord A Chimney in Each Room the Garret Not plaistered and at one End a Small Room partition'd of[f] with Plan'd Bord (Survey, 12 March 1765).

Wetherill estimated that the building was "about 2 or three Years Old" and he was correct. The Free School moved into the unfinished "new Buildings" in February 1763 and by the end of May a letter was sent to Provost Smith in England announcing the project's completion (Montgomery, 359). The first boarders arrived in 1764 (Turner, 183).

Earlier that year, Dr. Alison and Mr. Kinnersly visited the College of New Jersey at Princeton (Cat-

---

1. The dormitory is often referred to in Trustees' Minutes as the "New Building." Because this term was also used for the earlier College building (Academy/Whitefield Hall, Catalog #11), it will be employed here only in quotations from the minutes.

The buildings of the Charity School, Academy, and College were rendered in pencil, probably drawn around 1770 by Pierre Eugène Du Simitière, in whose notebook the drawing is mounted. Robert Smith worked on both buildings, remodeling the interior of the old school and later designing and building the new dormitory for the college. The contrast in style between the old-fashioned school and the Georgian college is striking. Library Company of Philadelphia.

alog #7) to view the student accommodations and assess the income potential of this new venture. A detailed report was made to the trustees in September with the recommendation that the "Economy of the House . . . be kept entirely on a separate Footing" (Minutes, 11 September 1764). A steward, matron, and cook staff were hired, but "the dormitory became a constant source of student complaint and financial loss" (Turner, 184). Eventually, the building was leased to a family, who assumed responsibility for the students' meals and housing.

The cost of the dormitory was estimated at £1500, but the Journal and Day Book of the College record payments in excess of £2000 to Robert Smith from 3 December 1761 through 11 September 1764, when the notation "paid in full," rather than "on Account," appears next to his name. His accounts were reported as presented and examined at the trustees' meetings of 12 June and 10 July 1764 and the Day Book notes payments of £50 on June 15th and £15 on July 27th, which probably correspond to expenditures authorized by the trustees. No receipt book for the relevant period survives, so that it is impossible to know if Smith was being paid the billed amount or a lesser sum. Not until 17 December 1765 did the minutes note his "account for erecting the New Buildings" as discharged.

Despite this presumed settlement of the account, there are other indications that bills were outstanding. On 20 December 1768, the minutes recorded that "Mr. Coxe laid before the Trustees Mr. Loxley's Account . . . for work done long since, and the same was ordered to be paid; and also an account of work done by Mr. Robert Smith, in the new Buildings, to be paid when the work is valued by two indifferent men, to be chosen by Him and the Trustees." Whether this "valuation" was for additional work, beyond the scope of the original plan, or represented the last hurdle before final payment is unclear. Additional requests for payments pertaining to the dormitory dragged on through the 1770s, but the exact nature of the work is unknown. An undated summary, labeled "Acct of the Cost of the Ground & Buildings," appears in the Day Book between 1773 and 1774, but it is obviously incomplete as it has only four entries. It may, however, be a summary of past expenditures because it includes a total payment to Robert Smith "for his Acct of Work" of over £2058, reflecting what he already had been paid. Benjamin Loxley had received £72. Possibly the building account for the dormitory remained unsettled until that time or some additional work was necessary

The carpenter, possibly Smith, was "ordered" to make shelves, cupboards, and "some little Conveniences as would be wanted" (Minutes, 8 February 1763). There may have been other requests that were not recorded. Some assignments appear in the Trustees' Minutes. In between completion of the dormitory and beginning work on the Provost's House (Catalog #51), Smith was hired to undertake various routine maintenance chores. He was asked "to make up a high Fence . . . and to repair the Front Fences" (Minutes, 13 September 1763), and also to repair the college roof, probably that of the earlier building (Minutes, 19 July 1771). "Mr. Donaldson's account of Boards delivered to Robert Smith for Repairs in the College," which was ordered to be paid in May 1772, was probably associated with this latter project (Minutes, 19 May 1772). No payments were made to Smith, however, until 4 April 1774, when

they were simply added to the outstanding balance for the dormitory. In February 1773, Smith had presented the trustees with an account "remaining unpaid for work done at the New Buildings" (Minutes, 16 February 1773). This was ordered paid, but no cash was forthcoming. With payment schedules like this, the financial difficulties evident in Smith's estate papers become understandable.

DOCUMENTATION:

Archives of the University of Pennsylvania. Account Book [Ledger], 16 January 1749/50-2 December 1779. Day Book Belonging to the Trustees of the Academy, 1749-1779. Insurance Survey, 12 March 1765, Philadelphia Contributionship. Journal A Belonging to the Trustees of the Academy of Philadelphia Anno 1749, [1749-1764]. Minutes of the Trustees of the College, Academy and Charitable Schools. 1, 1749-1768; 2, 1768-1791.

REFERENCES:

Cheyney, Edward Potts. *History of the University of Pennsylvania 1740-1940*. Philadelphia (1940); Montgomery, Thomas Harrison. A *History of the University of Pennsylvania from its Foundation to AD 1770* . . . . Philadelphia (1900); Nitzsche, George E. *University of Pennsylvania: Its History, Traditions, Buildings and Memorials* . . . . 6th edition. Philadelphia (1916); S&W, 2 and 3; Turner, William L. "The Charity School, the Academy, and the College." In *HP*; Watson (Hazard), 3; Westcott, Thompson. "Old Academy, Fourth Street." In *The Historic Mansions and Buildings of Philadelphia* . . . . Philadelphia (1877).

17

Purchase and Development of Second Street Property

Southwest corner of Second and Cedar (South) Streets, Philadelphia
1761

IN 1761, a year before the creation of the district of Southwark, Robert Smith bought a rectangular plot 256 feet deep with frontage on Second Street from the Quaker master builder Samuel Rhoads (Deed Book I-8:523, 30 March 1761). The two members of the

The site plan of Smith's Second Street property is illustrated in Book 11, page 228 of the Philadelphia City Orphans Court record pertaining to his estate. Smith and his family lived on Lot 1. Lot 10 was rented to a Captain Lake, and Lot 11 to John O'Neill, possibly a fellow carpenter, who worked on the cupola of Carpenters' Hall.

Carpenters' Company had worked together on the Second Presbyterian Church (Catalog #2), and later would collaborate on a house for Benjamin Franklin (Catalog #21) and the great city Almshouse (Catalog #29). That Rhoads respected and trusted Smith is evident by a £60 bond listed in Smith's estate accounts as "Contracted since the Year 1774."

Soon after purchasing the property, Smith built a house on the west side of Second Street, probably locating his lumberyard and shop at the rear, because later records indicate his subdivided lot was 151 feet deep. Smith's name appears in the 1767 and 1769 Southwark tax lists as owning a dwelling, horse and cow, and other property elsewhere. In 1770, his Second Street parcel was slightly enlarged as part of the proprietor's settlement of the city's southern boundary; and, sometime before 1772, Smith divided his land, probably into the eleven lots shown in the plat accompanying the estate papers (Patent Book AA, 12:9, 23 February 1770). He proceeded to sell some lots and develop others. Smith, his wife, and younger children lived on Lot 1. At the time of Smith's death, four brick dwellings faced Second Street, with a frame store attached to the corner house; these improvements are listed in the 1774 account attached to Smith's estate papers, as well as other documents related to the settlement of the estate.

DOCUMENTATION:

PCA. Orphans Court, Estate of Robert Smith. 11 February 1779 11:81, and 7 June 1782, 11:420-422. Bond of Administration. Account Inventory; Recorder of Deeds. 1 March 1772, D-17:437, 1 May 1772, D-68:429, 1 January 1773, EF-28:100, and Patent Book AA, Vol 12, 9, 23 February 1770. Register of Wills. Estate of William Williams, #227, 1794; Philadelphia County, Tax Lists, Southwark, 1767, 1769 and 1774. *Pennsylvania Evening Post*, 13 February 1777; *The Pennsylvania Journal and Weekly Advertiser*, 29 December 1763.

REFERENCES:
Tatman and Moss, 854-856.

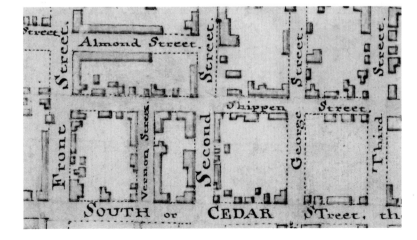

This detail of Charles de Krafft's 1790 copy of John Hill's 1788 map shows that by the closing years of the eighteenth century the lots along Second Street were fully developed. Courtesy Philadelphia City Archives.

Zion Lutheran School

325 Cherry Street, Philadelphia
1761, altered

THIS BRICK BUILDING is attributed to Robert Smith on the basis of style, patronage, and his later association with the Zion Lutheran Church (Catalog #26). The thirty-four by forty foot two-story school house sported "a small Turrett at the Top"

Zion Lutheran School, shown here in a nineteenth-century photograph, stood across Cherry Street from the Zion Lutheran Church. It served not only as a school, but also as a parish hall and early venue for meetings of the German Society. Courtesy Krauth Memorial Library, Lutheran Archives Center at Philadelphia.

(Philadelphia Contributionship), and such an ornament appears in nineteenth-century photographs. It seems to be a version, perhaps at somewhat smaller scale, of the top two stages of Smith's Christ Church spire. The corners of the building are articulated by shallow brick pilasters of the type that may have been used at the College of Philadelphia dormitory.

The congregation of St. Michael's Church acquired the property in 1760, and the school house was completed the following year at a cost of about £900 (Muhlenberg, 2 January 1762; S&W, 2:1422). (The same congregation commissioned the much larger Zion Lutheran Church in 1766, so that the school is referred to as Zion School.) The building effort was rooted in the German charity school movement, which prompted the construction of schools in outlying areas, such as Barren Hill in Montgomery County, as well as in the city. The German Reformed Church also sponsored a school, built around 1753, which once was thought to be a Robert Smith building.

Construction of Zion School is documented in histories at the Lutheran Archives Center and also in standard Philadelphia chronologies. The Rev. Henry Melchior Muhlenberg described its dedication, but those remarks are eclipsed by his disapproval of the expensive undertaking, which increased St. Michael's already burdensome debt (Muhlenberg, 27 July 1761 and 4 January 1762). The building was surveyed by Joseph Fox in October 1761. Although no policies have been found, the congregation held insurance on the school, as well as on St. Michael's and its parsonage (Muhlenberg, 2 January 1762).

DOCUMENTATION:

Krauth Memorial Library, Lutheran Archives Center at Philadelphia. "Einrichtung der schule," *Geschichte* (1876); "History—Zion School House" (1959); Muhlenberg, H.M. *The Journals of Henry Melchior Muhlenberg.* 3 vols. Translated by Theodore G. Tappert and John W. Doberstein. Philadelphia (1942-1958); Insurance Survey and Journal Entry, 6 October 1761. Philadelphia Contributionship. HSP.

REFERENCES:

Glatfelter, Charles H. *Pastors and People: German Lutheran and Reformed Churches in the Pennsylvania Field, 1717-1793.* Vol. 1. Breinigsville, PA (1980); Hogan, Edmund. *The Prospect of Philadelphia.* Philadelphia (1795); S&W, 2; Westcott, Thompson. "German Lutheran Church: St. Michael's and Zion." In *The Historic Mansions and Buildings of Philadelphia.* Philadelphia (1877).

19 A

Design Presbyterian Church

Princeton, New Jersey
1762, burned 1813

The only visual record of the original Presbyterian Church building at Princeton is this depiction on the church seal. It suggests that stylistically the building resembled Smith's other churches for Presbyterian congregations. Courtesy Princeton Theological Seminary with permission of Nassau Presbyterian Church.

NO DOCUMENTATION connects Smith with this building. However, what appears to be a relatively sophisticated design for its time suggests that he may have had a hand in its conception. When the church was begun in 1762, Smith still owned property in Princeton, and only four years previously had completed the President's House at the College of New Jersey. As late as 1760, he had presented a bill to the college for placing a fence around that building.

Although the College of New Jersey, essentially a Presbyterian institution, had settled in Princeton, the village had no church. It was midway between two towns, Kingston and Lawrenceville, where Presbyterian congregations had long been established. Princetonians, however, unless they wished to travel, attended services in the prayer hall of the college. In 1762, a group of citizens, in cooperation with the college, raised a subscription for building a church. The college donated land adjacent to and west of the President's House, and also loaned the congregation money. The church was begun that year, but not completed until 1766, evidently because of the difficulty of raising sufficient funds (Hageman 2:80-82).

The only view of the exterior of the building is on the church seal, originally struck in 1793. The present seal is thought to be an early nineteenth-century replication, made after a fire in 1835 destroyed the original (Egbert, n7). The building's proportions appear to have been good. Of a meeting house type, it was built of brick. The arched windows, pedimented doorways, oculus, and prominent cornice return all were part of the Middle Georgian vocabulary Smith employed at the Second Presbyterian Church and St. Peter's. An early pew plan shows the layout of the interior, although giving no hint as to its detailing (Hageman 2: facing 83). Two entrances faced north to the main street at either end. These led to aisles running north-south. To either side of the aisles were winding stairs leading to a gallery along the north wall. A center aisle led to a pulpit on the south wall.

Above this was a canopy, "an ample drapery of dark-colored stuff . . . which was held in festoons by a large, gilded, radiating, star-shaped ornament" (Collins [1945], 92). It had been presented to the church by Dr. John Witherspoon, then president of the college, and later a signer of the Declaration of Independence.

Although an attribution to Smith is plausible, it should be remembered that there were local builders, who may have observed his work at the college and absorbed the stylistic ideas Smith had introduced to the town. Among them was John McComb, Sr., father of the future architect of New York City Hall, one of three men called in to assess the severe damage done to the church during the Revolution (Inventory of Damages done to the Meeting House, Church Papers).

The building burned in 1813, and was rebuilt in different form, with some Gothic detailing, making it a very early example of the style in the United States (Egbert, 110-112). It burned again in 1835. At that time it was demolished. A much larger building was erected on the site in Greek Revival style, with a facade design provided by Thomas U. Walter. It has since had several alterations and additions, plus a change of name to Nassau Presbyterian Church.

DOCUMENTATION:

Nassau Presbyterian Church Papers. Deposited at Princeton Theological Seminary Archives; Shelley, Fred. "Ebenezer Hazard's Diary: New Jersey During the Revolution." *Proceedings of the New Jersey Historical Society*, 90, 3 (Autumn 1972): 169-179; Thomas Ustick Walter Papers, The Athenæum of Philadelphia.

REFERENCES:

Collins, V[arnum] Lansing. *Princeton Past and Present.* Princeton (1931, 1945); Egbert, Virginia and Donald. "The Gothic Revival in Princeton." *Princeton University Library Chronicle* 29, 4 (winter 1968): 109; Greiff, Constance M., Mary W. Gibbons, and Elizabeth G.C. Menzies, *Princeton Architecture.* Princeton (1967); Hageman, John F. *Princeton and its Institutions.* 2 vols. Philadelphia (1879); Link, Arthur. *The First Presbyterian Church of Princeton.* Princeton (1967).

Saint George's United Methodist Church

235 North Fourth Street, Philadelphia
1763, 1769-70; roof and ceiling burned 1865, rebuilt

THE BRICK BUILDING on Fourth Street, measuring fifty-three by eighty-two feet has been attributed to Robert Smith on the basis of some stylistic elements and the method of construction of the roof. A photograph, taken after a fire on 12 August 1865 destroyed the roof and ceiling, shows a truss structure not unlike that Smith used at St. Peter's in 1758 and at St. Paul's in 1760. Some of its interior arrangements also were similar in form to St. Paul's (Corson, 231). There is, however, no written reference to Smith's involvement, and the outside is plain and severe, and shows little or no resemblance to Smith's documented work.

Known as the "cradle of American Methodism," St. George's began life as a church for a splinter group of Reformed Presbyterians. These German Calvinists were an organized community for worship as early as 1732, and in 1748-49 had constructed a distinctive hexagonal church, visible on the Scull and Heap "East Prospect of Philadelphia" of 1754. Doctrinal disputes combined with allegiances to different preachers, and resulted in rival congregations claiming access to the church building.

"In 1762 a new church was organized in Philadelphia, and proved an unfortunate enterprise" (S&W, 2:1413). The congregation purchased land on the east side of Fourth Street, and undertook construction of a sizeable church. The members were poor, and also failed to gain affiliation with any established religious group. Six years after they had begun the project, the building was still unfinished, and the congregation was deeply in debt. Construction costs had exceeded £2000 and there was no money to pay anyone. Several church members served time in jail because of

The severely plain exterior differs from Smith's other churches and therefore makes attribution to him difficult. It is of course possible that plainness and severity were dictated by the client. Scharf and Westcott, *History of Philadelphia*, 2:1396.

the financial difficulties. It is said that when their acquaintances looked through the prison windows and asked, "For what were you put in jail?" the answer was "For building a church ....To go to jail for the pious deed of building a church became a proverb in the city of Brotherly Love" (S&W, 2:1413).

When the congregation disbanded in 1769, they petitioned the legislature for permission to sell the building at auction. Permission was granted and the sale advertised (*Pennsylvania Chronicle,* 13 and 20 February, 1 and 8 May 1769). Unfortunately, only £700 was realized. Subsequently, the Methodists purchased the shell of the unfinished church from the high bidder (Corson, 231-232). Joseph Pilmore preached in the new building on 24 November 1769, a few days after the Methodist purchase.

The roof span, established by 1763, is shorter than St. Peter's or St. Paul's. Although such a roof is something of a Robert Smith signature, by 1763 other Philadelphia builders could well have been aware of and using the same methods of truss construction. By this time, they would have been familiar with Smith's work at the two Anglican churches.

DOCUMENTATION:

Pennsylvania Chronicle; *Journal of Joseph Pilmore*. Philadelphia (1969).

REFERENCES:

Corson, The Rev. Bishop Fred Pierce. "St. George's Church: The Cradle of American Methodism." In *HP*, 230-236; Glatfelter, Charles H. *Pastors and People: German Lutheran and Reformed Churches in the Pennsylvania Field, 1717-1793*. Vol. 1. Breinigsville, PA (1980); Hogan, Edmund. *The Prospect of Philadelphia*. Philadelphia (1795); S&W, 2:1394-1396, 1411-1414.
HABS, PA-1473; Hammond, Joseph W. "Timber Framing Engineering of Robert Smith: Leading Builder/Architect of Colonial America." Paper presented at Robert Smith's Birthday, Philadelphia, 14 January 1995, and annual APT/DVC symposium on Historic Timber Framing, Philadelphia, 2 March 1996.

A photograph of the roof timbers of St. George's, made after a fire on 12 August 1865 shows a raised tie beam truss similar to those employed by Smith at other churches.
Courtesy St. George's Methodist Episcopal Church.

21

Build House for Benjamin Franklin

Franklin Court [Between Market and Chestnut Streets and Second and Third Streets, Philadelphia]
1766, demolished 1812

FROM the extensive, although scattered, record it is impossible to tell exactly who did what at Benjamin Franklin's house. With his wide interests in almost every form of knowledge, Franklin himself obviously played a major role in its design and accoutrements. Later he recalled that he had built "a good house ... contrived to my mind," and that the result was *"the Execution of my plan"* [emphasis added] (Franklin to Mme. Brillon, 19 April 1788, quoted in Smyth, 9:643; Franklin to John Smith, 31 August 1787, APS, 2:211).

Along with his many other skills and pursuits, Franklin had a long-standing interest in the building arts. His father, Franklin wrote in his *Autobiography*, fearing that his restless son might run off to sea, took the boy

to walk with him, and see joiners, bricklayers, braziers, etc., at their work, that he might observe my inclination, and endeavour to fix it on some trade or other on land. It has ever since been a pleasure to me to see good workmen handle their tools; and it has been useful to me, having learnt

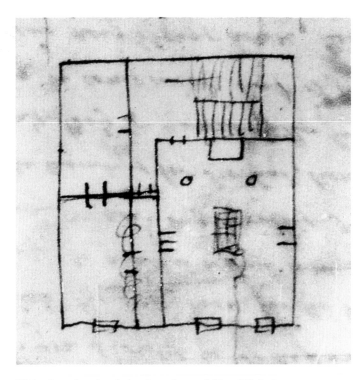

This tiny sketch of the first floor of Franklin's house may have been drawn by Franklin himself. Based on archaeological investigations of the foundations, it appears to be quite accurate. It shows the house with a side stair hall and an arch in the through passage. American Philosophical Society.

so much by it as to be able to do little jobs by myself in my house when a workman could not readily be got, and to construct little machines for my experiments" (Quoted in Van Doren, 12).

Sketches, believed to be in Franklin's hand, are among his papers at the American Philosophical Society. One may be a framing plan; two are plans of the first and second floors, the latter drawn on the back of a receipt dated 17 May 1764 (Cotter, et al., 90-91; Greiff, 197-198). They appear to be accurate according to later descriptions, although whether they reflect preliminary designs or decisions made later seems uncertain; materials already were being purchased for the project in 1763. The first floor plan seems to show a through passageway, a little off center, with two smaller rooms to one side, and a single large room and stair hall to the other. Yet these are crude sketches, obviously drawn by an amateur. It

would take a skilled designer/draftsman to give form to Franklin's ideas in order to execute them in brick and mortar.

That designer probably was Robert Smith, although Franklin's friend, Samuel Rhoads, oversaw the execution of the work, represented the Franklins, and disbursed the funds (Platt, 38-39). It was Smith who purchased the first materials for the house on 6 April 1763 (PBF, 10:237, n5). And it was Smith who appears to be responsible for rendering the final account, although he was delayed in doing so "because the house had not yet been measured." He did estimate that the final charge for materials would be £780. (Smith to Rhoads, 30 March 1767, PBF, 14:138, n6).

Yet in the long run, Franklin's house may have been a disappointment. In spite of all the worry and money expended, the project didn't turn out as well as he had hoped. Franklin and his lonely but devoted wife, Deborah, never lived there together. The house was begun while he was away on public business; his family moved in during his long-extended absence in public service abroad. He returned only after his wife's death, to spend his last, pain-filled years in the house in the design and building of which he had taken so much interest. Thus unlike his contemporaries, Washington and Jefferson, he cannot be remembered by a great house. They built on huge rural plantations then far from development pressures. Franklin fought a losing battle in a difficult urban environment that was tamed only by later generations. The pleasant aspect of the site today was created by Independence National Historical Park; it does not completely reflect its evolution on a somewhat inhospitable terrain.

The design and construction of Franklin's house began when, after some years abroad, Franklin returned to Philadelphia in 1762 and was ready to build a permanent home. By this time, the Franklins had lived in thirteen rental locations in the thirty-three years of their marriage (Cotter et. al, 87). Flush with cash from the settlement of his travel account with the Province of Pennsylvania, Franklin also brought back a lot of innovative ideas developed while he was in Britain.

The Franklins owned two adjoining lots fronting thirty-four feet on Market Street, one inherited from Deborah Franklin's father. Between 1734 and 1765, they bought other adjacent parcels along Market Street between Third and Fourth Streets, as well as some frontage behind other Market Street properties that they did not acquire. Their generous lot stretched back 308 feet, almost to Chestnut Street. The property had serious drawbacks. The whole neighborhood was then subject to noise from the traffic of the market and the stench of the long-established tanyards bordering Dock Creek, a branch of which ran next to or through the southwest corner of the property. It took many loads of fill to level their land, and a garden wall to close out Dock Creek. The house was located toward the south end of the lot slightly under 200 feet back from Market Street. This may have put it close to Dock Creek, but removed it from the noise and odors of the market shambles less than a block to the east. Franklin also probably intended to develop the valuable properties on Market Street for income-producing purposes, as indeed he later did.

Before the house was begun, Franklin was off on his travels as Postmaster General. During his long absences, it was Deborah Franklin who would suffer through the discomforts of building and worry about whether things would turn out to his satisfaction. Still, Franklin maintained a lively interest in the project's progress. He had asked his old friend, Samuel Rhoads, to oversee the project as manager. From New York City, en route to New England, Franklin wrote to his wife on 16 June 1763, "My love to Mr. Rhoads

when you see him, and desire he would send me an Invoice of such Locks, Hinges and the like as cannot be had at Philadelphia, and will be necessary for my House, that I may send for them" (PBF 10:291). Smith already had purchased some materials two months earlier.

Construction may have begun in the fall of 1764, when Rhoads noted the receipt of £200 from Franklin. The ubiquitous John Palmer was responsible for the brickwork. Robert Allison was paid £120 for assisting Smith with the carpentry. This was a substantial sum, and may indicate that he was responsible for the decorative interior woodwork. The work did not proceed as fast as Franklin wished, and he blamed Smith. On 4 June 1765, he wrote to Deborah, "I cannot but complain in my Mind of Mr. Smith, that the House is so long unfit for you to get into, the Fences not put up, nor the other necessary Articles got ready. The Well I expected would have been dug in the Winter or early in the Spring; but I hear nothing of it" (PBF 12:168). Probably Rhoads, who was inspecting the site work, shared part of the blame.

Deborah Franklin was able to move into the house in May 1765, but there still was work to be done (Riley, 149-150). By the summer of 1766, by which time Franklin was in London, the house was sufficiently finished to be evaluated for the Philadelphia Contributionship for the Insurance of Houses from Loss by Fire.

This drawing by archaeologist Barbara Liggett is a site plan of the Franklin property as it was when Smith had completed the house. Later, after Franklin acquired property fronting on Market Street, the driveway was shifted from the west end to the center.
Courtesy Independence National Historical Park.

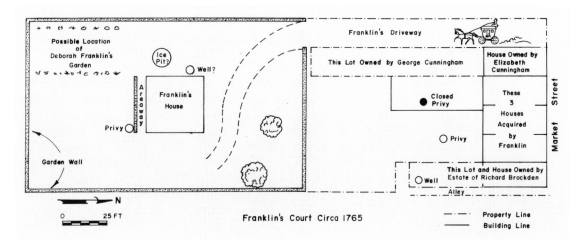

Survey^d Augt.5th 1766   N. 1148

A house Belonging to Benjamin Franklin, Situate on the South Side of high [Market] Street Between third & fourth Streets where his family dwells

34 feet Square—3 Storys high—14 & 9 inch walls—3 Rooms on a floor—pertitions in the Easternmost part of the house 9 inch Brick wall to the Garet floor in the westernmost part Studed & plaster^d.

East Room below wainscuted with frett Cornish [cornice] all Round,—four pedements with frett—Bedmold A Rich Chimney piece, 2 fluted Cullums & half pilasters with intabliture—the other Rooms and pasage below wainscuted pedistal high with frett and dintal [dentil] Cornish throughout one of s^d. Rooms has a Chimney piece with tabernacle frame pediment &^c.—All the Second Story wainscuted pedistal high, frett dintal and plain duble Cornish through the whole,—a Chimney piece in one of the Rooms with tabernacle frame pediment &^c.—Chimney Brests Surbass [chair rail] Scerting [skirting] and Single Cornish throughout the third Story—Garet plasterd a way out on Roof—two Storys of Stairs Ramp^d Brackited and Wainscuted—One—do Brackited—painted inside and out—Modilion Eaves—2 Large painhouses [pent roofs] with trusses at each end—all New—kitchen in Celler—

Gunning Bedford

£500 .. @30/per Ct. or if any higher Sum to be at 32/6.

From the survey it can be surmised that the elaborate interior woodwork was of an architectural level on a par with the mansions of Philadelphia's gentry. Deborah Franklin noted that "marbel fireplaces," by which she probably meant mantels, had been shipped from London. (Deborah Franklin to Franklin 8 January 1765, PBF 12:14). Despite the fine finishes and practical "contrivances," visitors did not seem impressed. Writing to his wife on 13 July 1765, Franklin complained, "you tell me only of a Fault they found with the House, that it was too little, and not a Word of any thing they lik'd in it" (PBF, 12:211). Besides what some considered its meager size, the house may not have put its best foot forward. It may have been designed to face south to Chestnut Street, although there is no evidence that the Franklins ever attempted to acquire that frontage. Visitors therefore always entered from the north, first coming though a rather narrow passageway.

The house was filled with innovative devices. Among them were various "contrivances" for the cellar kitchen, including those for carrying off smells, steam and smoke, and an iron "furnace" (Franklin to Deborah Franklin, 4 June 1765, PBF, 12:167). In-

stalling these unfamiliar items may have accounted for the delay in completing the house. Franklin worried that the chimneys would not be able to cope with these devices, but his wife assured him in October 1765 that "all the Chimneys that I have youused is verey good" (PBF, 12:298). So Smith had done well in designing his chimneys.

Undoubtedly there were Franklin fireplaces for heating. Colonel Robert Carr, who, in the 1790s served an apprenticeship with Benjamin Franklin Bache, recalled at least one coal grate in use.

The Doctor's office or study was on the first floor; and there was a coal grate, in which he burned Virginia or English coal. Below this grate, on the hearth, there was a small iron plate or trap-door, about five or six inches square, with a hinge and a small ring to raise it by. When this door or valve was raised, a current of air from the cellar rushed up thru the grate to re-kindle the fire (Carr, 59).

Carr also recalled that the doors were lined with green baize for quiet, and that some of them were on springs. In Franklin's bedroom, a pulley device could be operated from the bed to lock and unlock the door.

In 1767 the Franklins' only daughter, Sally, married Richard Bache, moved in with her mother, and in due course produced six children. Deborah Franklin died in 1774, shortly before her husband returned home from abroad in May 1775, and the Baches remained in residence. One of their children, Benjamin Franklin Bache, followed his grandfather into the printing trade, much to Franklin's pleasure. After Franklin's final return to Philadelphia in 1785, he built a print shop for young Bache between his house and the Market Street properties. Still active, although infirm, he made other expansive improvements. One corrected any perceived deficiencies in the size of the house, a sixteen-foot extension housing a large dining room on the first floor and library on the second, with chambers above. He also oversaw construction of three rental properties on Market Street, with a new, more direct entrance to his inner court between two of them, and a two-story brick coach house and stables. With Samuel Rhoads and Robert Smith both dead, Franklin must have supervised his building projects directly. "His faculties are still in their full vigor," wrote Dr. Benjamin Rush on 27 October 1786. "He amuses himself daily in superintending two or three houses which he is building in

Venturi and Rauch's design for Franklin Court represents the "ghosts" of the house and the print shop as steel frames. The concrete shelters in the foreground cover windows that look down into the excavated cellar. Courtesy Independence National Historical Park.

buildings were demolished, park service archaeologists investigated portions of the court in 1953, 1955, 1959, and 1960. Between 1970 and 1973, an extensive archaeological campaign covered almost the entire property (Greiff, *Independence*, 194-197, 206). None of the excavations ever found the bank of Dock Creek, but the archaeologists uncovered building foundations, privys, an ice pit, wells, and thousands of artifacts, as well as the probable location of Deborah Franklin's garden (Cotter et al., 90-96*)*. All these would be useful in interpreting the site to the public.

Park service supervisors already had determined that despite documentary and archaeological findings, there was not enough evidence to reconstruct the house (although they did restore the Market Street properties). Instead they decided to interpret Franklin and his property in terms of contemporary design (Greiff, *Independence*, 200-206). Franklin was a multi-faceted figure, and the property was small. They turned this difficult problem over to the architectural firm of Venturi and Rauch. In order to deal with all aspects of his life and career, Venturi and Rauch placed a museum and theater underground, leaving room on the surface to interpret what had been there. Steel frames, the now famous "ghost houses," were erected over the sites of the house and print shop. Today the court has an open, pleasing aspect, while still conveying to visitors an impression of its appearance in Franklin's lifetime.

DOCUMENTATION:

Franklin, Benjamin, *Papers of Benjamin Franklin* [PBF]. Ed. by Leonard W. Labaree. New Haven (1959-); *The Writings of Benjamin Franklin*. ed. by Albert Henry Smyth. New York (1906); American Philosophical Society [hereafter APS]. Franklin Papers; Bache Collection; HSP. Gunning Bedford, Insurance Survey, Policy 1148, 5 August 1766, Philadelphia Contributionship; Samuel Rhoads. Franklin's Receipt Book, 1764-1766.

REFERENCES:

Carr, Col. Robert. "Personal Recollections of Benjamin Franklin. *The Historical Magazine*. 2nd series, 4 (August 1868); Cotter, John L., Daniel G. Roberts and Michael Parrington. "Benjamin Franklin's Lost House." In *The Buried Past*. Philadelphia (1992); Greiff, Constance M. "The Second Wars of Independence." In *Independence: The Creation of a National Park*." Philadelphia (1987); Lopez, Claude-Anne. *Benjamin Franklin's 'Good House.'* National Park Service Handbook 114. Philadelphia (1981); Riley, Edward M. (with

the neighborhood of his dwelling house" (Quoted in Platt, 102). Franklin died in his house in 1790.

By the early nineteenth century, the neighborhood had become commercial, and was no longer desirable for residential use. The land had become more valuable than the old building. Franklin's descendants tore down the house in 1812, and opened Franklin Court for development (Lopez, 49). The entrance from Market Street was cut through to Chestnut, and named Orianna Street. Only the three large rental buildings on Market Street survived, and by the late nineteenth century they had been radically altered. By the time the National Park Service acquired Franklin Court in 1950 and 1951, nineteenth-century buildings covered all of the court except Orianna Street. As

Martin Yoelson et al.). "Franklin's Home." In *HP*, 48-160; Van Doren, Carl. *Benjamin Franklin*. London (1939).

Platt, John. "Franklin's House: Historic Structures Report." 29 November 1969. Independence National Historical Park Library.

22

Design and Build Two Houses for Mary Maddox

Third Street, east side, Philadelphia
1763, probably demolished

MARY MADDOX, widow of bibliophile wine merchant and Christ Church vestryman the Hon. Joshua Maddox (d.1759), contracted with Robert Smith to build two houses. The handwritten and signed agreement survives in the collections of the Historical Society of Pennsylvania and offers a detailed description of both the buildings and the business arrangements. While involved in the project, Smith borrowed £1000 from Mrs. Maddox. Papers documenting his indebtedness attest to his reliance on such loans to finance his business.

Widow Maddox was a woman of means, known for her enlightened conversation and conviviality. She was a faithful communicant at Christ Church and only left her adopted city during the Revolution, when she moved to New Jersey to be with her daughter; she died there in 1783 at the advanced age of 102 (Watson 2:617-18). Mrs. Maddox maintained an interest in her deceased husband's wine business and sought to improve her city properties to enhance their income potential. She lived on the east side of Second Street and the contract with Smith was for construction a block away on the east side of Third Street.

The contract, dated 1 January 1763, identified Smith as a "House Carpenter" and described the physical appearance of the buildings and terms of payment. Smith was to be paid £2250 for building two houses, which were scheduled for occupancy by 31 June 1764. The design elements and fundamental plan were based on the neighboring house, also owned by Mrs. Maddox. It was occupied by John Lawrence, possibly the same man who hired Smith in 1767 to work on his own dwelling (Stauffer Collection, 5:437). Lawrence's rental property had style and substance. Details specified for the Smith project reflect increasing attention to domestic niceties, such as brass locks, closets, a "genteel Marble Slab" for the front parlor, and good stone steps. The rear yards were to be enclosed with stone walls topped with brick and "neatly coped with wood." Provisions were made to handle water run-off from gutters and paving as well.

All in all, the building contract outlines construction of two houses suitable for the gentry. With the Powels, Willings, and Cadwaladers as neighbors, the Maddox houses were at one of the best addresses in pre-Revolutionary Philadelphia.

Articles of Agreement indented and made the first day of January Anno Domini 1763 Between Robert Smith of the City of Philadelphia House Carpenter of the one Part and Mary Maddox of the said City Widow of the other part as follows Viz.

First the said Robert Smith doth hereby for himself his Executors and Administrators covenant promise and agree to and with the said Mary Maddox her Executors and Administrators for the Consideration herein after mentioned that he the said Robert Smith his Executors & Administrators shall within the Time and in Manner herein after mentioned erect build and finish for the said Mary Maddox in and upon her Lotts of Ground on the East Side of Third Street in the said City Two three story Brick Houses of twenty one Feet Front each by Forty feet deep from the Street with a Piazza of fifteen Feet six Inches back from each House and therein make a good Staircase for each House up to the third Story and from thence by a smaller Stair into the Garretts and build a Kitchen of Twenty Feet long beyond the Piazza by twelve feet six Inches wide and two Storys high with good Cellars under the whole Buildings of eight feet deep from the Joists; The Storys of both Houses to be of the same Height with the Storys of the next House the property of the said Mary Maddox that Mr. John Lawrence lives in and to have the same Number of Windows and of the same Size with those in Mr. Lawrence's House with two Rooms on each Floor of both Houses and as many Closets in each room as there are in the said next house with proper Entrys and Passages through to the back Buildings and to the Several parts of the Houses The Rooms to be as well finished with outside Window Shutters Fastnings and in the same Manner and all the Work inside and out to be as much and as good [word crossed out] as near as may be with those in the said next House and the Stairs to be in the same Form with those in the said next House allowing for the Difference of the Plans The Back and Front Wall of the two Houses fourteen Inches thick and all the other Walls nine Inches thick except the Back of some of the Closets which may only be four Inches thick There is to be a genteel Marble Slab in each front Parlour with a good Brass Lock to both parlour Doors of each House and good suitable Hinges and Locks for all the other Rooms and Closets The whole Woodwork of the outside and inside to be well painted with three Coats of good Paint (except the Roof and the board Fences) The Yards to go back Seventy feet beyond the East End of the Kitchen and to be walled up with Stone and Lime and the Ground to be filled up and raised to a proper Heighth to give sufficient Fall for the Water and make Gutters out of both Yards into the nine Feet Alley between these and Mr. Lawrence's House and to have a nine Inch Brick Wall all around the Yards on the Top of the Stone Wall four feet six Inches high and neatly coped with Wood and make a Fence between the two Yards and an Alley with a Board Fence from the East End of the Northerly House into the said great Alley [text crossed out] There is also to be two double Brick Little Houses one in each Yard The Yards to be neatly paved with Bricks and the Street within the posts to be paved with Bricks and Posts also to be set there as usual There is to be good Stone Steps to the Doors and all the Workmanship as well as all the Materials are to be good of every kind and to be found and provided by the said Robert Smith in due time and Manner out of the Monies to be paid him by the said Mary Maddox as herein after covenanted and expressed [text crossed out] and the whole to be well plaistered painted and compleatly finished and ready for Tenants on or before the last day of June which will be in the Year one thousand Seven hundred and sixty four Provided always and it is hereby agreed that if any part of the Stone Wall that is designed to go round the Yard for supporting the new made Ground shall be thought unnecessary that then the Value of so much there of as shall be left undone shall be deducted in proportion to the Expence of the whole And the said Mary Maddox doth hereby in Consideration of the premises for herself her Executors and Administrators covenant and promise and agree to and with the said Robert Smith his Execrs & Admins that she the said Mary Maddox her Executors or Administrators shall and will well and truly pay or cause to be paid unto the said Robert Smith his Executors or Administrators the Sum of Two thousand and two hundred and fifty pounds lawful Money of Pennsylvania in Manner following that is to say Three hundred pounds now in hand Two hundred Pounds on the first day of April now next Two hundred Pounds on the first day of May next One hundred and fifty pounds more when the Joists of the first Floors of the Houses are laid Two hundred Pounds when the Second Floor is put on Two Hundred Pounds when the Third Floor is put on Two Hundred Pounds when the Roof is raised Two hundred Pounds when the whole Buildings are shingled in and all the Sashes glazed and put in Two hundred Pounds when one of the Houses is ready for plaistering Two hundred Pounds when the other is ready for Plaistering and the re-

maining Two hundred Pounds when the whole is finished. In Witness whereas the Parties aforesaid to these presents have interchangeably set their hands and Seals hereunto Dated the day and year first above Written eu ——

Francis Harris   Robt Smith [seal]
John Wallace

examin'd
    PWPeters [this name is difficult to decipher]

Smith probably entered into similar contracts for his other residential jobs, but the Maddox agreement is the only one known to survive. Payments to Smith in Samuel Powel's ledger refer to contracts for building houses, stores, and making alterations to Powel's Third Street house. Trustees' Minutes in the Archives of the University of Pennsylvania also refer to contracts with Smith for the Dormitory and Provost's House. But none of these contracts has been found. Certain agreements are recorded in the minutes, but the terms and format differ from the Maddox contract.

DOCUMENTATION:

HSP. Articles of Agreement ... Between Robert Smith ... and Mary Maddox ..., 1 January 1763. Wallace Papers, 5:30; Bond and Warrant, Robert Smith to Mary Maddox, 24 September 1764. Wallace Papers, 5:31; Invoice. Robert Smith to John Lawrence, Esq., 21 March 1767. Stauffer Collection.

REFERENCES:

Watson (1927).

23 A

Presbyterian Church of Lawrenceville

Main Street, Lawrenceville, NJ
1764, enlarged 1833 and 1853

THE TRADITIONAL DATE for the Presbyterian Church of Lawrenceville is 1764 (Tyler, 36). This date is inscribed in a stone in the front gable, installed when the church was enlarged in 1833. However, no church records survive from this period, and whether

Only the first two bays of the Lawrenceville Presbyterian Church were built in the eighteenth century. At that time the building was a meeting house type with its ridge parallel to the street. Courtesy Lawrence Township Room, Mercer County Library.

that is the date for the start or for the completion of construction is not known In any event, the Lawrenceville Church is a close contemporary of the original building of the First Presbyterian Church at Princeton and was similar in design.

Maidenhead, as Lawrenceville was known in the eighteenth century, was on the main road north from Trenton to New Brunswick. Most travelers between New York and Philadelphia combined this overland route with ferries across New York Harbor and the Delaware River. The town's proximity to Philadelphia gave it a connection to that city, and two eighteenth-century diarists, Elizabeth Drinker and Jacob Hiltzheimer, a friend of Robert Smith, recorded their visits to the town (Podmore, 51). Unfortunately, neither of them mentioned the church.

Originally a meeting house type, forty-five feet wide by thirty-two feet deep, with its ridge parallel to the main street, the building was lengthened to "church" form in 1833 and again in 1853. As a result, virtually nothing remains of the eighteenth-century interior. According to an architect who investigated the building, surviving original exterior features include the pedimented front entry, and the front windows, round-arched at the second level, and the octagonal cupola (Westfield 4,5). If indeed it is original, this cupola must have been moved when the building and its roof were re-oriented. It has been claimed that

it seems to be constructed in the same manner as Smith's cupolas at Christ Church, Philadelphia (Catalog #4) and Carpenters' Hall (Catalog #35) (Westfield). However, since those two are not constructed in the same manner, the comparison can hardly be valid. Furthermore, the roof of the cupola is a "pepper pot," rather than the hemispherical dome Smith favored.

The building has been attributed to Robert Smith on the basis of its style and his association with New Light Presbyterians in Philadelphia and Princeton. What is more certain than that he was the designer, is that he introduced the Philadelphia version of the Georgian style to the area. His influence seems clear, but a decade after construction of Nassau Hall, local builders may have been familiar with both his designs and his construction methods.

REFERENCES:

Presbyterian Historical Society, Philadelphia. Miscellaneous Papers and Notes, Klenke Collection; "Spirit of 76" (pamphlet), n.d.; Podmore, Harry J., ed. *The Presbyterian Church of Lawrenceville, New Jersey*. Second edition. (1974); Tyler, Donald H. *Old Lawrenceville (Formerly Maidenhead, New Jersey)*. Privately printed, [Lawrenceville, NJ](1965).

"Church Story Gives History of 250 Years." *Princeton Herald,* 13 October 1948; HABS-NJ53; Westfield Architects and Preservation Consultants. "The Presbyterian Church of Lawrenceville." August 1997.

24

Consult on New Building for the Land Office

1764, not built

ON 8 JUNE 1764 Thomas Penn expressed concern to his nephew John, then governor of Pennsylvania, about the possibility of losing vital records because of fire. He suggested that "Arched Offices" be constructed on one of the Proprietary lots. These arched rooms were to measure about twenty-four by fifteen feet. Undoubtedly in order to be fireproof, they were to have ceilings constructed of brick. Thomas Penn asked John to obtain a plan prepared by the "best Workmen" (Letter Book, 8:85-86). Several months later John Penn reported that he had "consulted Mr. Smith the best workman here." Smith thought it was too late in the year to begin the project. So John Penn suggested that his uncle obtain a plan in England, because then he could be "sure of having [the building] done to your own mind" (Penn Papers, official corr., 9:252).

Thomas Penn took his nephew's advice and announced that he would "get a plan settled by Mr Ledbetter an experienced Builder here [London]" (Thomas Penn to William Peters, 8 December 1764, Letter Book). Stiff Leadbetter (d. August 1766) was a competent, if unexciting, architect in the Palladian mode, who had done work at Penn's country house, Stoke Park at Stoke Poges (Colvin, 603-605). Penn proposed building the land office on Proprietorial land that had not been laid out for lots, suggesting sites on Chestnut, Walnut, and Pine Streets (Letter Book, 8:302). But nothing was done, and by October 1766 the land office opened for business in a new building built by James Tilghman, its secretary, on land he owned on the east side of Fourth Street, one building north of Market Street (Gazette, 16 October 1766).

Thomas Penn must have regarded this as a temporary measure. In November he promised to send Tilghman "the plan drawn for offices . . . by the first ship" (Letter Book, 7 November 1766). He duly sent the plan to his nephew in March 1767, asking him to "consult your best Architects . . . and inform me, what will be the expence of erecting such an one, either with, or without a story over it with his and your opin-

ion of it, or the form of any other . . . ." (Letter Book, 5 March 1767). If John Penn did consult the "best Architects," it seems likely that Smith would have been among them, given their previous discussions.

Although Thomas Penn gave elaborate instructions about such construction details as arches and brickwork, he was unable to settle on a site. By August 1767 he was considering whether the office should be part of a new courthouse proposed for the State House yard (Penn to Tilghman, Letter Book, 5 August 1767). Perhaps because of pre-Revolutionary political tensions, neither the courthouse nor a separate building for the land office was built. Instead, by the spring of 1769, some functions of the land office were back in one of its previous locations, the State House (Edmund Physick to Thomas Penn, 19 April 1769, Penn-Physick Papers, 3:9-13, Riley "Independence Hall Group," 15, n58). But Tilghman offered his building for sale as "the present land office" in 1770; it was not sold until the beginning of the Revolution (Gazette, 26 May 1768, 13 September 1770; James Tilghman to John Kaighn, 15 May 1777, Philadelphia County Deeds, D-1:91-93).

DOCUMENTATION:

HSP. Penn Papers. Official Correspondence, Thomas Penn Letter Book. Penn-Physick Papers; *Pennsylvania Gazette*.

REFERENCES:

Colvin, Howard. *A Biographical Dictionary of British Architects*. New Haven (1995); Riley, Edward M. "The Independence Hall Group." In *HP*, 1-42.

25

Measuring at Mount Pleasant

Mount Pleasant Drive, Fairmount Park, Philadelphia
1764-1765

CARPENTERS' COMPANY MEMBER Thomas Nevell (1721-1797) built a country house for Scotsman Captain John Macpherson on a bluff overlooking the Schuylkill River. Construction of Clunie, as Mount Pleasant was called originally, took nearly three

For a time Mount Pleasant was attributed to Robert Smith. But when Thomas Nevell's Day Book resurfaced at the University of Pennsylvania Library it became clear that the building was his. Smith did play a role, however, as one of two measurers evaluating Nevell's work. Photograph by Tom Crane.

years and occupied Nevell from August 1762 through May 1765 (Dickey, 3). Design of the stucco house, with its brick trim, projecting center pavilion, Venetian window, and other elements popularized by a reverence for the Middle Georgian Palladian style, was probably influenced by plates illustrated in Abraham Swan's *A Collection of Designs in Architecture* (London, 1757), a copy of which Macpherson sold Nevell when the house was finished (Moss [1998], 98).

Smith and John Thornhill, fellow members of the Carpenters' Company and Price Committee associates, were asked to value the carpentry work at Mount Pleasant before bills could be paid. In March 1764 they measured "a Frontish Piece Door in the Back front" of the house (Nevell, 30 March 1764). They returned in May to value two more frontispieces and a Venetian window, enabling Nevell to charge Macpherson for "the workmanship of ye Dineing

Room and Hall" (Nevell, 7 December 1764). The following July, Nevell submitted a comprehensive bill for £10841.7. for "All the Remainder of Carpenters work measured by [Messrs] Smith, Thornhill not hearetofore Charged" (Nevell, 24 July 1765).

As pointed out in the Introduction, three payment systems were in use in Philadelphia in the eighteenth century. These had been summarized by Christopher Wren as "by the Day, by Measure, by Great." It might be assumed that these were mutually exclusive, but documentation suggests that modified arrangements bridging the latter two systems were commonplace in Philadelphia.

Only carpenters at the upper levels of the profession, who commanded the respect of their fellows, were offered opportunities to act as measurers or valuers. They were compensated by being paid a percentage of the valuation, which might be as high as three per cent, "a tidy sum" (Moss [1972], 89). Nevertheless, it was not in their best interest to overinflate the values. Their fundamental purpose was to arrive at a price that was fair to everyone. The measurers generally worked in teams of at least two, adding another checkpoint to the process. Their valuation was subject to the scrutiny of both client and craftsman. In addition, as carpenter-builders, they would, in turn, have their work measured by others. It was the satisfactory combination of professional expertise, estimated cost, and independent valuation that made the system of "mensuration" a popular form of deciding the final price.

DOCUMENTATION:

Thomas Nevell. Day Book, 1762-1782. Wetherill Papers. Division of Special Collections, Van Pelt Library, University of Pennsylvania.

REFERENCES:

Moss, Roger W., *Historic Houses of Philadelphia*. Philadelphia (1998); ———. *Master Builders: A History of the Colonial Philadelphia Building Trades*. Ann Arbor (1972); Peterson, Charles E., intro. *The Rules of Work of the Carpenters' Company of the City and County of Philadelphia 1786*. Princeton, NJ (1971); Tatman and Moss, 790.
Dickey, John M. and Sandra M. Lloyd. "Historic Structures Report: Mount Pleasant for the Fairmount Park Council for Historic Sites." July 1987; HABS, PA-1130.

26

Design and Build Zion Lutheran Church

East Side Fourth Street (Southeast Corner Fourth and Cherry Streets), Philadelphia
1766, burned 1794, rebuilt, demolished 1869

BEFORE THE ARRIVAL of Henry Melchior Muhlenberg in Philadelphia, members of the German Lutheran and German Reformed Congregations shared worship space in a barn on Arch Street near Fifth. Efforts to build individual churches appeared to be thwarted by factions and divisions within the groups, but respect for Muhlenberg served to reduce strife temporarily among Lutherans in the city. Just

four months after his arrival, they purchased a lot on the east side of Fifth Street, and began construction of a church. St. Michael's was dedicated in August 1748, after construction lapses due to insufficient funding. The church was a rectangle, forty-five feet by seventy feet, with an impressive tower, which had to be removed in 1750 because its weight caused the walls to bow. Even after the tower was dismantled, the walls continued to spread and small "porches," similar to those at Gloria Dei, were added as buttresses (Westcott, 129-132).

Robert Smith was in Philadelphia by then, and he probably was aware of the tower episode. He was associated with two steeple projects in the early 1750s, Christ Church (Catalog #4) and Second Presbyterian (Catalog #2), but there is no evidence that he was consulted in the matter at St. Michael's. Smith was called upon a decade later, however, when St. Michael's proved to be too small to accommodate the congregation and the church council wanted guidance in exploring their options.

Even after overcrowding sent worshippers to services in the Zion Schoolhouse (Catalog #18A) and Whitefield Hall (New Building, Catalog #11), the congregation was cautious about undertaking a building project because they were still in debt. But conditions forced formulation of a plan for providing a larger facility. The council committed itself to eliminating the debt, and, on 13 September 1763, decided that when the indebtedness was paid "a new church shall be built with funds from the general treasury and the contributions of all the members of the church" (Haussmann, 1:43). Some parishioners opposed the prospect of building a new church, and proposed repairing and enlarging St. Michael's instead. This alternative seemed an expedient solution. Many in the congregation were not interested in founding a new parish, fearing a recurrence of the same divisiveness that had been a factor in the past, and that continued to plague the Germantown parishes.

The church council decided to keep their options open. To that end, Henry Keppele was appointed to examine a piece of land just a block away from St. Michael's at Fourth and Cherry Streets. It was thought that a new building, nearly in the shadow of the old, would reinforce the sense that they were really one congregation. Keppele reported to the vestry, but no decision was made about the site.

In October 1764, the congregation decided to enlarge St. Michael's to twice its original size, a course of action supported by Muhlenberg. On November 2nd, a committee was appointed, and instructed to "invite the celebrated architect, Mr. Robert Smith to inspect the church and then give his opinion" (Haussmann, 1:44). Seventeen days later, Muhlenberg noted that the committee "reported the judgement of the master builder, Robert Smith, concerning the church, namely, that it could not be enlarged, but must be torn down to the ground, etc." (Muhlenberg, 2:149). This evaluation, no doubt, caused distress. There was much discussion and lobbying, with one group, including Muhlenberg, continuing to support the prospect of enlarging St. Michael's and another eager to build a new church. The debt loomed large, which made people cautious, even as the congregation continued to expand and services were held in the church, the school house, and at the New Building owned by the College of Philadelphia (Hazard, 371).

While no particular course of action was authorized, the church council nevertheless pursued permission from the proprietors to build a church, so that they would be prepared to if that was the decision. When the plan to enlarge St. Michael's was finally abandoned in January 1766, they had in hand a charter from Thomas and Richard Penn, dated September 1765, authorizing the "erecting and supporting [of] one church more within the said city of Philadelphia or the liberties thereof for the better accommodating the said congregation" (*Deutsche Evangelisch*, 9; Westcott, 133). They also began a record book "containing the Minutes and Resolves . . . transacted in their respective Meetings begun on the 17th day of October Anno Domini 1765" (Vestry Book).

With Muhlenberg resigned to the necessity of a new building, the corporation made a resolution on February 19th to buy a lot on Cherry Street, opposite the school house, on which they would erect a "neue kirche" beginning in the spring (*Deutsche Evangelisch*, 9). Four days later, the congregation approved the expenditure of £1540 for a lot 96 by 128 feet, and immediately appointed "overseers and Managers of construction," including Henry Keppele and Jacob Graeff, Jr.[1] They were given power "to have a permanent and spacious new church built, to employ capable masons and carpenters and to keep an accurate account thereof" (Haussmann, 1:46).

Robert Smith's name first appears in the records associated with the building of Zion Lutheran Church in December 1766 when he presented his bill for woodwork. It is probable that he was paid because it was noted that the stone masons were not (Haussmann, 1:49). During that year, the walls had been completed as far as the roof and then construction slowed. The building, however, was noteworthy. When the cornerstone was laid in May 1766, it anchored a church 70 feet by 108 feet which, when completed, seated 2,500 people and was the largest and most beautiful Lutheran church in North America (*Deutsche Evangelisch*, 9).

Muhlenberg wrote about the cornerstone ceremony, and described a procession from St. Michael's to the building site, with sermonizing, hymn singing, an address by College of Philadelphia Provost William Smith, and an announcement "that anyone who wished to do so might place his mite upon it [the collection plate] as a thanks offering." Sixty-six pounds were collected and "considering the present hard times and the present shortage of money, this is to be regarded as an unexpected blessing, which the Lord in His grace vouchsafed to us" (Muhlenberg, 2:301-302). The hard times were reflected in the progress of the building project. Work was halted from time to time; even so, the debt continued to mount. Because Robert Smith continued to be involved in this and other large scale public and private projects, his financial situation must, at times, have been difficult. At Zion, the work proceeded in fits and starts, and Smith was requested to submit estimates, like one in 1767 "for plastering, the finishing of the cellar and the lower floor . . ., which called for an expenditure of £350, not counting the nails" (Haussmann, 1:49).

Work stopped again that summer. The debt exceeded four thousand pounds and St. Michael's Church needed repairs. Early in January 1768, Muhlenberg wrote that "in its present state Zion Church can not be of any use to us," and therefore Henry Keppele, Sr., and Jacob Graeff, Jr., should "go to the trouble of requesting the master builder, Robert Smith, to prepare an estimate of the costs of completely finishing the church" (Haussmann, 1:49-50). On January 9th, they recorded an estimate from "Architector Mr. Robert Smith" (Vestry Book, 128).

---

1. Jacob Graeff, Jr. served his church not only as a manager of construction but also as a participant. He was stonemason for Zion.

To finish Zions-Church from the Beginning of the Ground floor the Brick work in the foundation, and the Boards for the Floor excepted will cost—
To Carpenters Work for the Whole, except the Columns

to Scantling	£ 77	£ 1386
to Boards	187	
to Nails	40	
to Hinges	30	
to Stuff for Window Cases, Sashes, Venetian Windows Doors frontispieces etc		
	70	
to Glass	70	474
		£ 1860
to Glazeing and Painting		80
to Plaistering the Walls and Cieling of Galleries		80
		£ 2020

Smith must have been authorized to proceed. Progress, however, seemed to be very slow; whether this was due to the size and complexity of the building or to Smith's involvement with other projects is not known. In September 1768, Muhlenberg entered in the minute book of the church council an opinion that Zion church could hardly be finished before the winter, but work continued and decisions were made about placement of the pulpit and the position for an organ, if there should be money to buy one (Haussmann, 1:50). Once the news was announced in May that "Mr. Smith, the master builder, had promised to complete both the interior and exterior of Zion church within a month's time," a date was set for the dedication ceremony (Haussmann, 1:51).

Both St. Michael's and Zion Lutheran Church were included in the series of views by Thomas and William Birch published in the late eighteenth century. The progress of construction of the newer church was watched closely by Henry Melchior Muhlenberg. On 3 December 1767, he wrote to Robert Smith in English, describing him as the "Master-Builder or Architector of our new Church." Because many members of the congregation were immigrants and poor, Muhlenberg thought that permitting them to contribute work would add "Harmony and Unity" to the building program. He therefore hoped that Smith would permit some of them to lay the floor under his direction. Courtesy The Athenæum of Philadelphia.

Although unfinished, Zion Lutheran Church was consecrated on two successive days in June, with services in German on the 25th and in English on the following day (Muhlenberg, 2:399-404). The ceremony and festivities rivaled those held at the laying of the cornerstone, with the procession, once again, beginning at St. Michael's. The building was worth waiting for. "The roof and ceiling were supported by eight large columns, of the Doric order, which served for bases of the arches of the ceiling, which was ornamented and finished in a most magnificent manner, no expense was spared in finishing the inside of this church" (Hazard, 371). The exterior, with its Venetian windows and brick pilasters, was no less handsome. If indeed its original appearance was restored in 1795, the wall surfaces were enlivened by belt courses and arched windows with keystones and impost blocks. The cornices were richly carved; the doorways had pedimented frontispieces; and the roof was adorned with urns. In short, Zion was the most elaborately ornamented of Smith's churches.

A tower, which was to have been "erected simultaneously with the walls" and had its own cornerstone laid 11 June 1766, was not completed in time for the dedication in 1769, nor would it be finished when Smith died in 1777 (Haussmann, 1:48).

The great Zion Church served its congregation for less than ten years before the British occupied Philadelphia and gutted the building. "Zion Church...whose interiors alone cost more than £2500 was broken up and cleared out on the inside and was taken over as a hospital for wounded, crippled and dying soldiers" (Muhlenberg 3:625). The building reopened only on 21 December 1781, after Cornwallis's surrender at Yorktown, when a service of thanksgiving was held (Faris, 142). The repairs required after the Revolution must have been extensive, although it is not known who was retained to undertake them.

Although Smith was dead, a 1788 insurance survey by his fellow member of the Carpenters' Company, Joseph Rakestraw, is support for the validity of descriptions of the church, like Hazard's quoted above. Rakestraw found

22 Inch Walls—the Inside finisht With Wainscot—Pews below—and Board pland and Groved for the Pews—in the Galleries the fronts of Which is finisht With Wainscot and the Dorrick—Entablature at the Bottom and a fret in the Moulding under the Caping of the Rale—8 Large fluted Columns under Groin Centers With full—Plinths—Base and Capital—and 4 small Do under the Galleries—a Neat Pulpit and Conopy overd—2 pair of Plane Open Newell Stairs—one Story high Each—all the Windows Arch'd" (Philadelphia Contributionship, 4 February 1788).

He valued the building at two thousand pounds, considerably less than Muhlenberg's claim of its cost, but nevertheless evidence of the extent of its ornamentation and "handsomeness."

Its glory was not to last. On 26 December 1794, diarist Joseph Hiltzheimer heard "the cry of fire" while visiting a neighbor. Despite efforts to control the blaze, flames spread under the roof and "the whole beautiful building burned to the ground" (Hiltzheimer, December 26, 1794). Another diarist, Elizabeth Drinker, "was sitting in the back parlor reading near 8 o'clock [when she was] alarmed by the noise of a Fire Engine, and the ringing of Bells." Her husband went to investigate

and on his return informed us, that it was the unfinished steeple of the German Church in Fourth Street...Between 9 and 10 when we thought the fire was extinguished, heard the bells ringing again, and soon discovered the fire had got a head. I was apprehensive by the appearance that great and superb building, the new German Lutheran Church, called Zion Church would be entirely consumed" (Drinker, 255).

It was; only the brick walls remained standing.

The congregation decided to rebuild, and immediately engaged Carpenters' Company member William Colladay to do the work. He was listed as a "house carpenter repairing it at this time" in a 1795 description of "Sion Church," which also noted the steeple would be finished to a height of "about 200 feet" (Hogan, 44). Church finances must have improved since the days of Robert Smith because there were no lapses in the progress of construction. The building, its exterior rebuilt in its original form, was reconsecrated on 27 November 1796 and continued to serve not only the Lutherans but also the nation at large as the site of important public services and funerals. Before the fire, on 22 March 1791, a memorial service for Robert Smith's patron, Benjamin Franklin, was held there, and on 26 December 1799 the church was home to visiting dignitaries honoring the memory of George Washington (*Fest-Buechlein*).

The seventy-foot width of Zion evidently appeared

With its interior already virtually destroyed during the British occupation of Philadelphia, Zion Lutheran was consumed by fire in December 1794. Frederick Reiche, a member of the German community, recorded the catastrophic event in a copperplate engraving. The church was quickly rebuilt in its original form. The Historical Society of Pennsylvania.

daunting to Smith. He did not attempt to span it with his raised tie beam truss. Instead, he returned to a more conventional scheme for a large church with side aisles and a nave, all, from the description by Hazard, with arched ceilings supported by columns. By 1795, when William Colladay rebuilt the church, master carpenters, having learned from Smith's example, had more confidence in the strength of an iron-reinforced truss. Colladay probably did employ a truss similar to those Smith had used at St. Peter's and St. Paul's. An 1830 insurance survey describes the building as having a clear-span arched ceiling.

"Die Alte Zionskirche" closed on All Saints' Day 1868 and was sold in 1869; it was demolished the same year.

DOCUMENTATION:

Drinker, Elizabeth. *Extracts from the Journal of Elizabeth Drinker, from 1759 to 1807, A.D.*. Edited by Henry D. Biddle. Philadelphia (1889); Krauth Memorial Library, Lutheran Archives Center at Philadelphia. Haussmann, Carl F. "History of St. Michael's and Zion Congregation, Philadelphia, Pa. compiled from original sources in conjunction with the celebration of the two-hundredth anniversary of the arrival of Henry Melchior Muhlenberg in Philadelphia." 2 Vols. Typescript, (n.d., c. 1942); St. Michael-Zion German Lutheran Church of Philadelphia. Receipts and Expenditures, 1765-1775. Vol. 1; Vestry Book for the Corporation of St. Michael's Church, and German Lutheran Congregation . . . begun on the 17th day of October Anno Domini 1765. Vol. 1; Hiltzheimer, Jacob. Diaries, 1795-1798, microfilm at American Philosophical Society; Hogan, Edmund. *The Prospect of Philadelphia*. Philadelphia (1795); Muhlenberg, H.M. *The Journals of Henry Melchior Muhlenberg*. 3 vols. Translated by Theodore G. Tappert and John W. Doberstein. Philadelphia (1942-1958); Insurance Survey, 5 February 1788, Philadelphia Contributionship. HSP.

REFERENCES:

Deutsche Evangelisch-Lutherische St. Michaelis-und Zions-Gemeinde in Philadelphia. Philadelphia (1892); Faris, 137-143; *Fest-Buechlein zum 175 Jaehrigen Jubilaeum der Zions-Gemeinde 1742-1917.* Philadelphia (1917); Glatfelder, Charles H. *Pastors and People: German Lutheran and Reformed Churches in the Pennsylvania Field, 1717-1793.* Vol 1. Breinigville, PA (1980); Hazard, Samuel, ed. "German Lutheran Congregation of Philadelphia." In *The Register of Pennsylvania.* 4:24 (12 December 1829); "Old Zion Past and Present," [booklet] (1945); Tatman and Moss, 156; Westcott, Thompson. "German Lutheran Church: St. Michael's and Zion." In *The Historic Mansions and Buildings of Philadelphia . . . .* Philadelphia (1877), 129-140.

27

Design and Build Buck Tavern[1]

About two miles south of Philadelphia on The Five Mile
  Round, Moyamensing Township
1765, demolished

ROBERT SMITH owned land south of the city in Moyamensing and Passyunk Townships, which was suitable for grazing and had development potential. The property in Moyamensing was on the "Five Mile Round," a loop road linking the city with its outlying districts, making it a prime location for a tavern or way station. Smith built a substantial two-story brick house, welcomed friends, including diarist Jacob Hiltzheimer, to a "housewarming" on 16 March 1766, and advertised it "To be Lett" the following spring.

A description in the *Pennsylvania Gazette* of 26 April 1767 offers an enticing glimpse of landscaped grounds and substantial buildings

...on a pleasant spot of ground. A TWO STORY brick house of 45 by 31 feet, four rooms on each floor, three good rooms in the garret, a good kitchen, and cellars under the whole, a pump and excellent water, a garden and orchard of choice fruit trees; the ground is divided by fences in a regular uniform manner; two summer houses on each side of the entrance of an avenue, at the end of which is an arbour; the whole new and in good order.

The advertisement contained a further inducement to prospective tenants, suggesting many "agreed it is very fit for a genteel tavern," and asking "reputable person[s] fit to carry on that business... [to] apply to ROBERT SMITH, carpenter, on Society-Hill, Philadelphia." Apply they did because the place became the Buck Tavern and was known by that name a century after Smith's death. There was a tavern in the city on Second Street known as the Buck, which was, perhaps, the inspiration for the name of Smith's establishment *(Pennsylvania Gazette*, 1 January 1767). Advertisements related to both places appear in newspapers of the period.

Buck Tavern undoubtedly was a source of steady income, and also offered Smith a "country" property at which he could entertain his friends. A respected innkeeper helped make Buck Tavern a destination. On 6 July 1769, an advertisement appeared in the *Gazette* touting the buildings, surroundings, and proprietor. "DANIEL GRANT (who lived upwards of 7 years a Barkeeper to Mr. John Biddle, at the Indian King) HAS now opened a HOUSE of ENTERTAINMENT, at the Sign of the Buck, being the house built by Mr. Robert Smith, on the road the Five Miles Round, in Moyamensing." After describing the buildings, "calculated... for large entertainments," and gardens, Grant proclaimed that he "provided the best liquors of all kinds... [in addition to] the best tea, chocolate, coffee, &c.," which demonstrates his willingness to appeal to a wide spectrum of the tavern trade.

Grant was the proprietor when Gunning Bedford surveyed the property in 1770 for the Philadelphia Contributionship. The survey confirms the property's use as a tavern and records the name of the innkeeper. Bedford's description is consonant with Smith's "To be Lett" advertisement, and includes additional details, which describe the interior construction. "...2 pertitions Cross the house are 9 inch walls— the others plasterd—architraves & mantle Cornist to the Chimneys—Scirting Round the Rooms—Board Newel Stairs—Garot plasterd—pertitions in &c plaind Boards—2 ways out on the Roof and Iron Rails up—a kitchen in the Celler..." (Loose Survey #1389). The survey confirms that the building was new and well detailed. Smith clearly seems to have made this a viable income-producing property.

Charles de Krafft's plan of 1790, after Hill's survey of 1788 documenting improvements recommended in 1787, shows a proposed road through the property, and also the orchards, allées, "summer houses," and sundry outbuildings described in Smith's advertisement of twenty years earlier. This suggests that the complex and its buildings changed little during the intervening period. Indeed, after Smith's death in February 1777, his administrators acknowledged receipt of rent from Thomas Mushett, innkeeper since 1773 (Register of Wills, #52, March 1777, and Licenses for Marriages..., 74 [1773] and 241 [1775]). He planned to continue leasing the tavern and advertised it in the *Pennsylvania Gazette* of 9 April 1777.

Philadelphia was occupied by the British in Sep-

---

1. The *Pennsylvania Gazette* for 4 April 1765 carried an advertisement for a tavern for sale. It had been licensed for sixty years and was located a half mile south of the city, on the Passyunk Road. It is possible that Smith bought an existing operation and modified it, making it his own. However, the locations are disparate, and the probability is that this had no connection with the "Buck."

tember and John Smith, Robert's eldest son and one of the administrators of his estate, was absent from the city for nearly a year. When he returned and supplied an accounting of his father's estate to the court, expenditures of £64.7.6 were noted for repairs to Buck Tavern before it was advertised for sale. (Orphans Court Book 11, 17 June 1780). Estate records from the account given in 1780 acknowledge sale of the tavern property in 1778. A considerable sum (£2425) was realized, but it is difficult to determine the relative value of currency during the years of the war and immediately afterward. Gunning Bedford had valued Smith's tavern at £500 in an insurance survey made in 1770. This would have covered only the tavern, not land or outbuildings. The difference in value, however, is substantial, and probably is due to wartime inflation.

The property continued as a tavern after it was purchased from Smith's family. In 1781, "That Elegant House, known by the Name of the BUCK TAVERN" was offered for sale by John Levins "by Public Vendue." Describing it to attract potential buyers, Levins highlighted features that had been there since Smith's time—"three acres of choice land, with Kitchen, Sheds and Stables . . . in good repair: most of the land is made into garden; the whole abounds with fruit Trees of almost every kind, well enclosed with a fence made of two inch plank, five feet high. The house is pleasantly situated, and commands a fine prospect of the river Delaware" (*Pennsylvania Gazette* 11 April 1781).

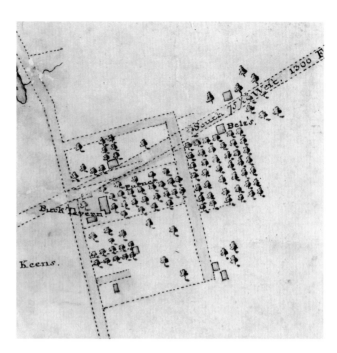

This detail of Charles de Krafft's 1790 copy of John Hills's 1788 map shows the desirable location of Buck Tavern on an important crossroads along the Five Mile Road. Courtesy Philadelphia City Archives.

DOCUMENTATION:

de Krafft, Charles. 1790 copy of John Hill's 1788 Plan of Southwark. Philadelphia City Archives; Hiltzheimer, Jacob. Diaries, 1765-1798. Microfilm at American Philosophical Society; Insurance Survey #1389, 3 March 1770, and Minute Book 6, 26 March 1770. Philadelphia Contributionship. HSP; Licenses for Marriages, Taverns, Peddlars [sic], etc. Vol 2, 1769-1775. HSP; Orphans Court Book 11:218-228, 17 June 1780. Philadelphia City Archives; *Pennsylvania Chronicle*, 27 April 1767, 8 March 1768; *Pennsylvania Gazette*, 1 January 1767, 30 April 1767, 6 July 1769, 10 August 1773, 9 April 1777 and 13 April 1781; *Pennsylvania Journal and Weekly Advertiser*, 10 August 1774.

REFERENCES:

S&W, 1; Thompson, Peter. *Rum Punch & Revolution: taverngoing & public life in eighteenth-century Philadelphia.* Philadelphia (1999).

28 A

Northampton County Courthouse

Center Square, Easton, Pennsylvania
1765, demolished 1866

DESIGN of the Northampton County Courthouse at Easton is attributed to Robert Smith for two reasons. The first, and most persuasive, is its resemblance to Carpenters' Hall in Philadelphia (Catalog #35). The second is the tantalizing documentary evidence that a trustee for the building project was paid "for Going to Philal [to] procure a bill of scantling" (Peterson, 99, n24; Commissioners' Minutes, 27 August 1765).

Jacob Hoffman was a landscape artist living in Philadelphia, whose views were published in the *Columbian Magazine,* the *Massachusetts Magazine,* and similar late eighteenth-century periodicals. This representation of the Northampton County Court House reveals its resemblance to the later Carpenters' Hall. Historical Society of Pennsylvania.

Land for a new county was appropriated from Bucks County in 1752, and in May surveyors Nicholas Scull and Williams Parsons laid out the town of Easton (Davis, 90-91). Parsons is described as a friend of Franklin in county histories and he may have been the link to Robert Smith. Another possible connection is George Taylor, who was something of an elder statesman in the newly formed community; he served as a trustee for the courthouse building project. Taylor travelled back and forth to Philadelphia, where he could have seen Smith's buildings and consulted with him for a tentative design (Metz, 1998).

After the county boundaries were decided, there was some disagreement about location of the county seat. Members of the Penn family favored Easton, at the confluence of the Lehigh and Delaware Rivers, but the citizens of the county were at odds, most wanting a central location, which would be more convenient for them. Despite their opposition, Easton

was chosen, and official county functions at first were accommodated in taverns and local residences. Building a jail was given priority because every county was required to have a prison, so it was not until March 1763 that the Commissioners made preparations to build a structure designated as the "Court House" (Commissioners' Minutes, 24 March 1763). A year later, the Commissioners decided to levy a tax on county residents "for Building a Court House & Defraying other publick charges of this County" (Commissioners' Minutes, 22 August 1764).

An additional county tax was memorialized in the Commissioners' Minutes of March 1765, and throughout the summer payments were made to George Taylor "to Discharge such Contracts as the Trustees" have negotiated (Commissioners' Minutes, 14 March 1765, 21 June 1765). In August, John Jones, who appears to have been a local carpenter, was paid "Expenses for going to Philadelphia," and on the same day "John Rinker one of the Trustees [was paid] for Going to Philal [to] procure a bill of scantling" (Commissioners' Minutes, 27 August 1765). A "bill" in this sense meant not an invoice, but an estimate. Scantling was a term for relatively small pieces of lumber. As part of the same trip, Rinker went "over the Mountain to the Sawmill," perhaps with the bill of scantling so the lumber would be properly cut.

In October 1765, "the Commissioners John Walker and Christopher Wagner Agreed that a County Tax shall be laid ... to defray the County Charges of Building a Court House," and it was agreed collection of the tax would begin in February. If extant records in the Pennsylvania Archives are representative of county policy, Northampton officials would have had to present a petition to the Provincial Assembly for permission to collect the tax. In 1766, one of the trustees was paid "for going Down with the petition to Philadelphia," a fact which could account for reimbursement for the earlier trips to the city, but not for the bill of scantling. (Commissioners' Minutes, 10 October 1766).

Nineteenth and early twentieth-century histories of the area acknowledge the resemblance of the Courthouse at Easton to Carpenters' Hall, but they fail to realize that the Easton building predated its Philadelphia counterpart. Carpenters' Hall may even have been designed in a hurry based on the existing plan for Northampton Courthouse. The format was unsuitable for an interior lot like the one in Philadelphia. The four equal gables certainly would be less surprising found in a public square approached from four sides, as at Easton, than heading up the narrow courtyard where it was actually built.

Certainly there were differences. Carpenters' Hall was built of brick, while the Courthouse was constructed of limestone, but geographical factors may have dictated the building materials. Also, the Philadelphia building carries more ornament, which may be a testament to the relative sophistication of the craftsmen, and their desire to show their finest skills in their own building. What remains, is the similarity of form and basic architectural detail, even though the decorative elements were not as rich at Easton. It is interesting to think that Smith, while engaged in other projects such as Benjamin Franklin's house and the rental properties for Mary Maddox, may already have been thinking of a design for Carpenters' Hall. This would not be unlikely because, as early as 1763 when the Carpenters' Company met to incorporate and adopt by-laws, they were considering the issue of erecting a suitable meeting place (Peterson, 98).

One hundred years later, arguments about location of the courthouse resurfaced and, in May 1860, a decision was made to move. "The venerable building at the Square was razed, the material removed, and the ground graded," obliterating any physical evidence of a Robert Smith building in Northampton County (Metz to A.S. Kichline, Peterson Files, n.d.).

DOCUMENTATION:

Commissioners' Minutes, 1755-1782. Northampton County Papers, Collection 456. HSP.

REFERENCES:

Davis, William W.H. *History of Bucks County, Pennsylvania.* Vol. 2. New York (1905), 91-92; Heller, William J. *History of Northampton County.* New York (1920); Peterson, Charles E. "Carpenters' Hall." In *HP*, 96-128.

Correspondence between Lance Metz and Charles E. Peterson. Northampton County Courthouse file. Peterson Files.

29

"Complete the Plan" for the Almshouse and House of Employment (Bettering House)

South side Spruce Street between Tenth and Eleventh Streets, Philadelphia
1766, demolished 1834-5

NEARLY THREE YEARS after the managers asked Robert Smith to "Complete the Plan and estimate the cost..." (Minutes, 29 and 31 May 1766), he was paid £30 "for his Services in Drawing Plans of the Alms House." At the same time, Smith was credited with two cash contributions of ten pounds each, one for himself, the other for his son John. This appears to have been customary practice. Most workmen affiliated with the project were also listed as contributors (Treasurer's Account, 10 January 1769). Similar contributions had been made a decade previously for construction of the Pennsylvania Hospital.

The Almshouse was another project in which Smith and Samuel Rhoads were intertwined, with Rhoads acting as manager and Smith as designer. In this capacity, Smith probably incorporated the ideas of those sponsoring the project into a comprehensive scheme for the complex of buildings that became the Almshouse and House of Employment. His design may in part have been inspired by James Horne's Foundling Hospital in London. (See Introduction.)

The buildings constructed between 1766 and 1767 on the western fringe of the city were authorized by an act of the Pennsylvania Assembly in February 1766. Two almshouses, a municipal refuge at Third and Spruce and a Quaker poorhouse on Walnut Street, had preceded this one. By the early 1760s, both had been overwhelmed by the needs of the destitute and downtrodden, and Philadelphia's Overseers of the Poor spent two years convincing the Assembly of the need for a new facility. The poorhouses provided care for the ill and insane, as well as for those unable to make their way or sustain themselves because of circumstance or misfortune. An organizations, such as the Saint Andrew's Society, raised money from its members to assist indigent Scotsmen and attempted to meet the needs of widows and orphans, as did the Carpenters' Company for its mem-

The two wings of the Almshouse, all that was ever completed of a larger scheme, bore
considerable resemblance to James Horne's Foundling Hospital in London. Similarities include
the bulky corner pavilions with hipped roof and prominent string courses, as well as the
interior arcades, noted in written descriptions, although not illustrated in this print.
Courtesy The Athenæum of Philadelphia.

bers. Still, the existing combination of public and
private assistance was insufficient to meet the need.
After construction of the East Wing of the Pennsylvania Hospital in 1755-1756, some of the medical
needs of the city's poor and mentally ill were met at
that location, which did serve to alleviate overcrowding at the poorhouse. Relief, however, was only temporary. With each ship's arrival, more people flowed
not only into the city's shops and trades, but also on-
to the streets. In many cases, their only place of
refuge was the poorhouse.

When the city acquired the block between Tenth
and Eleventh Streets and Spruce and Pine, accumu-
lation of building materials had already begun. Additional boards, stone, lime, bricks, and cedar poles
were delivered to the site while Joseph Allen's men

were digging the cellar. Names familiar in the building trades appear in the Treasurer's Accounts and it
seems fitting that men like Joseph Rakestraw, Samuel
Wetherill, Jr., Benjamin Loxley, and Thomas Nevell
would work on this important civic project. Robert
Smith was among those asked in June 1766 to "see
the work done agreeable to the Plan," but he was occupied with construction of Zion Lutheran Church at
Fourth and Cherry Streets, where the cornerstone
was laid in May (Catalog #26). Despite the absence
of his name as a routine participant in construction,
it is likely he appeared at the site to assess progress.
The buildings were erected with remarkable speed,
which suggests cooperation and coordination of effort
among all the craftsmen. Construction began in late
spring 1766 and by December the managers agreed

"that the East Wing of the building shall be finished with all convenient dispatch, the West Wing to be shingled, and the Windows & Doors Clos'd" (Minutes, 6 December 1766). The first occupants arrived in October 1767.

The almshouse was laid out in the form of an L, one hundred and eighty feet by forty, two stories in height, joined by a turret thirty feet square, and four stories high. The house of employment was on the west side of the lot, running south from Spruce, fronting Eleventh Street, also in the shape of an L, so that the range of buildings, enclosed on three sides a quadrangular space. A large central building was erected on Spruce Street, which stood between the L's (S&W, 2:1451).

The "turrets" were the monumental corner pavilions, with belt courses stressing the buildings' horizontal planes. Relief from the stern massing of the wings was provided by a "cloister of open arches" facing the interior courtyard. This colonnade, described as one story in height, introduced a touch of delicacy and rhythm to the sober demeanor of the place, while providing a sheltered, open-air place for the aged and infirm (S&W, 2:1451).

The central building evidently never was constructed, although it is shown both in a painting and a print derived from it. The painting probably was executed about 1767, but the print was not published until 1769 (Snyder, 81-82; *Pennsylvania Gazette*, 26 January 1769). However, these images, rather than depicting an existing building, may have been copied from a drawing, perhaps even Smith's own rendering. Almost certainly, the engravings of the Pennsylvania Hospital, executed in 1761, came from some such source. They show the complete hospital building with a central pavilion and two wings, when it is known that only one wing had been built at the time (Snyder, Figures 21, 22 and 70). In the 1790s, the central building of the Almshouse does not appear in prints by Malcom and Birch, although it surfaces again in rather fanciful form in 1815, as rendered by William Strickland, perhaps as an idea for the replacement building he later would design. Gunning Bedford's post-Revolutionary survey of what he describes as "The Northwest part of the house of Imployment [sic] & almshouse" seems to encompass only one building (Survey, 6 March 1786). A 1788 report described the "hospital" [by which the Almshouse was meant] as "constructed of bricks, and composed of two large buildings" (Hunter, *PMHB*, 50).

Had the Pennsylvania Hospital and the Almshouse both been completed as planned, they would have been companion pieces in an overall civic vision relying on the basic principles of classical symmetry. They are evidence that Philadelphia's civic leaders and architect-builders could plan on a large scale, incorporating contextual considerations into their designs.

The Almshouse served the poor for fewer than ten years before the southeast wing was appropriated for use by the military in October 1776. Injured soldiers arrived in the winter (Christopher Marshall Diary, 7 December 1776). The inmates were crowded into the remaining space. After the British occupied the city, the managers were asked to clear the buildings; at first they refused, but were unable to hold out for very long. The British removed the inmates to the Freemasons' Hall, Friends' Meeting House, and Car-

The Foundling Hospital (1742-1750) is depicted in William Maitland's *History of London*, published in 1756. Smith could have known it from this engraving, or could have seen the first wing, completed in 1745, and the partial construction of the second, completed in 1749, before emigrating.

penters' Hall. When the British left the city in mid-June 1778, the Almshouse again served as a hospital.

When the managers regained control of the Almshouse and House of Employment, the buildings were in deplorable condition, and the treasury was in a similar state. By 1781, the Legislature passed a law vesting the overseers with the power to incorporate. As Philadelphia expanded after the Revolution, it became increasingly obvious that a new, larger facility would be necessary. In 1829 plans for a new Almshouse designed by William Strickland were approved, although it was not completed until 1835 (Lawrence, 135). The old almshouse was demolished.

DOCUMENTATION:

HSP. Relief and Employment of the Poor. Contributors' Daybook, 1767-1768. Coll. #776; Insurance Survey, 6 March 1786. Philadelphia Contributionship; Christopher Marshall Diary; Thomas Nevell Day Book, 1762-1782, Wetherill Papers, Division of Special Collections, Van Pelt Library, University of Pennsylvania; Overseers of the Poor (Corporation of Contributors Relief of the Poor). Managers Minutes, 1766-1788. Treasurer's Accounts, 1766-1788. Philadelphia City Archives; *Pennsylvania Gazette.* 26 January 1769 and 25 January 1770.

REFERENCES:

Agnew, D. Hayes, M.D., *Lecture on the Medical History of the Philadelphia Almshouse.* Philadelphia (1862); Curtain, Roland G., M.D. "The Philadelphia General Hospital." In *Founders' Week Memorial Volume.* Edited by Frederick P. Henry. Philadelphia (1909); Hunter, Robert J. "The Activities of Members of the American Philosophical Society in the Early History of the Philadelphia Almshouse." *Proceedings of the American Philosophical Society,* 61,6 (1932): 309-319; ———. "The Origin of the Philadelphia General Hospital." *PMHB*, 57, 1 (January 1933): 32-57; Lawrence, Charles. *History of the Philadelphia Almshouses and Hospitals.* Philadelphia (1905); Morton, Thomas G., assisted by Frank Woodbury. *The History of the Pennsylvania Hospital 1751-1895.* Philadelphia (1895); Snyder, Martin P. *City of Independence.* Philadelphia (1975); S&W, 1:205-206, 260 and 2:1450.

Cliveden is another of the great Philadelphia Georgian country houses for which Smith served as a member of the measuring team. Here he was valuing master carpenter Jacob Knor's work. Photograph by Tom Crane.

30

Measuring at Cliveden

6401 Germantown Avenue, Philadelphia
1766

Benjamin Chew engaged Germantown carpenter Jacob Knor to build a country seat to his design. Chew also functioned as the general contractor, leaving Knor to hire the specialist masons, plasterers, and painters who would create the modified Palladian villa constructed to Chew's vision. The final plan was elegant and refined, and raised the standard of Philadelphia country house design beyond mere pattern book copying.

Chew's account books reveal that he had an "agreement" with Knor, but it is unclear just what tasks were included (Tinckom, 20, n36). Knor received additional compensation for measuring the work of other craftsmen, such as the painters, masons, and plasterers, who were unpaid until their work and itemized statements were satisfactorily evaluated by measuring by "outside" professionals (Cliveden Papers, 11 January, 6 September, and 12 September 1765). Two members of the Carpenters' Company, Robert Smith and John Thornhill, were called upon to evaluate Knor's work, thus attesting to its quality, and authorize payment. This team had worked together previously measuring Thomas Nevell's work at Mount Pleasant. The "certified" bill was presented to Chew in 1766, with a written acknowledgement that they had met Chew's request to "have measured & valued all the Carpenters work that Knor has done . . ." (Cliveden Papers, 20 December 1766).

DOCUMENTATION:

Cliveden Papers, 1764-1816. Chew Family Papers, Collection #2050. On deposit, HSP.

Philadelphia 1766

Benjamin Chew Esqr
To Jacob Knor ——— Dr

To 24 feet of Valley Gutter	ad 12	£1 : 4 : 0
To 2 Dorm. windows	ad 115/	11 : 10 : 0
To 52 feet of gutters to the Eves	ad 8	1 : 14 : 8
To 187 feet of Base & Sr Base	ad 18	21 : 10 : 6
To 7 Sets of Inside Shatters, 2 pair in each Set	ad 32/	11 : 4 : 0
To 7 Ditto	ad 30/	10 : 10 : 0
To 23 yd of wainscot Sr Base high	ad 6/6	7 : 9 : 6
Architrave — To 529 feet 8 in of Architrave	ad 10	22 : 1 : 4
To 86 feet of Ditto	ad 9	3 : 0 : 0
To Caseing & hanging of 26 wind.	ad 5/	6 : 10 : 0
To 8 Ditto Cased and hung double	ad 7/6	3 : 0 : 0
Wainscot — To 97 yd 3 feet of Wainscot	ad 6/6	31 : 12 : 8
To 218 feet 6 in of Base & Sr Base	ad 16½	15 : 0 : 5
Arch... — To 293 feet of Architrave	ad 10	12 : 4 : 2
To 34 Knees to Ditto	ad 25	3 : 10 : 10
Archit. — To 226 feet 6 in of Architrave	ad 10	9 : 8 : 9
To 13 Knees to Ditto	ad 25	1 : 7 : 1
Archit. — To 29 feet Architrave, large Ditto	ad 13	1 : 11 : 5
To 2 Knees	ad 32½	5 : 5
To 39 feet 8 in of Architrave	ad 10	1 : 13 : 0
To 78 feet 9 in of Base & Sr Base	ad 17	5 : 11 : 6
To 122 feet 10 in of Dentill Cornice	ad 24	12 : 5 : 8
Grounds — To 2 frames under Architraves	ad 4/	8 : 0
To 5 Pedements, one Tabernacle frame, and other work on a Chimeney		20 : 2 : 6
To 124 feet 10 in of Dentill Cornice	ad 24	12 : 9 : 8
To 57 feet 5 in. of Dorick Intablature	ad 2/9	7 : 17 : 10
To 116 feet 9 in of Collumns glewed up and flutted	ad 5/	29 : 3 : 9
To 24 feet of Bases, Capes, & plinths	ad 2/	4 : 16 : 0
To hanging 11 Sashes with hinges	ad 1/3	13 : 9
To 9 Pair of large six pane Shutters lined	ad 22/6	10 : 2 : 6
To 4 pair of Ditto Bead & flush on one side	ad 25/	5 : 0 : 0
To 291 Squares & 43 feet of measurable work	ad 18	262 : 5 : 9
To 3 Storys of Stairs, one story ramped and the wainscot ramped on the half pace of Ditto		68 : 18 : 9
To 52 Sqs of Work in Stables & Coach house and 82 ...	ad 5/	39 : 12 : 3
		£655 : 15 : 8

at the request of Benj.n Chew Esqr & Mr Jacob Knor
We have measured the Carpenters work of a House
at German Town, which is contain. in the above Acco.t
Measureing &c. ad 3 ... £ 19 : 18 f half £9 : 16 : 6

Rob Smith
Jo Thornhill

REFERENCES:

Garvan, Beatrice B. "Cliveden." In *Philadelphia: Three Centuries of American Art*. Philadelphia (1976), 82-83; Tinkcom, Margaret B. "Cliveden: The Building of a Philadelphia Countryseat, 1763-1767." *PMHB*, 88, 1 (January 1964): 3-36; Moss, Roger W. *Historic Houses of Philadelphia* (1998): 116-121.

31

Third Presbyterian Church ("Old Pine")

412 Pine Street, Philadelphia
1766, altered 1837, 1857, 1867, 1952

THE "Erection of a new Presbyterian Church (being a third in this City)" was authorized at a meeting of the General Committee of the First Church on 16 January 1766. At that time, over £600 had been raised for construction and "occupants for above 50 pews [might] remove to the intended new Church." As Philadelphia grew, overcrowding was one of the circumstances that had led the Christ Church Vestry to undertake building St. Peter's (Catalog #13), and similar conditions existed at First Church. That was not always the case. The evangelical movement of the 1740s had a direct impact on First Church; many of its members withdrew their support, and, after a bitter dispute, built their own house of worship, Second Presbyterian (Catalog #2). An influx of new members, principally from Scotland and Ireland, revitalized First Church; by the 1760s, the trustees again had to contend with overcrowding and the issue of an inconvenient location. First Church was on High [Market] Street, while most of the congregation lived in the rapidly growing southern part of the city. Therefore, in 1762, the trustees decided to acquire ground on Society Hill and formed a committee to consider options and alternatives. They agreed to approach the proprietors for a land grant, "undertake to raise by Subscription a Fund for Building ye said New Church," and arrange for use of a small house at Second and South Streets as a temporary worship space (First Presbyterian Church, Minutes, 24 June 1765; S&W, 1:1267).

Smith was the architect, although evidently not the builder, of the new church. Minutes of a meeting of "the Managers of the new Church building in Pine Street," on 2 September 1767, record their determination to complete the building, despite unpaid subscriptions and a depleted treasury. They appointed a subcommittee "to consult with Mr. Robert Smith, the architect, & settle the breadth of the galleries in order to lay out the places for the Pillars & the width of the Alleys" (First Presbyterian Church, Minutes, 2 September 1767). Church member and carpenter James Armitage was described in a subscription list as having "Employm[ent] in a very large Am[oun]t" and "Thomas Nevill Carpenter [as] put[ting] on [the] Roof & Ceiling" ("A List of Subscriptions actually received . . ."). An undated notation on the inside cover of Nevell's account book recorded an "Agreement for roof & cealing of New Presbyterian Meatin [sic] House" for £440 (Thomas Nevell Day Book). While Smith appears to have been the designer and Nevell the roofer, one Captain Condy was overseer of the work. When the building was completed, the congregation appointed a committee to meet with him "to try to learn how long he has been employd in their Service & make an Estimate what may be a sufficint recompence for his services that the Committee may pay him Accordingly" (Minutes, 14 August 1769).

Although the building has been altered almost beyond recognition, Smith's design influence is indicated by the surviving physical evidence of the raised tie beam roof trusses. He had introduced his variation on a British model and already used it successfully at St. Peter's and St. Paul's. The Pine Street Church span, like that of St. Peter's is approximately sixty feet.

Each truss has impressive iron straps at the heel joints and at the ends of the collar beam. Also, every truss has a vertical stirrup tying the kingpost to the collar beam, as well as a wrought iron yoke bolted to the underside of the long diagonals at the center of the truss. Interestingly, all of the iron straps seem to be incised with Roman numerals [but] if there was a pattern [to the numbers], it [does] not seem to correspond to the numerical markings on the wood truss members" (Pentz to Peterson).

The eighteenth-century trusses and shingles are intact beneath the present roof, which has been raised several feet to accommodate Classical Revival taste.

By the spring of 1767, the "large plain church" was still incomplete, being "nearly roofed, but no inside work, door nor window made or set up" (Minutes, 22 June 1772). The church still was unfinished when it

This seems to be the only image of the Third Presbyterian Church showing it before a series of major changes altered its appearance. The east side had already been modified by the substitution of two entrances for one. Nevertheless, with its Palladian window on the side facing the street, its pedimented doorways, and arched windows, it seems to have closely resembled the earlier Second Presbyterian Church. This view comes from a pamphlet issued by the church.

opened its doors for a service at the end of May 1768. During this period, it is almost impossible to assess the exact status of the building project. In December 1768, First and Second Churches joined forces to promote a lottery to discharge their debts. First Church allocated

the Dividend to be received from Said Lottery . . . toward paying the Debts that have accrued to us by Building the Church in Pine and fourth Streets—Reserving only Two hundred [pounds] towards paying the Debts that have accrued to us by repairing our Church in Market Street (First Presbyterian Church, Minutes, 22 December 1768).

Permission for the lottery was granted by the Assembly in 1769, enabling the churches to pay off the greater portion of their debts, and Third Church to complete its building (S&W, 2:1267).

The only known description of the original appearance of Third Church was published on the occasion of its centennial in 1868. The Rev. R.H. Allen listed architectural details remarkably similar to those used at Robert Smith's neighboring churches, and estimated the cost of the brick building at $16,000. Because it was a Presbyterian meeting house, Smith was not confined to a liturgical orientation, and could place the main entrance in the north gable end. He laid out pedimented entrances below Palladian windows on the north and south walls, and punctuated

the pedimented gables (and ventilated the roof) with bull's-eye windows. On the east facade there was a central doorway flanked by two windows on each side. Above these was a range of five round-arched windows. The west side of the church was a blank wall, except that immediately back of the pulpit, which was on that side, was a window (Allen, 1870).

Minutes document the building of the galleries according to a plan presented by Mr. Linnard in July 1792 (Third Presbyterian Church, Trustees' Minutes, 2 July 1792). Whether this means galleries had never been erected to Smith's plan, or that they were destroyed when the church was used as a hospital, and later a stable, during the British occupation of the city, is unknown (S&W, 2:1273). Other changes to the building also were made in the 1790s. The entrance centered on the east wall was bricked in and the array of openings was altered, creating three windows and two pedimented end doors.

A series of alterations from 1837, when the windows were "modernized" and the exterior stuccoed, through 1987 transformed the eighteenth-century meeting house into a Greek Revival temple. The columns, designed by John Fraser, were added to the Pine Street (north) wall in 1857. The roof was raised, and the building prepared for a complete interior remodeling, in 1867. Twenty years after that, additional exterior renovations were made. In the 1950s, architects Kneedler, Mirick and Zantzinger supervised a restoration program. Alterations were made to the lower level and entrance to the sanctuary in the 1980s, and a new interior decorative scheme devised. With all these changes, the only remnant of Robert Smith's design is in the roof trusses hidden above the later ceiling.

DOCUMENTATION:

Presbyterian Historical Society. First Presbyterian Church, Treasurer's Reports and Minutes, 1742-1772. Typescript. "A List of Subscriptions actually received . . . towards building a third Presbyterian Church in Philadelphia . . .," c. 1774; Third Presbyterian Church. Trustees' Minutes. Vol. 1, 1771-1796; Insurance Survey, Policy #1460, 24 June 1830. Pennsylvania Fire Insurance Company. HSP; Thomas Nevell. Day Book, 1762-1782. Wetherill Papers. Division of Special Collections, Van Pelt Library, University of Pennsylvania.

REFERENCES:

Allen, Rev. R.H., ed. *Leaves from a Century Plant: Report of the Centennial Celebration of Old Pine Street Church . . .* Philadelphia (1870); Faris, 53-58; Jeffreys, C.P.B. "The Provincial and Revolutionary History of St. Peter's Church, Philadelphia, 1753-1783." *PMHB*, 48 (1924): 338; Mackie, Rev. Alexander. "The Presbyterian Churches of Old Philadelphia." In *HP*, 217-229; Old Pine Street Church. Pamphlets (ca.1922, 1957). Order of service for rededication 20 May 20 1956; S&W, 2; Scott, John Wellwood. *An Historical Sketch of The Pine Street, or Third Presbyterian Church.* Philadelphia (1837).
HABS, PA-1374; Hammond, Joseph W. "Timber Framing Engineering of Robert Smith: Leading Builder/Architect of Colonial America." Paper presented at Robert Smith's Birthday, St. Peter's Church Philadelphia 14 January 1995 and 3rd Annual APT/DVC Symposium on Historic Timber Preservation, Arch Street Meeting, Philadelphia, 2 March 1996; Philadelphia Historical Commission, "Third Presbyterian Church," Brief of Title, 1765-44; Suzanne Pentz, Keast & Hood Co., to Charles E. Peterson, 6 October 1998. Peterson Files.

32

John Lawrence Project

Location unknown, probably Philadelphia
1767

DURING John Lawrence's tenure as mayor of Philadelphia (1765-1767), he engaged Robert Smith to carry out some type of building project. Whether Smith built a house for Lawrence or made alterations to an existing building is unknown. The only record of this transaction is that Smith wrote to Lawrence on 21 March 1767, requesting payment to one of his sub-contractors. "Sir Please to pay William Warner on order the sum of nine shillings for Boering the Collumns of the frontispiece to the front Door."

John Lawrence (1724-1799) had a number of connections with Robert Smith. He undoubtedly was familiar with Smith's work for Mary Maddox because his name is mentioned as one of her tenants in her building contract with Smith. A John Lawrence, probably this man, was one of the guests listed in Jacob Hitltzheimer's diary as present at the Buck Tavern housewarming (Catalog #27). Lawrence also was part of a circle of patronage related to Smith. His daughter married James Allen, the son of William Allen, who was active in the Third Presbyterian Church in Philadelphia (Catalog #31) and the First Presbyterian Church in Carlisle (Catalog #40). In 1773 Lawrence built a "very fine and stately dwelling" on the northeast corner of Sixth and Chestnut Streets (S&W, 2:882). The house was surveyed in 1785 and the written description attests to its elegance and ornament (Garvan, et al., 109-110). Could this be another Smith project? Unless further documentation surfaces, we may never know, but, given their connections, it is not unreasonable to conclude that when Lawrence was ready to either build or alter a house he would call upon Smith.

DOCUMENTATION:

Garvan, Anthony N.B., Cynthia Koch, Donald Arbuckle, and Deborah Hart. "Survey for Policy Number 146." In *The Architectural Surveys 1784-1794.* Vol. 1 of the Mutual Assurance Company Papers. Philadelphia (1976); HSP. Insurance Survey (James Glenn property), 16 March 1774. Philadelphia Contributionship; Robert Smith to John Lawrence, Esq., 21 March 1767. Stauffer Collection, 5: 437.

REFERENCES:

Keith, Charles P. *The Provincial Councillors of Pennysylvania...1733-1776*. Philadelphia (1883). Reprint, Baltimore (1997); S&W, 2: 882, 3: 1736.

33

Arbitrator for St. Peter's Church

Barren Hill, Whitemarsh, Montgomery County,
   Pennsylvania
1768, burned 1778, demolished 1849

AT BARREN HILL Robert Smith assumed a new role. In the course of his duties, he (and others) would measure the church, as he had other buildings. But his prime responsibility was as an arbitrator when the congregation encountered financial and legal difficulties.

In the eighteenth century, German Lutherans developed small congregations in outlying regions. As a result of a schism in the Germantown church, some Lutheran and Reformed members of that congregation joined to build a log schoolhouse in eastern Montgomery County in 1758. Initially this doubled as a church, with both Lutheran and Reformed services. Three years later, the Lutheran members of the congregation laid the cornerstone of a stone church, which was completed in 1763 (Doebler, 38; Glatfelter, 370). Because of his connection to Zion Lutheran Church (1766), Robert Smith's name has been associated with both these Montgomery County buildings. There is no documentation supporting his involvement with the school; however, his name appears in a manuscript record of 1767-68 related to the church. Smith was one of four men called upon to resolve a dispute over the costs of erecting the building.

Christopher Raben was chairman of the building committee for St. Peter's, with the Barren Hill school teacher, Selig, as accountant ("Muhlenberg Manuscript," 285). But funds proved difficult to come by. Although the congregations of Philadelphia's German churches were large, their members tended to be poor (Glatfelter, 414). Like its contemporary, St.

George's, the Barren Hill church was soon in financial difficulties.

When the church was completed, an enormous debt remained. Funding had been sought through a lottery in 1762, but it was unsuccessful, and by 1764 creditors were demanding their fees. Henry Melchior Muhlenberg, Henry Keppele, and others associated with St Michael's Church, were trustees of the church at Barren Hill. After attempts to raise money in Europe failed, Muhlenberg, Keppele, and the Rev. Dr. Wrangel of the Swedish Church assumed the debt. Control of St. Peter's was transferred to St. Michael's. Muhlenberg and Henry Keppele then demanded an investigation of the bookkeeping of Raben and Selig ("Muhlenberg Manuscript," 285-291). Four men were appointed as a Board of Arbitrators, among them Robert Smith. After deliberating for half a year, reviewing the bills, and measuring the building, they submitted a report in 1768.

The chosen Gentlemen Arbitrators Messrs Robert Smith Architect Jacob Graeff Master-Builder, Frederick Kuhl and Michael Hillegas Esqs having consider'd and compared all the Accounts, measured and computed the Building according to the common Rules, Prizes [prices] of Materials and Work, gave in the month of Decembr: 1768 the following Resolve and Settlement before their Award viz:

1, that the Cost or Charge of the whole Edifice according to the Measure amounted to 887£ 15 Shill: 9d.curr:

2, and the Contributions raised by Subscription and Lottery to 229£ 15Sh: 9d:

3, that Christopher Raben had in hand yet 20£ 6d; which he should repay to Henry Muhlenberg and Henry Kepp[e]le. Now add these 20£ 6d. to the Sum of 229£ 15Sh: 9d: You'l[l] have 249L 16Sh: 3 d: and

deduct of   887£   15sh   9d
               249"   16"   3"

Debt 637£ 9sh 6d there remains unto the year 1769, as more at large appears in a Writing of the Settlement, made by the above said Gentlemen Arbitrators.

Fortunately, large contributions from Europe, arriving in 1768 and 1770, could be used to pay the debt.

Henry Keppele, prominent in German circles, and familiar with Smith through the latter's activities at St. Michael's and Zion, may have been instrumental in requesting Smith's opinion as an arbitrator at St. Peter's. In any event, the choice of Smith to serve in this delicate matter attests to the respect in which he was held by Philadelphia's Lutheran community.

DOCUMENTATION:

Krauth Memorial Library, Lutheran Archives Center at Philadelphia. H. M. Muhlenberg. Balance Sheet of Barren Hill Finances, St. Peter's 1774; Narratives Concerning the Erection of the Schoolhouse & Church at Whitemarsh, now called Barren Hill; Renewed power of attorney for H. M. Muhlenberg in the administration of the Ebenezer-Salzburgers Congregation, 1778; Constitution of the Barren Hill Congregation, August 1765; Accounts of Barren Hill Church Building; Part of the History of St. Peter's at Barren Hill; Muhlenberg, Henry Melchior. *The Journals of Henry Melchior Muhlenberg.* Translated by Theodore G. Tappert and John W. Doberstein. 3 vols. Philadelphia (1942-1958); "A Muhlenberg Manuscript." *Bulletin of the Historical Society of Montgomery County, Pennsylvania,* 21 (1959):282-297.

REFERENCES:

Bean, Theodore W., ed. *History of Montgomery County, Pennsylvania.* Philadelphia (1884); Doebler, Harold F. *Saint Peter's Lutheran Church, Barren Hill, PA. 1752-1952.* Philadelphia (1952); Glatfelter, Charles H. *Pastors and People: German Lutheran and Reformed Churches in the Philadelphia Field, 1717-1793.* Breinigsville, PA (1980); S&W. 2:1422.

34

Samuel Powel Projects

Two houses on Second Street;
Alterations to Powel's house, 244 South Third Street Stores/ storehouses;
"Repairs at sundry Places," various locations, specific sites unknown, Philadelphia
1768-1776

ROBERT SMITH'S RELATIONSHIP with patron Samuel Powel was one of the longest of his career. Powel could afford the very best, so his choice is a testimonial to the quality of Smith's work.

Three generations of men named Samuel Powel rose to prominence in eighteenth-century Philadelphia. The family founder (d.1756), known as the "rich carpenter," amassed a sizeable estate with considerable real estate holdings in and around the city. A member of the Carpenters' Company, he passed his profession to his son; his wealth, however, was not merely derived from carpentry, but rather from inheritance and a prudent marriage (Tatum, 7-8). This made it possible for the first Powel and his son to pursue mercantile business ventures and invest in trading voyages (Tolles, 116). The second Samuel (d.1747) pre-deceased his father. His three children were comfortable financially, and, after their grandfather's death, wealthy.

The first documented association between Samuel Powel III (1738-1793) and Robert Smith occurred in 1760, when Smith supplied Powel with cedar plank. (Powel Family Papers, Ledger, 21 October 1760). Shortly after acquiring this lumber, Powel left Pennsylvania for an extended European tour, which lasted seven years. When he returned, he created a ledger page headed by Smith's name, evidence of Powel's anticipation of an ongoing working relationship. Powel may have been familiar with Smith through his grandfather's professional affiliation. He also probably was aware of Smith's work at the College of Philadelphia (Catalog #15), of which he was a graduate, and Saint Peter's Church, where he was a communicant.

The ledger refers to contractual arrangements for building two houses and "Stores," as well as "Repairs at sundry Places," and, most important, finishing a room in Powel's house. The contracts do not survive, but it is possible that they were similar in form to Smith's agreement with Mary Maddox. This suggests that Powel paid Smith fixed sums for these projects, rather than having the compensation valued by measurement, as had been the case at the Franklin House. Measuring still could have played a role, because the prices used in measuring completed work also could be used to estimate costs as the basis for a contractual agreement.

Samuel Powel's House

In 1769, two years after Powel returned from his European tour, he married Elizabeth Willing at Christ Church. Powel was born a Quaker but had converted to the Anglican faith while in England in 1764. The newlyweds settled into a newly purchased house on Third Street. Built for Charles Stedman in 1765, it adjoined the residence of Governor John Penn. It was described in a 1766 advertisement in *The Pennsylvania Gazette* as "large well finished [and] commodious" (Tatum, 6-7). Powel purchased the house in August 1769, just days before his wedding. Although it remained unsold between 1766 and Powel's

The Powel House, built for Charles Stedman in 1765, is the finest surviving example of a Philadelphia Middle Georgian town house. Although its interior was partially stripped and reconstructed in the Philadelphia and Metropolitan Museums of Art, its robust exterior has survived intact. Photograph by Tom Crane.

The reconstructed interior of the grand parlor or ballroom on the second floor of the Powel House reflects the finest Philadelphia mid-eighteenth century carpentry, plasterwork, and decorative carving. The original woodwork, considerably augmented to fit a large display space, is in the Philadelphia Museum of Art. Photograph by Tom Crane.

purchase in 1769, he paid the substantial sum of £3150 for the house, back buildings and stable.

Powel promptly insured the house with the Philadelphia Contributionship, and Carpenters' Company member Gunning Bedford valued the house at £1000 and the back building at £500. Powel entered into contracts with Smith "for finishing a Room in my Dwelling House" and for making alterations to the building. Although there is no documentation to support such a hypothesis, it is possible that Smith had built the house for Charles Stedman, and thus was the logical person to call on to enhance it.

The tasks called for are not specifically spelled out in the contract, so that no features can, with certainty, be attributed to Smith. Nevertheless, comparison of Bedford's survey with a subsequent survey of 1785 suggests that Smith was responsible for "finishing" the parlor on the second floor front, embellishing the room behind it, extending the elaborate mahogany stair from the second to the third floor, adding wainscot and cornices to the principal rooms in the back building, and strengthening the trusses at the third floor level (See comparative surveys reproduced in Tatum, 125-127).

The grand parlor runs the full width of the house and was one of the finest Georgian interiors in the country. Hercules Courtenay was paid £60 in the early fall of 1770 for carving, probably in the parlor and the room behind it, and James Clow received £31 for "stuccoing a ceiling." It was Clow who, after arriving from England in 1763, advertised his skills in the newspaper, and stated he could be contacted through Robert Smith, "builder," on Second Street. This suggests a collaborative association between the two men, and Powel's ledger documents their work on at least this project.

Smith's fee of £268 for finishing a room implies work of considerable importance and decorative embellishment, and one student of the building claims "there can be no doubt that the principal changes Powel made in Stedman's house were to this front room" (Tatum, 88). Smith was paid more than any other craftsman whose name appears in the ledger, and Powel specifically refers to "a" room, whereas the payments to Courtenay were "for carving in my dwelling House" (Tatum, 52). Even if it is assumed that Smith's fee covered finishing work throughout the house, the insurance surveys indicate that the major changes were made to the second floor front room. Thus, it is probable that Smith oversaw and participated in the transformation of that space. In addition to the rococo plaster ceiling, other embellishments of this room included full-height paneling, a richly carved mantelpiece and overdoors, and an elaborate cornice.

Possibly the room's anticipated function as a place for dancing necessitated the use of iron straps on the wall trusses over this room on the third floor level. These are similar to trusses illustrated in the *Articles and Rules* of the Carpenters' Company. Such trusses "might be used when the weight on the floor was expected to be unusually heavy or when there was insufficient support below" (Tatum, 109). Smith had repeatedly demonstrated his skill in adapting and modifying trusses; his practicality and ingenuity in this area of building design helped make his reputation as a leading builder-architect.

The other principal room on the second floor may have served as a card room and place for refreshment for those who were invited to dances. Because its ornamental features correspond to decorative elements in the front room, Smith probably had a hand in its overall alterations. (The original interiors of these second floor rooms are in the Philadelphia Museum of Art and the Metropolitan Museum of Art in New York; nevertheless, the recreated interiors in the house are indicative of the splendor of the originals and help to enliven the experience of contemporary visitors to the building, which is operated as a house museum.)

When Powel bought the house and insured it in 1769, the main stair, "bracketed and wainscoted . . . with a twist," and made of mahogany, ran from the first to the second story. Smith evidently extended the stair so that it rose from the second to the third story (Tatum, Appendix I).

Powel, known as the "Patriot Mayor," held the city's highest office before and after the Revolution. Before the war, he had been a member of the Common Council, and, as a gentleman of prominence, was host to city "grandees" and visiting dignitaries. Washington and Adams were regular guests, and the Powels were known for their hospitality. Robert Smith, and the other craftsmen, helped Powel integrate high style decorations into already "commodious" interior spaces, creating a fine Middle Georgian setting for Powel and his guests.

The Second Street Houses

Despite his extensive real estate holdings, documented in Grantee/Grantor indices, Powel's property records are fragmentary (List of Property, 1779). One parcel he owned was on Second Street between Walnut and Spruce, and this may have been the site of two houses built by Smith. The project cost £1956.5.6, with an additional building on one of the lots costing £373 (Ledger, 75). It is reasonable to assume that the houses were brick and featured some amenities, although their total cost was less than the £2250 specified in the Maddox contract of January 1763 for two three-story brick houses.

Robert Smith

17_8				
June 22	To Cash paid him	£ 150		
July 22	To d°	64		
August 4	To d°	103		
5	To d°	32		
17	To d°	102		
September 7	To d°	100		
October 9	To d°	66		
Novemb 28	To d°	50		
Decemb 16	To d°	40		
26	To d°	15		
1769		62		
January 20	To d°	30		
March 11	To d°	51	5	6
April 11	To d°	60		
25	To d°	14		
May 20	To d°	20		
31	To d°	56		
June 21	To d°	200		
August 15	To d°	200		
16	To d°	100		
Septem 22	To d°	35		
October 11	To d°	40		
27	To d°	15		
	To d° by withdrawing an Action against Trumbull	16		
Novem 10	To d°	15		
Decem 5	To d°	30		
16	To d°	15		
1770				
January 12	To d°	53		
26	To d°	39		
February 5	To d°	40		
27	To d°	18		
March 9	To d°	50		
May 4	To d°	10		
22	To d°	36		
June 22	To d°	21		
October 19	To d°	21		
Novem 3	To d°	6		
12	To d°	100		
1771		6		
January 9	To d°	9		
March 1	To d°	16		
18	To d°	21		
29	To d°	10	5	
April 12	To d°	27		
29	To d°	9		
May 17	To d°	13		
July 15	To d°	3	4	5
Aug 31	To d°	441	12	6
	To a Lott in second Street sold him	100		
1773				
April 22	To Cash paid him	100		
June 1	To d°	53		
Septem 10	To d°	25		
Nov 16	To d°	21		
Decem 15	To d°	82		
1774				
January 24	To d°	9		
1776				
January 5	To d°	13		
February 9	To 21½ Cords of Wood delivered to his Order	5	12	6
	To 24 white Oak Posts omitted			

	By his Contract for building two Houses in Second Street	£ 1000		
	By his Contract for an additional Building to one of said Houses	343		
	By his Account for additional Finishings to said Houses	56	5	6
	By his Contract for finishing a Room in the Dwelling House	260		
	By his Account for Alterations in said House	49	19	3
	By d° for Repairs at sundry Places	15	7	2
	By his Contract for building Stores	382		
	By his Contract for raising Stores	132		

See Folio

A page in Samuel Powel's account book records his dealings with Robert Smith. Usually Smith worked for him on a fixed contract, receiving monthly progress payments. But this arrangement could be modified, as it was for two houses on Powel's property on Second Street, where Smith was awarded further contracts for "an additional Building" and "additional Finishings" for one of the houses.
Library Company of Philadelphia, on deposit at Historical Society of Pennsylvania.

At the same time that Smith was building these houses, he entered into an agreement of sale with Powel for "a Lott in second Street," which, possibly, adjoined the parcel being developed by Powel (Catalog #41).

Stores

The amounts listed in the ledger as paid to Robert Smith from April 1773 through January 1774 correspond to entries in Powel's receipt book. Powel recorded Smith's "Contract for building Stores" (£382) and "Contract for raising Stores" (£132) in the ledger, but it is six entries in the receipt book that date the building project, and confirm the contracts. The final payment "Received January 21 1774 of Samuel Powel Eighty Three Pounds in full for building Stores making with sundry other Payments Three Hundred & Eighty Two Pounds the Sum for which I contracted to build & finish said Stores" summarizes the arrangement. The ledger lists no payments to Smith in 1772, but it is reasonable to assume that the contract for raising the stores was charged against Smith's £441 purchase of the Second Street lot, recorded in Powel's ledger in 1771.

The location of the stores is unknown. Powel inherited "... three Messuages or Tenements with the Stores, Wharff & Lott of Ground thereunto belonging ... situate on the East Side of Plumb Street" from his father in 1747, and, possibly, he expanded development of the site (Estate Book, cited in Dashiell). There is no other mention of "stores" in his papers. It is more likely, however, that he built new stores at an entirely different location.

In addition to dating construction of the stores, the entries in the receipt book document a master/apprentice relationship between Smith and his nephew by marriage Robert Jones (1758-1802). Jones received the November and December 1773 payments for the stores in his uncle's behalf. An isolated payment of nine pounds, for some other project, was received by Jones in January 1776 and acknowledged as "on Account for my Master Robert Smith" (Powel's Receipt Book, cited in Dashiell).

"Sundry Job[b]ing"

Smith also performed minor tasks at some of Powel's properties, and sold him building materials, for which a bill totaling £26.9.6 1/2 was submitted in January 1774. Despite the onset of the Revolution, Powel made a partial payment of £9.0.0 in January 1776. Powel was one of the clients who generally paid Smith promptly. Neverthelesss, the last invoice for this work is another symptom of the possible reasons for Smith's financial difficulties. Although Powel must have made additional payments, after his father's death John Smith submitted an accounting to Powel in 1781, and acknowledged receipt of a final £0.16.2 (Powel Papers. Samuel Powel section, 20 October 1781).

DOCUMENTATION:

Library Company of Philadelphia, on deposit at HSP. Powel Family Papers. Samuel Powel Section. Samuel Powel Account Book 1760-1776. Estate Book. Ledger 1760-1793. Receipt Book 1773-1776. List of Property 1779.

REFERENCES:

Bridenbaugh, Carl and Jessica. *Rebels and Gentlemen: Philadelphia in the Age of Franklin.* New York (1942); Moss, Roger W. *Historic Houses of Philadelphia.* Philadelphia (1998); Tatum, George B. *Philadelphia Georgian: The city house of Samuel Powel and some of its eighteenth-century neighbors.* Middletown, CT (1976); Tolles, Frederick B. *Meeting House and Counting House: The Quaker Merchants of Colonial Philadelphia, 1682-1763.* Chapel Hill,NC (1948).
Dashiell, David A. Unpublished notes (January 1995). Peterson Files.

35

Design for Carpenters' Hall

320 Chestnut Street, Philadelphia
1768

CARPENTERS' HALL is one of this country's outstanding Georgian buildings. Tucked away in its own small court off Chestnut Street, it once was entirely hemmed in by other buildings. Most passersby probably were unaware of its existence until the National Park Service tore down the surrounding buildings in the 1950s in the course of creating Independence National Historical Park. Although Carpenters' Hall is small, it is monumental. This impression is heightened by the approach through a narrow alley, which is flanked by the reconstructed Fawcitt House and New Building. The sudden opening into Carpenters' Court, with the hall looming up in the foreground, makes the building appear larger than it is and distinctly imposing.

The original design employed a range of typical Georgian detailing in a sophisticated manner, particularly in the handling of the balustraded, arched windows in the second story. These handsome windows, however, serve no functional purpose, lighting as they do the upper landing of the stair and the hallway. They lend some credence to the hypothesis that Carpenters' Hall was an adaptation of the design for the Northampton County Courthouse. There such windows would have added dignity to the court room, a facility traditionally located on the second floor. Because members of the Carpenters' Company constructed their own hall, the quality of workmanship is high. The roof is topped by the octagonal cupola with domed roof so often employed by Robert Smith.

The Carpenters' Company of the City and County of Philadelphia is probably the oldest trade organization in the United States. In the eighteenth century its members were master carpenters. Today they are principals in architecture, engineering, and construction firms. When the company was incorporated

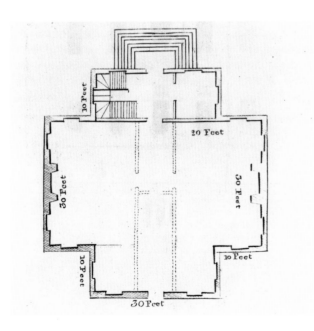

The elevation of Carpenters' Hall was drawn by Thomas Nevell, perhaps on the basis of a drawing by Robert Smith. Along with the plan of the hall, and other plates illustrating carpenters' work, it was engraved by Thomas Bedwell, and published in 1786 in the *Articles of the Carpenters [sic] Company of Philadelphia and their Rules for measuring and valuing House-Carpenters Work*, commonly known as the *Rule Book*. The design may have been derived from one Smith had prepared for one of the courthouses needed as new counties were being created in the province of Pennsylvania. Its cruciform plan would have been more appropriate on the open square of a county seat than in the hemmed-in enclosure of Carpenters' Court. It is not clear whether the dotted lines designate partitions removed from the first floor or were intended to indicate the plan of the second floor.

in 1790, its founding date was remembered to be 1724, although a minute book (now lost), kept by Joseph Fox, indicated a date two years later (Hall, 26; Moss, 44). The existing company records do not go back farther than 1763, when the Company began planning for its own headquarters. Previously they had rented tavern rooms in which to meet, for which the cost included "fire and candles."

The members did not act, however, until 1768, when they selected a building site on Chestnut Street just a few hundred feet away from Benjamin Franklin's new house. Modern tastes would have found both sites intolerable. The whole area was fouled by long-established tanyards, reeking with the stench of animal wastes and the smoke of burning tanbark. It was to be several years and a lively public controversy before the area was upgraded. The building of both architectural landmarks may well have been an act of faith. Philadelphia was soon to suffer a great war and there is reason to believe that many of those involved were consciously preparing for it. Major Thomas Proctor, also a member of the Carpenters' Company, built the nearby City Tavern just in time for the First Continental Congress (1774) and the Walnut Street Jail (Catalog #48, 1773) was completed in time to house prominent prisoners of war, Tories, and patriots, as the fortunes of war shifted.

On 3 February 1768 three leaders representing the company—Benjamin Loxley, Thomas Nevell, and Robert Smith—bought the site from Quaker George Emlen (Deed Book 14:146). It was 66 feet wide and extended south 255 feet to Howell's tanyard on Dock Creek, as shown on a manuscript plat. (Peterson [1953], 98). The terms of the deed called for the Company "to Build on the Sd Lott 2 or 3 Story high 36 by 22 of Brick or Stone" within three years time. They also agreed not to tear down any of the existing structures without replacing them. The consideration was £66 per year ground rent with the right of purchase for 3520 dollars.

Existing buildings occupied the Chestnut Street frontage. These were a frame house (the "front" or Fawcitt house, built 1713), a shop, an office, and two kitchens. They were separated by a fourteen-foot alley leading to two gardens, one of them in the use of Samuel Pleasant, a neighbor. These buildings were let separately by the Company, and rent was collected from the tenants. Under the direction of Joseph

Rakestraw, a member, the company immediately made repairs to the house. Benjamin Loxley furnished some of the men and part of the materials, including nails, spikes, HL hinges, a well chain, and glass and glazing. In the meantime, money was being pledged for the new headquarters (Uselma Clarke Smith Papers).

Fortunately, Loxley kept a small, now somewhat tattered memorandum book that offers details showing some changes made by 1768. To the east was John Breitnal's property alongside Hudson's (or Whalebone) Alley. On the west stood a Quaker meeting house and school house, both relatively new. The "Old Plan" showed the existing small shop and a house located on the public street.

Loxley proposed a new layout, in which the old buildings on Chestnut Street would be removed and replaced by two symmetrical houses still separated by an alley, which would now lead to Carpenters' Hall. This is the first representation on paper of the new hall. It is somewhat similar in shape to the unusual design submitted by Robert Smith two weeks later, but with a shallower projection in front.

On 18 April 1768, "Mr. Smith exhibited Sketch for a Building to be thereon Erected & the Members Were desired to Consider When Will be a proper time to Begin the Building &c." The time came two years later. On 30 January 1770, the company decided to proceed with construction and a list was opened entitled "Subscribers, Names and Sums for a Hall." Smith was one of the largest contributors. It is worth quoting here because it contains the names of some of the most prominent builders of Philadelphia and differs somewhat from other lists (Loxley memorandum book). Loxley's spellings have been retained.

Joseph Fox (6 shares)	£ 24.0.0
Robert Smith (5 shares)	20.0.0
John Goodwin (4 shares)	16.0.0
Abram Carlile (3 shares)	12.0.0
Patrick Craigehead (1 share)	4.0.0
Joseph Reakstraw (3 shares)	12.0.0
James Pearson (4 shares)	16.0.0
Benjamin Loxley (5 shares)	20.0.0
Levi Budd (1 1/4 shares)	5.0.0
Richard Armit (3 shares)	12.0.0
James Bringhurst (3 shares)	12.0.0
William Lowance (1 1/2 shares)	6.0.0
Thos. Shoemaker (3 shares)	12.0.0
Isaac Coates (5 shares)	20.0.0
George Wood (1 1/2 shares)	5.0.0

Saml Powel (1 share)	4.0.0
James Armitage (2 shares)	8.0.0
John Thornhill (3 shares)	12.0.0
John Hitchcock (1 1/4 shares) £	5.0.0
Thos. Nevel (3 shares)	12.0.0
Silas Engles (1 1/2 shares)	6.0.0
William Colladay (1 1/2 shares)	6.0.0
James Worrel (5 shares)	20.0.0
Willm Robinson (1 1/2 shares)	6.0.0
Willm Roberts (1 share)	4.0.0
James Davis (2 1/2 shares)	10.0.0
Isaac Lafever (1 1/2 shares)	6.0.0
John Trip (1 share)	4.0.0
Saml Wallis	
Joseph Rhoads (3 shares)	12.0.0
James Potter	4.0.0
Robert Carson	8.0.0.
Saml Griscome	6.0.0
Benjn Mifflin	4.0.0
Andrew Edge	3.0.0

Because this campaign did not produce all the money needed, the company decided "to apply to Several Others who are intimately Connected with them in the Building Business and from whome they have had great Encouragement and kind offers of Assistance . . . as they are willing to give either money or work or materials, which they promise to pay to Joseph Fox Esqr, Master and Treasurer of the sd Company." This produced a few more contributors as follows:

John Roberts Miller £	5.0.0
William Anderson plaistr	2.0.0
Francis Gerrigues	5.0.0
Jno Allen	5.0.0
Hercules Courtney work £	20.0.0
Charles Woolfall 100 ft	
[?] pf & used at Hall	
Andrew Read, Iron Backs	5.0.0
Robert Wright p. day [?]	5.0.0

Although Smith had undoubtedly drawn the plans, he did not supervise the construction, in which many members participated. Loxley noted that on 13 February 1770 "We Mett & Examin'd the Drafts again & agreed then Appointed Each member of the Committee to his particular Charge in Collecting Materials & Building the Carpenters Hall 50 ft by 50 ft." He also gave the intended vertical dimensions as follows:

Cellar	9.6	Roofe	. . . .
1st Story	15.0	Cupola	. . . .
2d Story	12.0	Doome	. . . .
2 floors	2.0	Spindle	. . . .
	38 ft 6 in		

The accounts show that Loxley appears to have held primary responsibility for construction throughout the building season of 1770. Among other items at this time he supplied "Rum & Nails for Digers" and lumber (boards, planks, scantling, joists and scaffold poles) and he hauled various materials to the site. In addition, he furnished the work of half a dozen men and worked personally, for which he billed 6.6 per day. Other members also provided labor and materials. While all the details have not survived, the individual accounts of Carpenters' Company members Abraham Carlisle and James Worrell are substantial. Carlisle who was a heavy subscriber to the building fund handled some of the early work. His bill for 1771 ran as follows:

[Jan?]y 12th The Carpenters Company to Abraham Carlile [sic] Dr.

To Diging & Walling @ nessery of 15 feet Deep & 9 feet 2 wide @8/	6.0.0
To arching & laying the foundation	1.10.0
To 96 feet of oak scantling	0.7.6
To 18 lbs of 20d nails @10d	0.15.0
To one Read Cedar post for the nessery floor	2.6
To 38 feet of oak scantling for 2 jois in hall	0.3.2
To 4lb of nails for do	0.4.0
To 20 Read Cedar jambs for Cellr windows	1.18.0
To 35 Read Cedar Cills for upper windows	5.16.0
To Cash for shugar &c wen puting on floor	0.3.8
To Cash paid michel nick for pileing stone &c	0.7.0
To Cash paid John Skiner for Scaffold poles	5.0.0
To Cash paid for hauling 2 old girders	0.1 6
To Cash paid David hughs for hauling 2 loads of Sash boards from sellars	0.6 0
To 119 feat [sic] of 3 1/2 Cedar plank @	2.4.7
To 960 feet of Ceder boards @ 9/	4.2.6
To Cash paid georg pepper for hauling plank	0.2 6
To six pices of Read Ceder for Checks and sills for the Celler Doors	1.10.8
To one pice of Read Ceder for the terret [the turret or cupola]	0.4.0
To Cash paid John hitchcock Coch [?]	0.7 6
To Cash paid John harper for 13 Loads of ballast stones	2.12.2
	£ 33.16.5
To Cash paid Robert Right to two bead plains and Repairing a cornish plain	0.17.6
	£ 34.13.11
To my subscription	12.0.0

by Robert Rights gift to the hall received
   by me Abraham Carlile   5. 0. 0

                            £ 17. 0. 0

(CCCCP, Miscellany,etc., Series 8 Item 23: 18).   17.13.0

Great progress was made at the site. It was customary to get a building under roof before winter weather; the records show that the cellar excavation, foundations, cupola, roof shingling, cornice and weather vane were all in place by the end of 1770. With the building under protection the flooring, doors and window glazing could proceed.

Work in the following winter included eight days carpentry on the "kechen" in the cellar done by Worrel, Coe and Scot. Eden Haydock got £1.4.0 for painting the twenty-four nine-inch by eleven-inch sash lights and a nine-light sash to be fixed in the inside cellar door. Hugh Roberts & Son provided £1.6.6 of hinges, latches and lath nails, Philip Wisman ten pounds of 10d and 20d nails and Abraham Usher 10s for "Closing Lox." The account closes on January 9, 1773 with Scot, Garrott and one Nelson "puting up fencing a Long the Hall Ally with Sundry other jobing work £ 2/4/0" and a pair of hinges bought from Adam Stricker for 3.6.

Philadelphia was nervously aware of the hostilities in Boston. To hurry progress on the new hall £300 was borrowed early in 1773 from Carpenters' Company Master Joseph Fox to finish the construction. The plastering was done by April 1774 and the stairs were installed in August. The building was insured against fire by the Philadelphia Contributionship by the end of the year.

The insurance survey by Gunning Bedford, value totalling £750, describes the building.

50 feet Square having a 10 ft Brake [break] in each Corner thereof two Storys high 14 inch walls—two Rooms and passage below—3 Rooms & passage, in Second Story plasterd. pertisions—two Storys of open Newel Stairs—Rampd. and Bracketed—Straight Joint floor in first Story the Rooms finishd. very plain Glass 12 by 0 [?] a frett in Bedmold of Eaves Cornish. A Cupola on the Roof New."

The building of the hall had been a risky financial venture for the company. A move to share the cost led to renting the whole second floor to the Library Company of Philadelphia, under an agreement made on 26 October 1772. Thomas Nevell was engaged to do the elaborate joinery, which included carved cabinets and bookshelves guarded by wire latticework. The windows were fitted with inside shutters and the rooms warmed by hickory wood burned in open fires, later changed in favor of stoves. A dozen Windsor chairs, six brass sconces and two chandeliers were also provided. The Library Company moved in on 6 September 1773.

The next year the country was moving toward war. An act of Parliament closed the port of Boston and shocked the New England colonies. Pennsylvania was slower to react, but, on 18 June 1774, radicals in Philadelphia began to organize for action. A group of "Freeholders and Freemen" met to agree that the Boston situation was a common threat and set up a subscription for the relief of that town. The minutes of the meeting list prominent citizens, including "Robert Smith, carpenter," and he was appointed to The Committee of Forty Three, charged with beginning the subscription. The Forty Three printed handbills, and rushed them to newspapers up and down the coast, calling for a general congress at Philadelphia. Although Smith did not attend subsequent meetings, Gunning Bedford was at the meeting of July 6th. In general, artisans became politically active in the immediate pre-revolutionary period (Olton, *passim*; Ryerson, 186).

On 5 September 1774 delegates to the First Continental Congress gathered at the new City Tavern on Second Street, walked up to inspect Carpenters' Hall, and agreed to convene there. That bitterly disappointed the Pennsylvania lawmakers who had invited them to use the State House. Samuel Rhoads, Esq. was among the eight Pennsylvania delegates (*Journal of the Proceedings*). The Congress sat for seven weeks, adjourning October 26th. In a gesture of hospitality the Province of Pennsylvania treated the departing delegates to a dinner at the City Tavern.

All of these events got wide coverage in the colonial press. But at the close of the year 1775 a secret meeting of the utmost consequence took place in the library upstairs in Carpenters' Hall. The French nation, which had suffered the humiliation of losing

Canada a few years earlier, was watching for an opportunity of striking back at Britain. In 1775, Louis XVI's government sent a spy, Achard de Bonvouloir, to Philadelphia to see if the Americans could and would fight against the mother country. Bonvouloir sought out Benjamin Franklin, and Franklin and Committeeman John Jay of New York met the spy after dark on three occasions. The librarian of the Library Company, Francis Daymon, who was French, translated.

The Americans exaggerated a bit, it seems, and assured Bonvouloir that their countrymen were anxious to throw off the British yoke and eager to fight. This was speedily reported back to France in a written manuscript that has survived (*Papers of Benjamin Franklin*, 22:310-318; "French Spy at Carpenters' Court"). Eventually the French agreed as a starter to send military supplies through the West Indies.

When the Americans won their stunning victory against General Burgoyne at Saratoga, the French declared war. In due course General Rochambeau marched down from Newport to Yorktown, Virginia, meeting General Washington on the way. The fleet of the Comte de Grasse bottled up British General Cornwallis in the York River. Thus the great victory at Yorktown, signaling the end of the Revolutionary War, was achieved with considerable help from France, help that may first have been broached as a possibility in a meeting at Carpenters' Hall.

In late June of 1776, the Provincial Conference convened in Carpenters' Hall. It defied the old Pennsylvania Assembly, and, becoming more radical and aggressive, extralegally seized the government of the province. Colonel Thomas McKean, of the Philadelphia City Committee, dominated the Conference. The official roster included Benjamin Franklin, who was ill and not present, and veteran Captain Benjamin Loxley of the Carpenters' Company who did attend. This group clearly endorsed independence, and helped make possible the Declaration two weeks later (*Proceedings of the Provincial Conference*).

With war at hand, Carpenters' Hall was first occupied by refugees and wounded Americans. When the British took the city in September 1777, it was used as an infirmary by their troops, and also as a refuge for inmates of the Almshouse, displaced when the British used that building as a barracks (Catalog #27). It would be many years before the Carpenters'

The section reveals the concealed second floor wall trusses with doorways in the trussed frames, and iron strapping at the base of the queen posts. It is not known whether these were part of Smith's original plan or were added when the first floor partitions were removed at an early date. They allow the existence of a twenty-nine foot clear-span ceiling on the first floor. A similar truss is illustrated as Plate XV of the 1786 *Rule Book*, and there also is a truss of this type in the garret of the Powel House. Edmund Woolley had used a wall truss in 1733 for the long gallery on the second floor of Independence Hall. Drawn 1999 by J.S. Winterle, principal delineator under Suzanne Pentz. Courtesy Keast & Hood Co.

Company managed to occupy their own building[1] When the Americans recaptured the city, the basement and first floor of the hall became a commissary, while the Library Company continued as a tenant on the second. The Library Company moved out in 1790, and some major alterations took place. These included new steps and a frontispiece on the north front and probably removal of the partitions that had formed a central hallway on the first floor. (The south doorway received a new frontispiece in 1792-1793.) A new tenant, the First Bank of the United States, took occupancy of the entire building in 1791. Increased income enabled the Carpenters' Company to build the so-called "New Building" on the west side of the alley leading to the hall. This also was a rental property, as well as the venue for the company's meetings.

The bank stayed for a decade, until completion of its own majestic building on Third Street. The bank was followed briefly by the U.S. Land Office, and then by the Bank of Pennsylvania, which moved into its handsome building, designed by Benjamin Henry Latrobe, in 1801. The Custom House was the next major tenant, remaining until 1819. Again it was completion of a larger building, this one designed by William Strickland, that led to a move. Toward the end of its tenure, the Custom House may have shared the hall with the Second Bank of the United States, which took over Carpenters' Hall when the Custom House moved out. Following its predecessors, the bank left in 1821, moving a short distance west on Chestnut Street to its marble temple, also designed by Strickland. In the next several years, various tenants, generally charitable and cultural institutions, rented parts of the hall. In 1828 a long-term tenant appeared. C. J. Wolbert & Co., Auctioneers, then occupied part of Carpenters' Hall, and by 1838 the entire building.

"What a desecration!" author Benson Lossing exclaimed, after visiting Philadelphia around 1850 as part of the preparations for his *Field Book of the American Revolution*. By this time many Americans were beginning to view the surviving buildings of the colonial and Revolutionary period as shrines, especially those closely associated with the lives and activities of the founding fathers. As the site of the first meeting of the Continental Congress, Carpenters' Hall certainly was in that category. Aware of this, as well as their group's long history, the members of the Carpenters' Company shared the sentiments of those who wished to commemorate the past. A few years after Lossing's book appeared, at a meeting in January 1856, they asked the Managing Committee "to inquire into the expediency of removing to the Old Hall." When the report was favorable, the members voted to undertake renovations, with "especial care to be taken to preserve, as much as possible, every feature in said Hall as it now exists indicative of its original finish."

Although the members of the Carpenters' Company considered their 1857 undertaking a restoration, it is now looked on as preservation. The work included adding gutters and painting the exterior, laying out walks, and planting a garden. On the interior, a new furnace was installed in the basement, and a custodian's apartment was created on the second floor. The large room on the first floor received an elaborate decorating scheme very much of its period. It included a stylish Minton tile floor, papered walls, a frescoed ceiling, heavy draperies, and elaborate gasoliers. Proud of their accomplishment, the company mounted the name "Carpenters' Hall" in large letters in the front pediment, along with the legend "The Company Instituted in 1724," and its crest. Theirs was a very early preservation effort, coming only four years after the foundation of the Mount Vernon Ladies' Association of the Union (Moss, *Historic Houses*, 1-19).

Soon after the Carpenters' Company moved into its refurbished hall, the City of Philadelphia took an interest. The city already had demonstrated fervent respect for its past as the birthplace of the nation. It had "restored" the steeple of Independence Hall in 1828 and the Assembly Chamber in 1831, fitting up the latter as a museum in 1855. In 1859, the company was asked whether it would be willing to sell the hall to the city. In declining, the company wrote:

... we cannot under any circumstances receive favourably any propositions involving the sale of Carpenters' Hall. We in common with our fellow citizens venerate it not only for its associations with the stirring events of the Revolution "[sic] But we also hold it as a sacred trust committed to

---

1. The following summary of the later history of Carpenters' Hall is based on a more comprehensive account in Charles E. Peterson, "Carpenters' Hall," in *HP*, 104-115, where citations of sources can be found.

us by our predecessors, which nothing shall ever induce us to part with." Also that having fitted up the Room Occupied by the first Congress as near as possible as it was originally finished we intend as heretofore to keep it open for the inspection of all who may wish to visit it.

And so they have. Carpenters' Hall remains the headquarters of the venerable company, as well as a tribute not only to those who founded the nation, but also to those who designed and built Philadelphia.

DOCUMENTATION:

Carpenters' Company of the City and County of Philadelphia [hereafter CCCCP]. Antiques and Curiosities, Minutes, Miscellany, 1683-1857. Warden's Book, 1769-1781. On deposit at the American Philosophical Society; Deeds, Philadelphia City Archives; *The Papers of Benjamin Franklin*. Vol. 22. Ed. by William B. Wilcox. New Haven (1982); HSP. Uselma Clark Smith Papers, MSS #1378C. Insurance Survey, 22 December 1773. Philadelphia Contributionship; Loxley, Benjamin. Memorendum [sic] Book . . . Begun 6th of June 1768. Dilks Collection; Baumann, Ronald A. *Proceedings of the Provincial Conference of Committees, of the Province of Pennsylvania: Held at the Carpenters Hall at Philadelphia, (18 June-25 June 1776)*. Facsimile edition. Philadelphia (1984); Wolf, Edwin II. Introduction. *Journal of the Proceedings of the Congress Held at Philadelphia*. Facsimile edition. Philadelphia (1974).

REFERENCES:

Alsop, Susan Mary. "The French Spy at Carpenters' Court, 1775." In *Yankees at the Court*. Garden City, NY (1982); Hall, Louise. "Loxley's Provocative Note." *Journal of the Society of Architectural Historians,* 14, 4, (December 1957): 26-27); Moss, Roger W. "The Origins of the Carpenters' Company of Philadelphia." In *Building Early America*. Edited by Charles E. Peterson. Radnor, PA (1976); ———. *Historic Houses of Philadelphia*, Philadelphia (1998); Olton, Charles S. *Artisans for Independence: Philadelphia Mechanics and the American Revolution*. Syracuse, NY (1975); Peterson, Charles E. "Carpenters' Hall." In *HP*, 96-128; Ryerson, Richard Alan. *The Revolution is now Begun*. Philadelphia (1978).

36

Advisor to Observatory Committee, American Philosophical Society

State House Yard, between 5th and 6th Streets, south of Chestnut Street, Philadelphia
1769, taken down and sold 1783

IN THE INTEREST of promoting scientific knowledge and clarifying surveying data, the American Philosophical Society planned to participate in formal observation of the transit of the planet Venus on 3 June 1769. Astronomer David Rittenhouse was among those proposing that the planet be viewed from three different eastern locations (the western site was Fort Pitt), and the results compared. Plans were underway to use Rittenhouse's observatory at Norriton and the lighthouse at Cape Henlopen when the Philosophical Society petitioned the Pennsylvania Assembly for financial assistance and permission to erect an observatory on the grounds of the State House.

Eager to begin, the society appointed a Transit Committee on 17 February 1769 whose members were Samuel Rhoads, Jr., J.M.D. Pennington, and Robert Smith. They were directed to employ a workman to erect an observatory "for a sum not exceeding £60 . . . if they cannot find among the houses belonging to the Assembly, one fit for the purpose" (*Early Proceedings*, 31-32). No suitable building was found and they engaged James Pearson, a house carpenter, to "erect the Observatory to a plan delivered him" (*Early Proceedings*, 36). David Rittenhouse probably stipulated the requirements for supporting the instruments and sheltering the observers. He may have prepared a plan (Bedini, 161).

It seems more likely, however, that one of the builder-architects on the committee designed the structure to house the instruments. Whether or not this was Smith is uncertain. He had been elected a member of the American Philosophical Society on 8 March 1768. He signed the rollbook "Robert Smith, architect," but never attended any meetings. During this period, attendance was recorded by the secretary and the society met every two weeks to hear members' papers on issues of practical interest. Because Smith was inactive in society business matters, it is possible he was only minimally involved in Transit Committee activities. He almost certainly would have reviewed Rittenhouse's specifications, making suggestions about the supporting structure and housing for the instruments, but his exact role in the project is unknown.

The observatory remained in the State House yard, serving as a speakers' platform and storage house for military equipment (Bedini, 167). Robert Smith was summoned to attend to repairs in February 1771, which suggests he played a part, however minor, in the earlier project, but there is no record of the nature of his work (*Early Proceedings*, 62).

DOCUMENTATION:

Early Proceedings of the American Philosophical Society. Philadelphia (1884); *Pennsylvania Archives*, 8th Series, 7:6356-57 and 8:7206-08. Harrisburg (1935).

REFERENCES:

Bedini, Silvio A. "That Awful Stage (The Search for the State House Yard Observatory)." In *Science and Society in Early America: Essays in Honor of Whitfield J. Bell, Jr....* Philadelphia (1986).

This sketch of the James City County Court House was drawn in 1930, when it was thought that its design might be the work of Robert Smith

37 A

James City County Courthouse

Market Square, Williamsburg, Virginia
1769, restored

THE ISSUE of the *Virginia Gazette* for 23 March 1769 announced that a plan of the proposed courthouse, shared by Williamsburg and James County, could be seen at Mr. Hay's, as the reconstructed Raleigh Tavern was once known (Whiffen, 154). The new brick courthouse, with its portico, was unlike any other Virginia public building of the time. It was judged "more sophisticated" and "a building whose designer one would like to name" (Whiffen, 152).

Although some of the classical details made the building distinctive, it shared a T-plan with other Virginia courthouses, making it an interesting hybrid of current style and familiar form.

Unfortunately, there is no documentation of the courthouse project. James City County records were destroyed during the Revolution; those that survived into the nineteenth century were destroyed during the Civil War (Weisiger, 1998).

The building's classical front required stone unavailable in the region, and it was ordered from England. Stone for the steps arrived by 1772, when a London merchant was thanked by the president of the Council, but it is likely the columns were not erected until 1911 when they were added during a renovation (Whiffen, 157; Guidebook, 38). The renovation was necessitated by a fire that destroyed the roof and cupola. The latter feature was restored as an octagonal cupola, which closely resembled those designed by Robert Smith and led to an attribution to him.

It is only remotely possible that Robert Smith had a hand in the design, although there were also many social and political connections between Williamsburg and Philadelphia through which Smith's name could have become known in Virginia. Also, during the year the courthouse was under construction, he submitted plans for the "Hospital for Idiots and Lunatics" (Catalog #43) at Williamsburg.

On the basis of more recent study, the cupola has been re-restored with a different appearance, and it is no longer considered that Smith had any role in the design of the building (Lounsbury, 1999).

REFERENCES:

Colonial Williamsburg Foundation. "Courthouse of 1770." In *Colonial Williamsburg Official Guidebook*. 7th edition. Williamsburg (1972), 37-38; Gaines, William H., Jr. "The Courthouses of James City County." *Virginia Cavalcade*, 18, 4 (1969):20-30; Whiffen, Marcus."The Courthouse of 1770." In *The Public Buildings of Williamsburg, Colonial Capital of Virginia: An Architectural History*. Williamsburg (1958).

Lounsbury, Carl L., Colonial Williamsburg Foundation. Conversation with Constance Greiff. June 1999; Weisiger, Minor, Archivist, Virginia State Library. Letter to and conversations with Maria Thompson. November and December 1998.

38

Plan, Elevation and Model for a Covered Bridge over the Schuylkill River

Near the west end of Market Street, Philadelphia
1769, not built

NO PERMANENT BRIDGE over the Schuylkill River was erected until 1798-1805. As early as 1751, however, the Pennsylvania House entertained a petition to span the river and improve access west of the city. Various locations were investigated and "sundry Plans of Bridges and Computations of the Expense of building them" were considered (*Papers of Benjamin Franklin*, 181).

Eighteen years later, on 31 January 1769, "A Representation from Robert Smith, Master-Builder, of the City of Philadelphia," was presented to the House and set forth that

...the said Smith, being informed of the public spirited Concern in the House to amend the Roads, and improve the Communication between the trading City and the remote Parts of this Province, for the general Utility; and that the principal Obstruction to this useful and necessary Work, respecting the Western Counties, is the Difficulty of bridging the River Schuylkill near this City, he has been induced to attempt an Improvement on the Designs of wooden Bridges raised on Stone Piers, with Hopes that one might be constructed with equal Security, and much less Expense than any heretofore published;—that in this Attempt he had been so happy as to succeed, in the Opinion of some Persons of approved Judgement and Knowledge in Architecture, by a simple Method, suspending the Platform below the Arch that sustains it, by which Means the

Piers are better secured than by any other Method, and applying the Arch in the Side to strengthen it, and the Whole well covered to secure it from the Weather, thereby saving a great expense in the Frame, and lessening the Height;—that he has drawn a Plan and Elevation of such a Bridge, made a Model of one arch and two Piers, and, with great Respect to the Honourable House, begs leave to present the same to them, in Hopes that the ingenious may turn their Thoughts to the Subject, and make such further Improvements thereon, as may render it of some Service to the Public, whenever the Legislature shall find the Province in a Capacity to execute a Design of such Utility and Importance to the whole Community" (*Votes and Proceedings*, 134).

Two weeks later, on February 11th, Smith's "Representation" was read again, debated, and "referred to further Consideration" (*Votes and Proceedings*, 145). The project languished and nothing came of it until December 1774 when, due to the "prosperous state" of public funds, the Assembly was again petitioned to consider the advantages of a bridge over the Schuylkill. It is possible that Robert Smith's plan was resubmitted, and that he was the "workman of Character and Experience [who] offered...to erect a substantial Bridge, with Stone Piers, and a wooden superstructure, well covered and secured against the Injuries of the Weather" (*Pennsylvania Archives*, ser. 8, 8:7179).

The designer claimed the bridge "shall stand unhurt by Ice, Freshes and other Obstructions." A committee was appointed to select a suitable location for the bridge and they were charged to report at the next meeting, at which discussion reiterated the deplorable condition of roads west of the city and the difficulties of access to the metropolis from that direction (*Archives*, ser. 8, 8:7181). Debate continued through March 1775 when "Several Plans of Bridges [were] laid before [the] Committee" (*Archives*, ser. 8, 8:7205). Nothing happened, undoubtedly because the Assembly had more pressing matters to consider.

Unfortunately the plan, elevation, and model have disappeared, and it is not clear from the description whether Smith intended the deck to be suspended from the arches or attached to the superstructure in some other manner. In any event, the idea of a multi-arched bridge with covered superstructure was highly advanced. His submission of such a scheme indicates his interest in solving complex engineering issues with an innovative technological approach.

During the Revolution, a floating bridge was constructed by the British army; it was rebuilt after being swept away by a freshet, only to meet the same fate as its predecessor. Not until 1798 was a plan adopted for a permanent bridge over the river. The wooden multi-arched bridge, with a protective wooden covering and two statues carved by William Rush, opened 1 January 1805, thirty-six years after Robert Smith had proposed such a span.

DOCUMENTATION:

Papers of Benjamin Franklin: Assembly Service, 1751-64; Pennsylvania Archives. 8th series, 7:6335-6336, 6359. 8th series, 8:7179-7181, 7204-7205. Harrisburg (1935); *Votes and Proceedings of the House of Representatives of the Province of Pennsylvania Beginning the Fourteenth Day of October 1767...Philadelphia* (1776), 6:134, 145.

REFERENCES:

S&W, 1

39

Design Christ Church

Broad Street and Sycamore Avenue, Shrewsbury, New Jersey
1769, altered

OVER THIRTY YEARS AGO, Donald R. Friary recognized that the design for Christ Church, once thought to have been provided by Provost William Smith of the College of Philadelphia, had actually been supplied by Robert Smith (Friary, 318). The basic design and style of the building, as well as its distinctive roof trusses, confirm Friary's discovery.

In April 1760, the Reverend Samuel Cooke (1723-1795), rector of Christ Church, Shrewsbury, attended a convocation of Anglican clergy in Philadelphia (Friary, 318). There had been considerable discussion in his home parish of the need for a new church building and two lotteries had been held to raise funds. While Cooke was in the city, it is probable that he visited St. Peter's Church (Catalog #13), then under construction and ready to receive bells from Philadelphia's Christ Church. Another matter, the founding of St. Paul's Church (Catalog #14), would also have been a major topic of discussion during Cooke's stay. The choice of Robert Smith to design several aspects of St. Paul's, especially its roof, could hardly have escaped Cooke's notice.

Cooke had come to New Jersey as a missionary from the Society for the Propagation of the Gospel in Foreign Parts in 1751. He corresponded with clergy in London, apprising them of his activities at Shrewsbury and elsewhere in Monmouth County. He also was known in Philadelphia and, in 1768, was offered a position as assistant at Christ Church there, which he declined in favor of remaining in New Jersey (Friary, 319). When the vestry at Shrewsbury was ready to undertake a building project, Cooke knew where and to whom to turn for assistance with the design.

Vestry minutes of 27 January 1769 noted:

Mr. Cooke produced a Subscription amounting to Four hundred & fifty Pounds for rebuilding of Christ's Church in Shrewsbury: Whereupon it is unanimously agreed, that the Work shall immediately be set about. Mr. Cooke at the same time produced a Draught of the Building, 60 by 36 feet in the clear, which is agreed to."

That the proposed interior would be "in the clear," consequently free of columns or other visible means of support for the roof, concerned a vestry member, Josiah Holmes, who disapproved so strongly that he furnished an alternative design using more conservative carpentry practices (Hammond, section 7:6). For two months, the vestry debated the issue and on Easter Tuesday "Ordered that the building of the Church shall be carried on, and that the Roof, &c. shall be framed according to the Draught of Mr. Smith of Philadelphia" (Vestry Book, 29 January 1769). Vestryman and Clerk of the Congregation Holmes resigned in disgust (Hammond, 7:6).

The roof trusses specified by Smith were similar to those he used for the larger spans of St. Peter's and St. Paul's. Because the thirty-eight foot span of Shrewsbury was so much shorter, Smith called for only one iron bolt to secure the junction of each of the large diagonal braces with the raised tie beam, rather than two, as he had, for example, at St. Peter's. He also omitted the iron straps and bolts he had used in larger churches (Hammond, 8:2). He, or the carpenters executing the work, provided more traditional means of stiffening, with timber braces rising from be-

Christ Church has not changed since this photograph was taken c. 1870. One of the alterations that had been made by this time was the insertion of colored glass with Gothic-arched muntins, a nod to the Gothic Revival. Courtesy Christ Church.

low the plate to engage the major diagonals, and short vertical timbers between the major diagonals and the tie beam. Thus Smith clearly had modified his more or less standard truss design to meet the requirements of a smaller, timber-framed building.

Another Smith signature at Shrewsbury is his distinctive domed octagonal cupola. That he was responsible for the entire design of the building is signified by the Articles of Agreement entered into by local carpenters in June 1769.

The Roof to be built & framed agreeable to the Plan given herewith from Mr. Smith of Philadelphia." The men also agreed to "follow his Directions thro'out the Work . . . [and] to Frame, Raise & enclose with Shingles from Top to Bottom, with a Cupola agreeable to the Plan deliver'd herewith" (Friary, 791).

Because it requires the workmen to follow Smith's directions, this contract is the most complete record of his role in the design of a building.

The Shrewsbury church is situated on an east/west axis, with a large Venetian window over the altar at the east end of the building. Two doors on the west have elaborate pedimented surrounds in the Doric order, which complement the treatment of the Venetian window. These evidently are the only known colonial examples of one of the classical orders in Monmouth County. They are so well executed that it has been suggested that they were shipped to the site from Philadelphia (Hammond, 8:3). An alternative is that Smith may have sent fairly detailed drawings, which enabled the local carpenters to achieve detailing superior to what was common locally. Four round-headed windows, with heavy moldings and keystones, are evenly spaced along the north and south walls. Other characteristic details of Smith's churches also are present, such as a cornice return creating a pedimental gable with an oculus in the center. These architectural features combine with a cove cornice to create a visual impression atypical for the region.

The men engaged to build the church were to be paid in New York currency, a reminder of the close connection between East Jersey and New York. All of the carpenters were church members, which may have added another dimension to their involvement with the project. The June agreement referred specifically to designs for the roof and cupola, requiring the workmen to build "agreeable to the Plan," but they were "to make the Window Frames, sashes, Doors,

Inside & outside Cornish . . . all in a good, substantial & neat Manner" (Friary, 2-3). It would not have been unusual for the period had the details of the moldings and interior appointments been the responsibility of the carpenters.

Smith's role, however extensive, appears to have ended with submission of the plans, although the provision of the contract that the carpenters would "follow his Directions thro-out the Work" is a tantalizing hint that he may have provided some construction supervision.

The Reverend Mr. Cooke estimated the cost of the building at £800. There is no record of what part of this sum, if any, went to Smith. Work was to be completed by November 1770, but shortages of cash and materials led to work stoppages. It was not until April 1774 that Cooke could write to the Society for the Propagation of the Gospel that "the accounts are all settled, the materials all paid for, and the Workmen satisfied to the uttermost farthing" (Quoted in Hammond, 7:4).

There have been many alterations, including the insertion of stained glass in the windows and the removal of the cupola from the center of the ridge to the west end. Nevertheless, the building has retained an amazing degree of its eighteenth-century fabric. Its fundamental size and shape survive, with the only additions a small tower against the west elevation, containing a new entrance; and a ten-foot extension to the rear of the chancel. Even a number of the long, round-butt shingles are original. Unusual for a colonial building is the existence of a cornerstone in the southwest corner, inscribed S C M [. . .] 1769. On the interior Smith's arched ceiling remains, although now covered with pressed metal, along with canopied pews flanking the chancel. In sum, next to St. Peter's in Philadelphia, Christ Church is the best preserved of Smith's churches.

DOCUMENTATION:

Christ Church Archives. Vestry Book, 1747-1854. Treasurers' Records. Loose documents.

REFERENCES:

Friary, Donald Richard. The Architecture of the Anglican Church in the Northern American Colonies.... Ph.D. diss. University of Pennsylvania (1971); HABS, N J-37; Hammond, Joseph W. Christ Church (Episcopal), Shrewsbury. National Register of Historic Places Registration Form. April 1995.

An engraving in Sherman Day's *Historical Collections of the State of Pennsylvania* (1843) illustrates Carlisle's public square. The court house, town hall, and Methodist Church face the main street (and the railroad) on the left. The Episcopal church is at the far right, with the Presbyterian Church slightly right of center.

40

Design the First Presbyterian Church

North Hanover Street
The Public Square, Carlisle, Pennsylvania
1769, altered

ABOUT one hundred miles west of Philadelphia, across the Susquehanna River, is a stone Presbyterian meeting house, for which Robert Smith received five pounds for providing a plan in early 1769 (Loose receipt in church vault). No record survives of Smith ever visiting Carlisle, but in 1766 he had been involved in the design of the Third Presbyterian Church in Philadelphia (Catalog #31), and this activity may be the link with like believers to the west.

Cumberland County, on the edge of Indian territory, was created in January 1749/50. James Hamilton, Governor of Pennsylvania, approved of the westward expansion, but was saddled with the task of mediating locally among the newly appointed commissioners and, at another level, between the commissioners and proprietor Thomas Penn about the location of the county seat. The squabbles consumed considerable time and it was with relief that Hamil-

ton wrote to Penn in November 1752 that "The Commissioners appointed by Act of Assembly . . . have at length by new Management been induced to recommend to me the Town of Carlisle . . . and I am very well pleased to have got rid of that Controversy" (J. Flower, 16).

With the location agreed upon, new areas of disagreement arose concerning the layout of the town and its central square, but eventually these too were resolved. By July 1753, "there [were] Six very good Stone Houses, several good Frame Houses and a Large Number of Log Houses in all making the Number Sixty Five Houses, upon the whole [the town] made a much better appearance than expected" (J. Flower, 17-18). Development of the central square was another matter. It was intended to be the site of public buildings, but the jail was built elsewhere, and the French and Indian War delayed plans for additional buildings (J. Flower, 27). Limited prosperity returned after the war and with it came several building projects. Soon there were a courthouse, market house, and an unfinished Anglican church on the square.

In September 1764, Governor John Penn wrote to his uncle, the proprietor, about Thomas Penn's agreeing to grant a lot for a meeting house to the Presbyterians (J. Flower,44). Two years later, a warrant was issued for a survey of "a Lot of Ground one hundred and eighty feet by two hundred feet the Remainder of the Center Square in said Town to accommodate them with a Site for a Presbyterian Church or Meeting House" (Quoted in Flower, 44). A patent from Thomas and Richard Penn, dated 20 September 1766, granted ownership of the lot to trustees appointed by the Presbyterians. Among them were Philadelphians William Allen and Adam Hoops (J. Flower 44).

Even before Carlisle's Presbyterians received ownership of the lot on the square, they had proceeded with fundraising. A "small and easy lottery" for "erecting a [Presbyterian] house of Worship" in Carlisle was advertised in the *Pennsylvania Journal* in June 1761. The prizes were described, the managers listed, and the "Frontier town and county, where many of the inhabitants have been sufferers in the late calamities" was depicted as worthy of the assistance of the "generous and well disposed." Although advertised for almost a year, the lottery was unsuccessful, perhaps because so many other Prebyterian groups—Brandywine, Lancaster, Newtown, and Middletown—started lotteries at the same time (*Pennsyl-*

vania Gazette, 1 October and 17 December 1761, 6 May and 15 July 1762). An act of the Pennsylvania Legislature was required to settle the accounts of the manager, who brought suit for recovery of funds. (*Pennsylvania Gazette*, 25 September 1766; *Pennsylvania Archives*, 8th series, 7:5935)

Despite this setback, the Carlisle Presbyterians proceeded. Robert Smith may have been approached for a suitable design when ownership of the lot was assured. Plans certainly were available before 1768, because a surviving subscription record of that year begins with the following statement:

The Presbyterian congregation at Carlisle Under the Pastoral care of the Revd. Mr. John Steel being under the Necessity of Erecting a House of Publick Worship and Notwithstand'g The said Congregation have contributed largely towards Building the same yet part of the Work is Unfinished and are obliged to apply to their Friends for Assistance" (Quoted in Landis, 14).

Robert Smith is listed among the contributors. His one pound was among those raised from other Philadelphia supporters like William Allen, Thomas Willing, Henry Keppele, and Joseph Fox.

What sort of building did Smith design for the Presbyterians in Carlisle? No plans survive, but the church itself, though altered and reoriented, is testimony to his classical approach to a meeting house. The rich deposits of stone, including limestone, in the area were the source of the "Ranged Work" specified for the south front and east end of the building in a February 1769 building contract. The south and east fronts are laid in quarry-faced ashlar; a nineteenth century addition conceals the north side. Besides specifying the "Ranged Work," the contract called for "the A[r]ches over the Windows to be of Cut White Stone and a Belt Round the said Building of the same kind of Cut Stone" (Quoted in Murray, 50-51). Contractor John McGlathery (possibly related to Matthew McGlathery, who was a member of the Carpenters' Company) was to "Compleate and Finish the Shell . . . the Dimensions of Seventy feet Front and Fifty feet Deep in the Clear." Further instructions specified the dimensions of the walls and payment schedule.

As in most of Smith's churches, this fifty-foot span was to be "in the clear," that is, no columns supported the arched ceiling. Unlike them, however, the ceiling was not hung from a raised tie beam truss. Instead, Carlisle's is a king post truss with intermedi-

This photograph was taken c. 1865 to 1870 before the church had been altered. It shows a belt course and rusticated window heads similar to those at Zion Lutheran Church in Philadelphia. Their smooth finishes create a strong contrast with the quarry-faced range work. The clear window glass has since been replaced by stained glass with pointed-arched mullions in the Gothic Revival taste. Courtesy Cumberland County Historical Society

ate posts. Like the raised tie beam trusses, it bears a strong resemblance to an illustration in Francis Price's 1733 publication, *The British Carpenter,* in this case to Plate G,B. Just as the iron strapping in the American raised tie beam trusses was modified, so it was here. The truss illustrated in Price has iron straps securing the tie beam and top of the king post to the principal rafters. The tie beam and intermediate posts also are strapped. The Carlisle truss has omitted the straps at the intermediate posts and the top of the tie beam, but added a strap at the king post, extending to an iron plate across the bottom of the tie beam. Support for the arch of the ceiling is provided, as at Shrewsbury, by knee braces. The adaptation of the iron strapping is similar to the solutions Smith employed in his raised tie beam truss. Without firmer documentation, however, it is impossible to determine whether Smith or McGlathery designed the roof system at Carlisle.

McGlathery failed to finish the job, whether because of funding difficulties or other causes is unrecorded. Another contract, with a different mason, was agreed to in April 1771. This one called for the mason to "Complete and Finish the Shell of a Stone Meeting House," repeated most of the specifications of the 1769 contract and added "there is Rabits to be made in the Walls to receive the Window bases Agreeable to the plan Drawn by Mr. Robert Smith of Philad'a." (Quoted in Murray, 52). The document is evidence that Smith's design was followed, and, most importantly, that it included elevations as well as a plan.

The 1771 contract also failed to produce a finished building, and it appears that the congregation decided to oversee the job themselves. No order of service or dedication record survives, but accounts suggest the building, though unfinished, was available for services by fall 1773 (Original Register). The Revolutionary War intervened, and in 1786, when two Carlisle congregations decided to join forces, one of their tasks was to "finish our meeting-house from its present state, according to the original plan" (Quoted in Murray, 39).

Over the years, the church has been trebled in size, and converted from what essentially was a meeting house to a more church-like appearance. In 1874, an addition equal to the size of the original building was added to the north, and a square bell tower was erected at the southwest corner, while the entrance shifted from the south to the east. Probably the communion table then was moved to the west. At about the same time, stained glass windows were installed in the nave. A perpendicular addition of 1951 now extends south of the tower (Dan Deibler to Constance M. Greiff, 3 August 1999). Nevertheless, the solidity and dignity of Smith's design is still evident.

DOCUMENTATION:

First Presbyterian Church, Carlisle. Original Register, 1756-1920 (typescript). Special Collections, Dickinson College; Murray, Rev. J.A., D.D. "Local History-A letter to Hon. J.C. Lamberton," *Carlisle Herald,* 31 July 1884; *Pennsylvania Gazette,* 25 September 1766; *Pennsylvania Journal* (Philadelphia), 11 June 1761.

REFERENCES:

Day, Sherman. "Cumberland County." In *Historical Collections of the State of Pennsylvania* . . . . Philadelphia (1843); First Presbyterian Church, Carlisle. Anniversary Programs, September 1934, September 1957, September 1959; Flower, James D. *The Planning of Carlisle and Its Center Square.* Carlisle (1983); Flower, Milton E. *Carpenters' Companies and Carlisle Architecture.* Carlisle (1955); Landis, John B., Esq. *The Old Stone Meeting House 1757-1832* . . . Carlisle (1904); Murray, Rev. Joseph A., D.D. *An Historical Address at the Semi-Centennial of the Second Presbyterian Church* . . . *12 January 1883.* Carlisle (1905); *Pennsylvania Archives.* 8th series, Vol. 7. Harrisburg (1935), Wing, Rev. Conway P., D.D. *A Discourse on the History of Donegal and Carlisle Presbyteries* . . . *October 14, 1876.* Carlisle (1877); ———. *A History of the First Presbyterian Church of Carlisle, Pa.* Carlisle (1877).

41

Design and Build a Brick House

East side Second Street between Walnut and Spruce, Philadelphia
1770, demolished

SMITH'S first documented business relationship with the affluent Samuel Powel (1738-1793) was in the fall of 1760 when he supplied a quantity of cedar plank. Their association grew after Powel returned to Philadelphia from Europe in 1767 and engaged Smith to work on a series of projects.

In 1768, Powel sold Smith a lot on the east side of Second Street between Walnut and Spruce Streets (Brayton Papers) A deed, dated 28 March 1770, and recorded in 1774, transferred the lot to Smith for £441.13.6 1/2 (Deed Book I-11:544, Powel Ledger, 75). Smith developed the property, building a "brick messuage and tenement," which he promptly sold to John Martin for £1500. It is possible Martin's house was part of a row. Powel owned the property south of the parcel sold to Smith and this may be the location of the two brick houses on Second Street that Smith built for Powel (Catalog #34).

Smith is identified in both the 1768 parchment deed and document recorded in 1774 as a "House Carpenter." His expertise and reputation could have made what was probably a speculative undertaking a profitable enterprise. Clearly, Smith was interested in this type of venture in the early 1770s because, at about the same time, he was negotiating with the vestry of Christ Church for the purchase of a large parcel on Spruce Street (Catalog #47).

DOCUMENTATION:

Deed, 17 August 1768. Brayton Papers. HSP; Philadelphia City Archives. Deeds I-11:544; Samuel Powel Ledger, 1760-1793. Powel Family Papers. Library Company of Philadelphia, on deposit, HSP.

42 A

College Edifice [University Hall]

Rhode Island College [Brown University] Providence, Rhode Island
1770

ALTHOUGH SPONSORED by Baptists, Rhode Island College has an interesting early connection with the Presbyterian College of New Jersey at Princeton. It is on the strength of this relationship that Robert Smith has been given credit for influencing the design of the "College Edifice." The first president of the Rhode Island College, the Reverend James Manning, was a Baptist preacher. He had graduated from the New Jersey institution and seems to have cherished fond memories of his alma mater.

In the fall of 1762, Manning undertook a tour of New England and the Middle Colonies to assess the residents' receptivity to his Baptist message. The Philadelphia Association of Baptists also charged him with evaluating the possibility of opening a college in Rhode Island. Manning accepted a pastorate near Providence and opened a Latin school. Time was ripe for pursuit of his collegiate mission, and, by September 1764, a corporation for founding and endowing a college had its first meeting. Manning was appointed president, and the college accepted students a year later (Kimball, 335-347).

The college moved to Providence in 1770 and funds raised in the colonies, England, and Ireland were earmarked for its building. Account books belonging to Nicholas Brown, whose family advanced nearly four thousand pounds to the college treasurer, record an expenditure of one shilling four pence on 7 April 1770 "To Postage of a Letter from the Architect of Philadelphia." Because of this entry, Carl Bridenbaugh and others identified this architect as Robert Smith, but a letter discovered in the archives at Brown University in the late 1950s cast doubt on this assertion. In this March 1770 letter addressed "To The Corporation of the College in Road-Island Government," Joseph Horatio Anderson described himself as "Architect at Philadelphia"(*JSAH*, 26). Anderson was responding to an advertisement which appeared in the Philadelphia papers at the end of February, and his letter is an exercise in self-promotion; its existence appears to remove the evidence cited to justify the claim that Robert Smith had a hand in the "draught" of a plan for the college.

A careful examination of the sequence of planning and construction, however, restores Smith as a definite influence and possible participant in the building's design. Manning received authorization from the Browns for the "removal [of the college] to Providence" in mid-November 1769. A building committee was appointed, consisting of Manning, Stephen Hopkins and Joseph Brown, brother of the chief patron of the college and a talented gentleman-amateur architect (Downing, 297).

More than one scheme must have been considered. A plan of 9 September 1769 in the archives at Brown proposed a building not exceeding sixty-six feet in

Smith may not have provided a design directly, but the debt of Brown's building to Nassau Hall is evident. Although the Providence building has four stories above the basement rather than three, and the placement of the entries is slightly different, the basic design with its pedimented central pavilion is much like its predecessor. Combined with the similarity in dimensions and James Manning's statement that it was to be "the same plan as that of Princeton," Robert Smith's influence seems clear. John Hay Library, Brown University Libraries.

length (Bigelow to Peterson, 31 October 1952). Another plan, undated and unsigned, shows the "Whole length from outside to outside" at 108 feet, but differs from the building as actually constructed not only in dimension, but also in the number of windows and placement of doorways. Its fundamental scheme, however, is that of a long rectangle with a projecting center pavilion, not unlike Nassau Hall.

In February, before advertising in the Philadelphia newspapers for an architect, some basic decisions had been made about the size and shape. A brief description of the building was recorded: "That the House be one hundred and fifty feet long and forty six feet wide with a projection of Ten feet on each side and that it be four stories high" (Brown Corporation Records, 9 February 1770). The trustees must soon have had a plan in hand. On 21 March 1770, a freshman student, Solomon Drowne, wrote in his diary, "This day they began to dig the Cellar for the College" (Hall to Peterson).

Manning remembered his days at Nassau Hall (catalog #7) and wrote to Hezekiah Smith, a Baptist minister in Haverhill, Massachusetts, noting the resemblance of the two buildings:

The College edifice is to be the same plan as that of Princeton, built of brick, four stories high, and one hundred and fifty feet long. I wish I had a draught to send you but it is not in my power. They determine to have the roof on next fall, and to cover it with slate, as they are now able (12 February 1770).

Despite recent correspondence with university archivist Martha Mitchell, who found claims of the existence of a plan signed by Smith to be erroneous (Cohen, 30, n.20), it is possible he provided preliminary guidance or "draughts" for the college building, even though "the details of the structure to be seen on the campus at Providence today do not have the flavor of Smith's work and were obviously executed by a builder (probably local) with ideas of his own" (Peterson, 1990, 20). What is likely is that Nassau Hall served as a model, as it did for many later college buildings: Hollis Hall (1762-1763) and Stoughton Hall (1805) at Harvard, Dartmouth Hall (1790), and, closer to the original, John McComb, Jr.'s Queens College (1811) at Rutgers and Alexander Hall (1813-1814) at the Princeton Theological Seminary. The actual designer probably was Joseph Brown (Downing, 297), but, as at the Williamsburg Public Hospital (Catalog #43), the skills and taste of local workmen determined the details.

DOCUMENTATION:

Brown University. John Carter Brown Library. Joseph Horatio Anderson to The Corporation of the College in Road-Island [sic], 13 March 1770; Plan, n.d. University Hall Papers; John Hay Library. Nicholas Brown Accounts, Rhode Island College. Miscellaneous Papers; Brown Corporation Records. James Manning to Hezikiah Smith, 12 February 1770.

REFERENCES:

Cohen, Jeffrey A. "Early American Architectural Drawings and Philadelphia, 1730-1860." In *Drawing Towards Building.* Philadelphia (1986); Downing, Antoinette F. "Joseph Brown." In *Macmillan Encyclopedia of Architects.* Edited by Adolf K.

Placzek. Vol 1. New York (1982); Guild, Reuben A. *Early History of Brown University*. Providence (1897); Kimball, Gertrude Selwyn. *Providence in Colonial Times*. Boston (1912); Peterson, Charles E., ed. "American Notes," *Journal of the Society of Architectural Historians*, 17, 2 (Summer, 1958), 26; Peterson, Charles E. FAIA. "Philadelphia Carpentry According to Palladio." In *Building By the Book-3*. Edited by Mario di Valmarana. Charlottesville (1990).

Bigelow, Bruce and Lawrence Wroth, Brown University to Charles E. Peterson. October-November 1952. Peterson Files; Hall, Louise to Charles E. Peterson. 1952. Peterson Files.

43

Design Hospital for Idiots and Lunatics [The Public Hospital], Eastern State Hospital[1]

Williamsburg, Virginia
1770, built 1771-1773, burned 1885, reconstructed 1981-1985

THE PUBLIC HOSPITAL for "Idiots, Lunatics and Persons of Insane Mind," designed by Robert Smith and constructed in Williamsburg, was unique in colonial America. It was the first institution in the New World built solely for the treatment of mental illness. Why Governor Francis Fauquier decided to found the hospital in 1766 remains something of a mystery, although there must have been some concern in Virginia for the care of the mentally ill. In 1769, William Byrd III of Westover corresponded with Mayor Thomas Willing of Philadelphia about four lunatics in the Williamsburg Public Gaol, who were eventually accommodated in the Pennsylvania Hospital, which cared for the insane as well as the physically ill (*House of Burgesses*, 303-305).

There is no evidence that Smith ever visited Virginia. His involvement in the hospital project is known only from his written description copied into the hospital's Court of Directors' Minutes. Although Smith's connection with Williamsburg is undocumented, it can readily be accounted for. William Byrd III is the person who must have been the catalyst. Byrd was well acquainted with Philadelphia, having married Thomas Willing's sister in 1761 and lived in

the city from then until 1764. Willing was a trustee or subscriber to at least three buildings designed or built by Robert Smith: the College of Pennsylvania, Christ Church, and the Presbyterian Church in Carlisle. He also was a subscriber to the Pennsylvania Hospital, for which Smith was, at the least, a design consultant. There were other connections. Mary Willing Byrd's uncle was William Shippen, who had played a role in the design of Nassau Hall; her brother-in-law was Samuel Powel, for whom Smith worked extensively, most notably on his Society Hill House. Undoubtedly, Byrd would have known Smith's reputation personally.

Sparse but telling documentation establishes that Smith had been chosen as the designer even before the project was authorized. He submitted "A Description of the Plan and Elevation of a Hospital for Virginia" dated 9 April 1770, which predates both the act establishing the institution in June 1770 and the appointment of a committee to determine the design in July (ESH Minutes, 13-15). Smith's description was quite detailed, and accompanied by three small sketches, the only documented drawings from his hand.

The Plan consists of a Hall for a Staircase, behind There is the Keepers apartment, and 12 other Rooms chiefly for the Reception of mad People, The Stairs begin near the front Door and lands on passages in the second Story, The second Story has 12 Rooms the same Dimensions as those in the first Story, and a Room over the Keepers Apartment which may serve the Managers of the Hospital to meet or may be divided which will make two other Rooms for Patients

The Hall is design[e]d to be open as far as the landing of the Stairs the whole hight of both Storys, The Cellers should be about eight feet high between the under sides of the Joices [joists] and the Surface of the Celler floor, And the foundation must go 12 Inches lower which will make the whole height of the Celler Wall on which you lay the first floor 9 feet, This Wall shou'd be 19 Inches thick either of Stone or very hard Brick and the Partition Walls shoud be 14 Inches thick, The first floor is designed 3 feet above the Surface of the Ground which will require The Wall about 2 feet or a little more raised above the said Surface, This part from the ground up to the top of the first floor shou'd be cased with hard Brick if the Celler Wall be of Stone, unless you go to the Expense of hewn Stone for this part which will be better; After the Wall is worked up as high as the first floor to the full Demensions of the plan sett off about 4 Inches for the finishing of the plinth or Water Table which may be of Moulding Bricks.

---

1. This entry is partially based on an essay generously supplied by Travis McDonald, Jr. for Colonial Williamsburg.

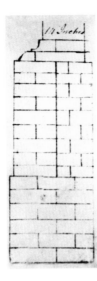

The first Story is ten feet high from floor to Cieling. The outside Walls all round 14 Inches Thick and the partitions nine Inches thick of Bricks. The second Story is designed the same thickness and to be Nine feet six Inches high. The Windows are 6 lights of Glass 10 by 8 Inches for the hight and 3 for the Width, there must be a grate of Iron to the inside of each Window which may be fixed in the follow Manner Suppose this to be the Jaums of a Window and Irons fixed ready to receive the grates when the Building is finished.

I would have 2 eyes of Iron made like the rough Scratch above, which shou'd be made of Common flat bar Iron with a hole of an Inch diameter to receive a hook which will be fixed to the Grate, the other End split and turned up or down one Inch and built in the Brick work. These two Eyes shou'd be fixed about eight Inches above the bottom of the Window and two more fixed about the same distance from the top of the window, the Grate having four hooks to fit into those eyes May be set in and a hasp fixed to the Grate at top that will fall on a Staple drove into the lintel over the Window head fix on a padlock the whole will be safe.

See this rough sketch.

Dimensions of the Plan

	feet	In:
The Keepers Apartment		22 feet
6 Rooms on one side	11.9	70.6
2 End Walls	14	2.4
6 Ditto	9	4.6
2 Water Tables	4	.8
Whole length of Build		100.-

	feet	In:
2 Room	10.9	each 21.6
1 Passage	6.2	6.2
2 Walls	14 thick	2.4
2 Ditto	9 Do	1.6
2 Water Tables	4 Do	.8
Whole Width of Building		32.2

NB The middle part projects 3 feet

If there shoud be occasion for Fire to warm the common Rooms, there may be Stoves fixed in the Partition between two Rooms—with the Mouth open to the Passage, by which means they make fires and the mad People cannot come at them They shou'd be fixed about two foot above the floor for fear of the Patients falling against the Stoves. See to the left hand on the Plan the place of two Stoves. This Building will require about Two hundred thousand Bricks each Brick about 8 3/4 Long 2 3/8 Thick and 4 1/4 Broad about 13 of such Bricks with Mortar will make one foot Superficial of a Nine Inch Wall or 19 1/2 of such to a fourteen Inch Wall. The Bricklayer must order it so that the Chimneys come one in the Roof at Equal distance from the middle otherwise they will have a very ill Effect. This may be easily done.

About 40 Thousand feet of Scantling will be wanted Superficial, which we reckon at one Inch thick 12 such feet makes one foot Cubical Measure.

16 Thousand feet of plank for Doors and floors about 1 1/2 Inch thick 2 Thousand feet of plank very good for Sashes &c.

5 Thousand of Inch Boards for Cornice to the Eves and other finishing besides Boarding the Roof

The above hints and a careful inspection of the plan may be sufficient to perform any part of the Building
Philadelphia April 9th 1770   Robt Smith
(ESH, 13-15)

Smith's design for the hospital falls into a pattern he employed for institutional public buildings rather than being specifically related to its function. Nassau Hall, the Public Hospital, and the slightly later Walnut Street Jail are functionally indistinguishable in exterior form, even though they were intended for a college, a hospital and a prison. The hospital and the prison, although they were new building types in

This photograph shows the hospital as it was reconstructed by the Colonial Williamsburg Foundation between 1981 and 1985. The gauged brick window surrounds are more typical of Virginia than of Smith's work and reveal the hand of the conservative local builder. By the time the hospital was built such details were considered old fashioned. Courtesy Colonial Williamsburg Foundation.

Like Nassau Hall, the Williamsburg Hospital was a simplified version of generic British public buildings, such as William Adam's Watsons Hospital, shown as it appeared in *Vitruvius Scoticus*. The Adam building was actually an orphanage, not a hospital, but this type of plan, with its double-loaded corridors, could be made to serve for any institution housing a number of people, whether students, patients, or prisoners, as Smith used it at the Walnut Street Jail.

P.151

The North Front of Watsons *Hospital at Edinburgh*

Extends 100 feet

Plan of the Lodging Story

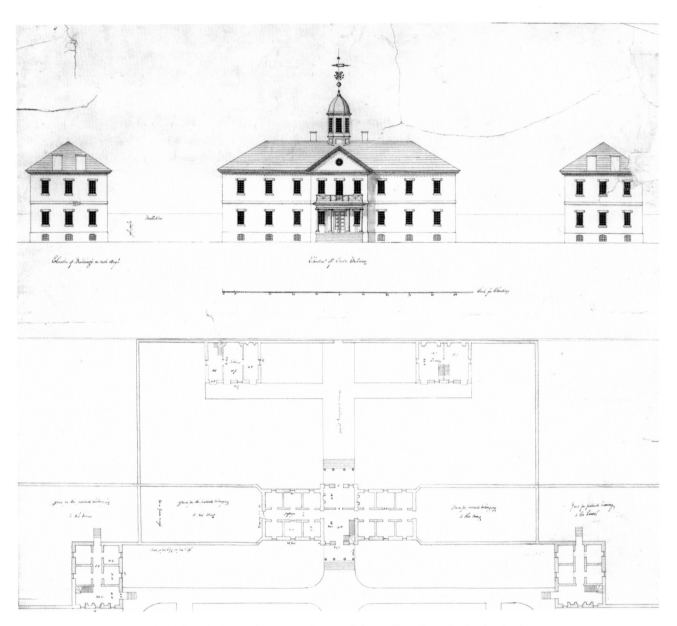

The elevation and plan of the hospital was drawn in 1829, and is attributed to the institution's physician and keeper, Alexander Dickie Galt. By this time side pavilions had been built, linked to the main building by walls, as had two outbuildings at the rear. A portico and balcony had been added at the front entrance. Courtesy Virginia State Archives.

America, depended like Nassau Hall on eighteenth-century British school or college building forms, in which long rectangular facades were broken by a projecting central entrance pavilion. As at Nassau Hall, a bull's eye marked the hospital's pediment. The detailing lacked, however, some of the refinements shared by the college and the jail, such as rusticated doorways and windows with keystones. It is not known whether this was because of a tight budget or the capabilities of the local contractor who constructed the building.

The public call for construction proposals ran in the *Virginia Gazette* on 2 August 1770.

The Committee appointed here, in Pursuance of the above Order, agreed on a Plan for the HOSPITAL, and are ready to treat with all Undertakers [contractors], who may be inclined to engage in the Work. It is to be a large commodious Brick building, and to be erected in or as near the City of *Williamsburg* as conveniently may be.

A prominent local builder, William Powell, was chosen to erect the hospital for the sum of £1,070. At least part of the time, he substituted local practices for what Smith had specified. Smith had expressed a preference for stone for the foundation, probably not realizing that none was locally available. Powell used brick. Smith had also stated that "the plinth or Water table . . . may be of Moulding Bricks." He must have thought this important, for a profile of this feature was one of the three small sketches included in his "Description." Powell instead used a simple one-part bevelled water table brick common in Virginia.

But it was Smith who set the interior arrangements. Unlike William Adam's Royal Infirmary, where the central pavilion housed a grand stair, the equivalent space in Smith's buildings was at least partially occupied by the most important public and administrative uses. At Nassau Hall, these were the prayer hall and library. At the Public Hospital somewhat less was made of this area. While the stair took up part of the central space on the first floor, the rest was occupied by the keeper's apartment on the first floor, with the Court of Directors' meeting room above.

Inmates' cells flanked central corridors in both wings. In the legislation the founders of the hospital had expressed two concerns: fear and cure. In calling for such a hospital as early as 1766, Governor Fauquier had recommended that "a legal Confine-

ment and proper Provision, ought to be appointed for these miserable Objects, who cannot help themselves. Every civilized Country has a hospital for these People, where they are confined, maintained and attended by able Physicians, to endeavor to restore to them their lost reason" (*House of Burgesses*, 12). The arrangements of the Virginia hospital, however, appeared to favor confinement over cure. No room was specified for a physician. Primarily the hospital functioned to remove the inmates from society, and also to separate them from their keepers and one another. It was intended that prisoners would be kept in separate cells, in which their meals were served. Smith would have been familiar with the Pennsylvania Hospital, where other means also were used to exert control over the patients: fetters, strait jackets, locked and bolted doors, and barred windows and transoms. The importance of the latter were discovered in the early days of the Pennsylvania Hospital where, in 1758, "It appearing by the Reports that several of the Lunaticks have made their Escape owing to the iron bars of the Celles being too slender. Tis agreed that the Monthly Committee employ the same Smith [i.e. blacksmith] who made them to make them stronger and more secure" (MBM, 2 April 1758). Robert Smith must have been well aware of these problems. The only sketches he submitted with his "Description," aside from the brick water table, were for iron window and transom grates.

To provide some exercise for the patients, while maintaining security, Powell erected a ten-foot fence in 1773 to enclose a yard.

The hospital stayed in operation during most of the Revolutionary War, but only barely. Forced to close in 1781, it reopened in 1786. Smith's plan was soon altered, with staircases at either end of the wings leading to the exercise yard installed in 1790. Ten years later, the yard was enclosed in brick. Over the course of the nineteenth century, Smith's building was engulfed by alterations and additions, until it burned in 1885. Colonial Williamsburg demolished its replacement in 1969, and reconstructed Robert Smith's Public Hospital in 1981-1985.

DOCUMENTATION:

A Description of the Plan and Elevation of a Hospital for Virginia, 9 April 1770. Eastern State Hospital. Court of Directors' Book of Minutes, 10 December 1770-23 July 1801 [hereafter ESH Minutes]. Virginia State Library; *Journal of the House of Burgesses*. Edited by John P. Kennedy. Vol. 11. Richmond (1906); *Virginia Gazette*, 2 August 1770; Minutes of the Board of Managers, Pennsylvania Hospital. Vol. 2, 1757-1764 [hereafter MBM].

REFERENCES:

Blanton, Wyndham Bolling. *Medicine in Virginia in the Eighteenth Century*. Richmond, VA (1931); Dain, Norman. *Disordered Minds: The First Century of Eastern State Hospital* . . . Williamsburg (1971); Gaines, William H., Jr. "The Public Hospital for Disordered Minds: How Virginia Pioneered in Caring for the Mentally Sick." *Virginia Cavalcade*, 3, 1 (1953):34-38; Gibbs, Patricia A. and Linda H. Rowe. The Public Hospital, 1766-1785. Research Report. Colonial Williamsburg Foundation, 1974; Jones, Granville, M.D. "The History of the Founding of the Eastern State Hospital of Virginia." *American Journal of Psychiatry*, 110, 9 (March 1954):644-650; McDonald, Travis C., Jr. The Public Hospital: Architectural History and Chronicles of Reconstruction. Typescript. Colonial Williamsburg Foundation, 1984; Zwelling, Shomer S. *Quest for a Cure*. Williamsburg (1985).

44

Repairs to the Steeple of Christ Church

Second Street between Market and Arch Streets, Philadelphia
1771, Steeple (For original construction, see Catalog #4)

THE PROUD NEW STEEPLE of Christ Church was in trouble almost immediately after its construction in 1753. On 22 November 1756, minutes record that the vestry appointed a special committee "to examine that part of the Steeple which is like to be injured by the Weather & to call in what Tradesmen who they thought proper and agree with them on the best Terms for having it speedily repaired." Six years later they ordered that the steeple "be immediately repaired and painted" (Minutes, 2 June 1762). Still nothing much was done, and by the spring of 1771 the situation had become alarming. Robert Smith, designer of the steeple, was called back and conducted an inspection on May 7th. He found the wood sills on top of the brick tower decayed and the shingle walls leaking. He asked that some of the brickwork be removed for a closer inspection (Loose mss). The vestry pressed him for his attendance at the site, and

he reluctantly consented to undertake the work on July 1st or sooner (Minutes, 20 May 1771). A week later members of the vestry climbed the scaffold with the architect and were appalled at what they saw. "The Ends of the great Timbers [were] so rotten as to be a mere Powder, and the other Parts likewise very much decayed" (Minutes, 4 June 1771).

To signal the start of the repair program, on July 3rd a large order of lumber was delivered by Arthur Donaldson. For the first time in the surviving records of the church there is a clutch of detailed vouchers, starting with blacksmith Samuel Wheeler's large bill for furnishing spikes, nails, screws, and the repair of tools. Thomas Cuthbert furnished poles and spars for scaffold and hoisting; Wetherill & Cresson more lumber; Joshua Humphreys oak scantling; John Inglis a double block and rope. On August 1st, Robert Smith wrote that he "shu.d be pleased to see some of the Vestry now and then at the Steeple to see how we go on. I have a very difficult piece of Business. I think it is more so than any I Ever had before" (loose mss.). How many climbed the dizzy heights to look is not recorded.

Eden Haydock provided 320 1/4 pounds of sheet lead and Arthur Donaldson supplied shingles already dressed. By October 14th it was all over but the painting, which was done by Barrett & Fling. Smith wrote recommending that "the Painters to paint the spindle Black of A dark Couler." The painter's bill for three or four coats came to the large sum of £123.3.10 1/2, from which £8 was deducted as a contribution. (Many other participants also contributed.) The painters charged steeplejack prices. Included was an item for "Smalting the Cap of the Spire"—adding a coating of tiny glass beads that would glitter in the sunlight. Robert Smith then reported the steeple "as strong as it Ever was."

What is probably evidence of the repairs still survives. Two sets of eighteenth-century tiedowns with heavy iron straps remain. These served to anchor the wooden steeple to the masonry of the tower. Possibly they were installed to hold down a temporary roof on the tower until construction of the steeple could begin. This was the case at Independence Hall, where a shallow roof covered the tower after it was necessary to remove the original steeple. More likely Smith had to cut off the original tiedowns when he returned to repair the bottoms of the original timber columns

Two sets of tiedown anchors, reinforced with iron strapping, probably represent both of Smith's construction efforts. The original on the right does not engage the present timbers of the steeple; rather the T-shaped hardware at its base engages the bottoms of timber spars embedded in the masonry. The replacement tiedown anchor on the left does engage the existing steeple. George Eisenmann photograph.
Courtesy Keast & Hood Co.

and sills (Suzanne M. Pentz to Constance M. Greiff, 21 July 1999).

It says a great deal for Smith's reputation among his contemporaries that he was called back to correct the error made in the original construction of the steeple. The truth of the matter was that Philadelphia had no experience with steeples and did not understand their construction. Both those of the State House and the Presbyterian Church were soon to fail structurally and be taken down.

DOCUMENTATION:

Christ Church Archives. Loose Manuscripts. Vestry Minutes, 1761-1773.

45

Consultant and Measurer for the German Reformed Church

South Side of Race Street below Fourth Street, Philadelphia
1771 (Consultation); 1775 (Measuring); demolished 1836

THE CUPOLA of the first church built for the German Reformed congregation of Philadelphia is visible in Scull and Heap's 1754 East Prospect of the city. The church was a distinctive building, hexagonal in form, but, despite its architectural features, served its congregation for only about twenty years. Various schisms and reunifications probably made property maintenance a secondary consideration; by 1771 the building was in a state of disrepair. On July 1st, the Church Council, or Consistory, met in the school house to consider construction alternatives. Should they build anew or repair? Should they move or rebuild on the same lot? They decided to hold a parish meeting to discuss proposals (Minute Book, 1 and 15 July 1771). Various opinions were aired. A majority favored demolition, and building a new church on the existing lot. To resolve their dilemma, they called on Jacob Graeff and Robert Smith for advice.

After the Church Council of our High German Reformed Church has taken into consideration the present state of the church and has found that the building clearly is not only dilapidated but also too small to accommodate the growing number of members comfortably, its thinking is as follows: (especially as the lot and house adjoining the church have been bought and paid for), it should come to a decision about building [a new church]. Since, however, there are different opinions of the Council, it was resolved unanimously on July 1, 1771 (as the only way to keep peace and concord is to ascertain the opinion of the Parish) to call together all the members of our parish, to acquaint them lovingly with the state of the said church and to listen to their opinions, so that the God of Peace, to whose honor the building is to be erected, will bless all of us with his grace.

My worthy brothers! Two experienced builders were consulted, namely Mr. Robert Smith and Mr. Jacob Gra[e]ff, to give their opinion regarding the demolition of the church as well as the adjoining house and kitchen, which they did and it is as follows:

1. The material from the church, as far as it
   is usable for building is worth   £221/12
   Cost of breaking up the church   £ 92/18

   Leaving a balance for the parish of   £128/14
2. The material from the house and kitchen,
   as far as it is usable for building   £198
   Cost of breaking up the house and kitchen £ 45/2

   Leaving a balance of   £153/4

The above cost includes £9/12 for moving the rubble, which, however is to be used as fill. Accordingly, when the church, house, and kitchen are demolished, there remains a balance of £291/10

Adding to the [above] sum   £208/18

One gets a total of   £500/—

For above £500, the parish can build a school house, because the present one is too small to comfortably accommodate the growing number of young people, and the present [school house] can be made into a home for the preacher at little expense. Moreover, enough land remains to build a church as large as is necessary. Thus it will be much easier to spend £208/10 than to lay out £1160 for another lot, which would only saddle the parish with a debt of £900, but would also cause our descendants with great damage and trouble (Minute Book,15 July 1771).

Smith's role on this project was not unlike his initial consultation at St. Michael's Lutheran Church, where his advice was sought about enlarging the building. There he "disapproved of the plan," and wound up with the job of designing a whole new church (Catalog #26). That would not be the case with the German Reformed Church.

Discussions about the relative merits of the proposal generated by Smith and Graeff's investigation continued through July. Finally building on an alternative site on Arch Street was dismissed as too costly. Early in August, the Church Council met in the school house to elect a committee of parishioners to oversee construction of the new building, and, a few weeks later, named William Colladay as builder (Minute Book, 4 and 19 August 1771).

Colladay, a member of the Carpenters' Company, was a master builder active in civic affairs, who, three years later, would serve with Robert Smith as a Regulator of Party Walls, Buildings, and Partition Fences (Tatman and Moss, 156; Catalog #50). But this project was his pre-Revolutionary plum. He weathered the congregation's dissension about the orientation of the building—east/west vs. north/south, steeple vs. no steeple—and was rewarded on Saturday, March 21st, with the unanimous decision to "carry out the design submitted by Mr. William Colladay for building the new church." Less than a month later the "foundation stone" was laid, and a celebratory service was held April 20th (Minute Book, 21 March, 10 and 20 April 1772).

Colladay went on to suggest modifications to the carpentry work (Minute Book, 8 June 1772). Members of the Church Council solicited funds, made arrangements for adding to their property, and debated the relative merits of organ placement (Minute Book, 10 and 12 May 1773). On the first day of May, 1774, the newly built church was dedicated (Minute Book).

It has been suggested erroneously that Robert Smith was the designer of the German Reformed Church (Hammond, 1995). This assumption was based on descriptions of exterior design motifs and the presence of an arched ceiling (S&W,2:1415), described in an 1830 insurance survey, and salvaged "roof truss elements." But by this time, thirteen years after the design of St. Peter's (Catalog #13), Robert Smith surely was not the only Philadelphia builder familiar with a raised tie beam truss, and capable of modifying it to suit the needs of a particular site. At St. Peter's Smith had adapted the raised tie beam truss illustrated by Francis Price in *The British Carpenter,* adding supplementary iron straps and bolts. His introduction of this truss type and its adaptation to New World conditions, was an important step forward, expressing his creativity and practical ingenuity. But other builders must soon have been able to emulate him, as William Colladay did in this instance.

Smith subsequently played a different role at the German Reformed Church—that of measurer, a position he could not have held had he been the designer or builder. In February 1775, a team composed of Gunning Bedford, Joseph Rakestraw, Abraham Carlisle, and James Worrell, all members of the Carpenters' Company, "measured and valued all the Carpenter's Work done at the Calvinist Church." Some dispute must have arisen, because a second team of evaluators was called upon. Smith, Joseph Fox, and James Pearson, another Carpenters' Company triumvirate, "carefully examined the aforementioned Work, and assisted in settling the prices thereof" (Quoted in Hammond, 1995).

DOCUMENTATION:

Survey, 11 February 1830. Franklin Fire Insurance Company. HSP; Hills, John. Plan of the City of Philadelphia and its Environs. 1796; Minute Book of the German Reformed Church (extracts translated by Dr. H. Karl Frensdorff, 1995) [records on deposit, but unprocessed and unavailable in 1998]; Biddle, Clement. *The Philadelphia Directory*. Philadelphia (1791); Hogan, Edmund. *The Prospect of Philadelphia*. Philadelphia (1795).

REFERENCES:

S&W, 2; Tatman & Moss; Wilson, Robert H. *Freedom of Worship: Meeting Houses, Churches and Synagogues of Early Philadelphia*. Philadelphia (1976); Yeomans, David T. "British and American Solutions to a Roofing Problem." *Journal of the Society of Architectural Historians*, 50 (September 1991): 266-272.

Hammond, Joseph W. The German Reformed Church in Philadelphia: An Important 1772 Addition to the Works of Robert Smith. Typescript, 1995. Peterson Files.

46 A

St. Peter's Episcopal Church

31 Throckmorton Street, Freehold, New Jersey
1771, altered

LOOKING AT St. Peter's Church today, it is difficult to recognize it as an eighteenth-century building, so changed has it been by nineteenth-century Gothic Revival alterations. But it was in fact begun in 1771. It was the second building of the local parish, replacing a church deemed too small, in poor repair, and inconveniently located. The congregation already owned land in the Monmouth County seat, which they believed more suitable for the new building.

Although the building was begun in 1771, construction languished, and only the envelope and small tower were built before the outbreak of the Revolu-

tion put a stop to all work. The church was not completed until 1793-1794. Originally, the entrance, now at the west end, was on the south, with a door at each end. The interior was a meeting house type, with the pulpit along the north wall and a peripatetic communion table, planned first for the raised chancel at the east, and finally placed at the north (Friary, 801; Hammond and Gavin, 7:5).

St. Peter's has been attributed to Robert Smith on the basis of three factors: the close relationship of the St. Peter's congregation to that at Shrewsbury, New Jersey (Catalog #39); a drawing showing a roof truss with raised tie beam, reinforced by iron straps and bolts; and the resemblance of the small tower, particularly the cupola, to documented Smith designs, such as Nassau Hall (Catalog #7) and Christ Church, Shrewsbury.

Certainly the congregation at Freehold had close ties to that at Shrewsbury. The two had shared missionaries until 1766. When St. Peter's acquired its own rector in 1767, he was a man who would have known Robert Smith's work. William Ayres was educated at the charity school in Philadelphia, and by 1755, when Smith was altering the school's building (Catalog #11), became a member of its faculty. He also was on the faculty of the College of Pennsylvania when Smith was architect for a new dormitory (Catalog #16; Hammond 7:3).

On the other hand, the drawing tends to argue against Smith's involvement. For one thing it is crude in comparison to the plan of Carpenters' Hall (Catalog #35), or, for that matter, to any of the drawings in the Carpenters' Company rule book. The poché is uneven and the manner in which some of its lines cross those defining the wall is sloppy. Furthermore, although the inscription is in an eighteenth-century hand, that hand does not appear to be Smith's. The manner in which the capital "C" and the numerals "1" and "7" are formed seems to be unlike Smith's customary penmanship. The span of the ceiling at Shrewsbury, where Smith also employed a raised tie beam, is thirty-eight feet, that of the Freehold church only thirty-two feet. At Shrewsbury, probably confident of his knowledge of structure, Smith called for far less iron than shown in the drawing for Freehold. Strangely, although evidently executed in 1771, the drawing resembles nothing so much as Plate VII of the Carpenters' Company rule book, a truss in-

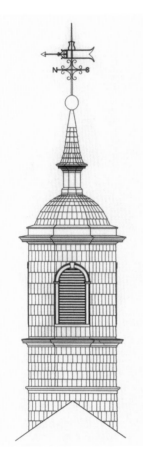

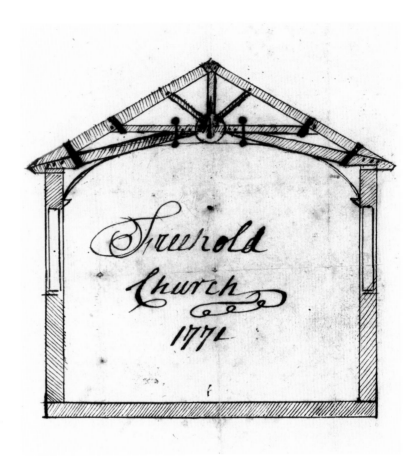

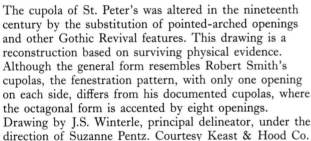

The cupola of St. Peter's was altered in the nineteenth century by the substitution of pointed-arched openings and other Gothic Revival features. This drawing is a reconstruction based on surviving physical evidence. Although the general form resembles Robert Smith's cupolas, the fenestration pattern, with only one opening on each side, differs from his documented cupolas, where the octagonal form is accented by eight openings.
Drawing by J.S. Winterle, principal delineator, under the direction of Suzanne Pentz. Courtesy Keast & Hood Co.

It is not possible to attribute St. Peter's to Robert Smith on the basis of this drawing. Although it titled in an eighteenth century hand, the writing is quite different from documented examples of Smith's penmanship, particularly in the formation of the capital "C" and the number "7." Nevertheless, it is of great interest as an extremely rare example of a drawing of a section from this period. Monmouth County Historical Society.

tended for a sixty-foot span. The drawing also shows the bolts connecting the tie beams and the diagonal braces as protruding through the ceiling. Surely Smith's aesthetic sense would not have accepted such a solution.

The building's small tower is contemporaneous with the structure of the roof. Therefore, if, as the documentation suggests, the building was under roof by 1771, the cupola also must at least have been

framed, and undoubtedly enclosed, at that time. Thus a date of construction during Smith's lifetime seems correct, and the design, consisting of a square base and octagonal cupola, is, as noted above, similar to that employed by Smith on a number of buildings. The scale of St. Peter's is different from that of other surviving Smith cupolas, such as those at Christ Church, Philadelphia, or Shrewsbury, so that it is difficult to make comparisons. The framing of each of the three cupolas is different. Thus there is not enough similarity in construction technique to support an attribution to Smith on that basis alone (Suzanne M. Pentz to Constance M. Greiff, 16 July 1999).

Without written documentation, it is impossible to attribute St. Peter's to Robert Smith. What seems most likely is not that he provided plans for it, but that local carpenters, of some skill, but less sophistication about structure, emulated his design of the Shrewsbury church.

REFERENCES:

Friary, Donald R. The Architecture of the Anglican Church in the Northern American Colonies.... Ph.D. diss. University of Pennsylvania (1971); Garlick, Rev. Bernard M. *A History of St. Peter's Church, Freehold, New Jersey, 1702-1967.* Freehold (1967); "Old St. Peter's Church, on the Battlefield of Monmouth, New Jersey." *The American Messenger.* 60, 7 (July 1902).

Hammond, Joseph W. and Caroline Gavin. St. Peter's Episcopal Church. National Register of Historic Places Registration Form. August 1997; Keast & Hood Co. St. Peter's Church, Freehold NJ. Site Visit Memorandum, April 1996. Peterson Files.

47

Purchase and Development of Spruce Street Property

North side of Spruce Street between Fourth and Fifth Streets, Philadelphia
1771

AT THE TIME of his death, Smith owned most of the north side of Spruce Street between Fourth and Fifth Streets. He had gained possession of the property through a 1771 agreement with the Christ Church vestry, which required payment of ground rent and construction of "good brick houses." The exact status of the project when Smith died in 1777 is not entirely clear, but estate papers and other documents help unravel pieces of this venture in speculative residential development.

The tale begins with a 1732 bequest by Englishman Edward Jauncy directing the purchase of land in Philadelphia "for support and maintenance" of the ministers of Christ Church (Dorr, 372). It was some time before locals and overseas officials of the Society for the Propagation of the Gospel devised a suitable plan which honored all aspects of Jauncy's bequest, so the funds were set aside and invested. When plans for St. Peter's Church (Catalog #13) at Third and Pine Streets were shown to the vestry of Christ Church in June 1750, the subject of funds available for support of the minister resurfaced. Accordingly, in February 1759, a letter "To the reverend Doctor Philip Bearcroft, secretary to the incorporate society for propagating the Gospel in foreign parts" requested distribution of the money to "be immediately laid out in a piece of land, and let to tenants on ground rent..." (Dorr, 114-15). It was two years before the plan was approved in London and Bearcroft authorized the vestry to proceed with the purchase. Bearcroft's decision was acknowledged in January 1762 and the vestry promptly arranged with the agents of proprietor Thomas Penn for a suitable lot on the north side of Spruce Streets between Fourth and Fifth Streets. In addition, they developed a plan of income allocation, designating three-fifths of the proceeds for the benefit of Christ Church and two-fifths for St. Peter's (Dorr, 372-373).

Vestry minutes show that four years later a committee was appointed "to make a Plan of the Ground ... and to divide the same into lots to be let out to such Persons as shall offer the best Ground Rent," but several more years passed before the project moved forward. Vestrymen were preoccupied with raising funds to discharge debts associated with building St. Peter's, installing a new organ in Christ Church, routine maintenance of buildings and churchyard, and "other matters of importance." No mention was made of the Spruce Street lot until 1770 when, in April, a new committee was appointed "to treat with any persons who may incline to become Purchasers." Whether Robert Smith was among this initial group of prospective buyers is unknown, and the minutes are silent about any aspect of the project or reasons for the continued delay. Location of the lot may have been an important consideration. The 1762 Clarkson-Biddle map of Phildelphia shows little development on the north side of Spruce Street west of Third, and this alone may have contributed to caution on the part of the vestry and potential buy-

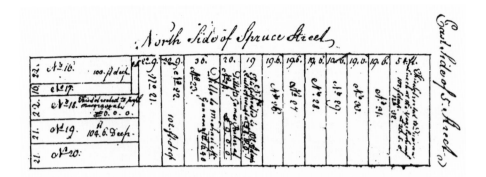

The layout of Robert Smith's Spruce Street property was drawn, like that of his Second Street holdings, to establish the location of lots involved in the distribution of his estate. It appears in Book 11, page 228 of the Philadelphia Orphans Court records. The sketch and related documents suggest that Smith may have completed one house on the property and begun two others before his death.

ers. By the first of June 1771, however, the vestry decided that "Mr. Robert Smith's proposal to take the Church lot on Spruce Street upon Ground Rent for ever should be accepted."

Despite the positive tone of this vote, the issue was not resolved, and Smith was confused about the status of his proposal. He wrote the rector on June 28th that he had no "answer with regard to that Lot of the Church," and restated the agreed upon financial terms. Apparently, a competitor proposed a different arrangement because Smith somewhat testily declared, "I believe you will find on considering this Affair I have made the best bid of any you have had." The vestry concurred and on July 13th "again considered Robert Smith's proposal," approving it after review on August 2nd.

Smith received an indenture transferring ownership of the ground on the north side of Spruce between Fourth and Fifth Streets the same day, subject to ground rent, and immediately tapped its income potential. He sold a double lot at the corner of Fifth Street to Duncan Leach; the deed was recorded September 21st (Deed Book D-5:505). Between 1774 and 1776, Robert and Esther Smith sold three contiguous lots [#s 23, 24, and 25]. Because Smith held only a leasehold, all the lots still were subject to ground rent (Deed Book M,R-5:150-153, 19 May 1774; Book I-15:481, 1 February 1776; Book D-72:273, 30 March 1776). No development occurred on Leach's parcel,

and exactly what occurred on many of the other lots sold before Smith's death is open to question.

By 1773, Smith was occupied with work for Samuel Powel (Catalog #34) and probably also was busy at the jail (Catalog #49), which could account for his apparent lack of activity in Spruce Street. Nevertheless, he certainly began a house on Fourth Street and may have begun or built two others. In September 1778, Esther and John Smith, administrators of his estate advertised one for sale:

To be SOLD by Public Vendue, On Saturday the 3rd day of October next. An excellent unfinished three story brick HOUSE, situate three doors above the corner of Spruce street in Fourth street, twenty two feet Front and thirty one feet three inches deep, it is finished all to plaistering except the entry, and the work is prepared for that ready to put up; the lot it stands on is twenty-two feet front and one hundred and ten feet deep, with the privilege of a four feet six inches alley; Subject to a ground rent of 6l. per annum; Late the estate of Robert Smith, house carpenter, deceased. Those who chuse to purchase may view the premises, apply to the subscribers living below the New Market....By order of an Orphans Court.

ESTHER SMITH, Administratrix
JOHN SMITH, Administrator

In 1780, John Smith listed, as cash received a year earlier, "£1950 for "the House in fourth Street." This can be identified as the Joseph Musgrave property. The Orphans Court Docket records the sale to

Musgrave of a "messuage and lot" near the corner of Fourth and Spruce on September 13th (Orphans Court 11:141). Musgrave's name also appears on the map filed with papers pertaining to partition of the Smith estate, where he is shown as owning the third lot down from Spruce Street, with a twenty-two foot frontage.

Another cash influx in 1779—£225—came from George Meade. This was far more than the cost of a lot, but far less than had been realized from the sale to Musgrave. Perhaps this was a building Smith had begun, but not carried to the same state of completion as the Musgrave house. The value of his estate included "Buildings on Spruce Street and 4th as they now stand unfinished," estimated at £1000 and "400 feet of Ground Rent in Spruce Street" at £3600 (Orphans Court Docket, Estate of Robert Smith). If the building was incomplete, it must have been finished shortly. This property was at the corner of Spruce and Fourth Streets. A house on that corner, "occupied by George Meade," was advertised for sale in the *Pennsylvania Gazette* of 22 July 1780. Five years later, George Meade appeared in Macpherson's 1785 directory, living on Chestnut Street. What is puzzling is that Charles Thomson (1729-1824) is sometimes spoken of as residing on the Spruce Street corner. Did he lease the house and then buy it from Meade? The diarist Elizabeth Drinker noted that Thomson's house burned down in 1777, so he may have needed to establish himself elsewhere and, why not on Fourth Street. He is listed as insuring the corner property in 1795.

Smith may have completed a third house before his death. This was located on Fourth Street, adjacent to the Meade property. At the partition of his estate in 1780, Lot 17 went to his son, Henry, who soon would be lost at sea. At the time, it contained "A certain Three Story Brick Messuage or tenement and Kitchen..."

In the 1780 partition, John Smith received lots 20 and 28, while lots 26 and 27 went to his brother-in-law William Williams. Except for Lot 28, they were not included when the remainder of the lots, and the house on Lot 17, were advertised as on the block at the sheriff's sale that ended the disposition of Smith's real property (*Federal Gazette*). Williams built two houses on his inheritance, at 425 and 427 Spruce Street, which survive as fine examples of Philadelphia Federal period houses. The first (425) was sold to An-

thony Butler in 1792. Antoine de la Forest, the French Consul General to the United States, bought the second at about the same time. It was resold in 1795 to Don Joseph de Jaudenes, Commissary General and Envoy from the King of Spain (Tatman and Moss, 855).

At Smith's death, his debts exceeded his assets. Among them, listed in the estate account prepared before the partition was one pertaining to Spruce Street. This was "Debt Contracted since the Year 1774" of £100 "To Ground Rent for the Church Lot." This must have been an ongoing problem, for Christ Church vestry minutes of November 1772 lament the absence of Smith's £100 annual payment, and complain that they have received nothing from him since undertaking the transaction a year before (Vestry Minutes, 16 November 1772).

DOCUMENTATION:

Office of the Recorder of Deeds. Estate of Robert Smith, deceased. Orphans Court hearing (File B.r. 84). 17 June 1780. Book 11:141 and 218-228. Philadelphia City Archives; *Federal Gazette and Pennsylvania Daily Advertiser*. 2 April 1790; *Pennsylvania Gazette*. 15 September 1778; Minutes, 1761-1834. Vestry of United Congregations [Christ Church and St. Peter's]. Christ Church Archives.

REFERENCES:

Dorr, Rev. Benjamin, D. D., *A Historical Account of Christ Church Philadelphia . . . and of St. Peter's and St. James's, until the separation of the churches*. New York (1841).

48

Measuring at Jacob Hiltzheimer's Kitchen

Possibly on the east side of Seventh Street below Market, Philadelphia
1773

GERMAN-BORN Jacob Hiltzheimer (d.1798) settled in Philadelphia about the same time as Robert Smith. Hiltzheimer was briefly apprenticed to a silversmith, but found his real calling as a farmer and owner of a livery stable on Seventh Street near Market. His advertisements in issues of the *Pennsylvania Gazette* in the late 1760s through 1778 extol the virtues of horses for sale and appeal for the return of those that had strayed or been stolen. His pasture at the "upper end of Spruce Street," described as near the hospital, was not the only place he kept his livestock. He also owned land south of the city, possibly in the vicinity of Smith's Buck Tavern (Catalog #27).

Hiltzheimer was a friend and associate of Robert Smith. They "dine[d] on Beefstakes with about 24 or 25 Gentlemen," shared "some of my Big Steer named Roger at Mr. Mullins on the Bank of the Schuylkill," met for jaunts to Greenwich Island, and had an occasional punch at the Buck Tavern (Diaries, 6 November 1773, 12 February 1774, 12 June 1774). Both men "Supped at the new Gaol opposite that State house yard" on 10 September 1774, the day the roof of the building was raised, when one of their hosts was Joseph Fox, a manager of the Walnut Street Jail project. Fox was a master builder, member of the Carpenters' Company, a prominent leader of fellow craftsmen "on the eve of the Revolution," and a surveyor for properties to be insured by the Philadelphia Contributionship (Tatman and Moss, 278). He was also active professionally as a measurer. It was in the latter capacity that he and Robert Smith went to Jacob Hiltzheimer's on a cloudy, cold day in December 1773 to "value" the kitchen (Diary, 22 December 1773).

The practice of measuring or valuing the work of another craftsman has been explained in the Introduction. Generally, to insure fairness, one of the measurers was chosen by the workman and the other by the client. Perhaps, in his mind, Hiltzheimer's association with both Joseph Fox and Robert Smith provided extra assurance that the kitchen would be valued fairly.

DOCUMENTATION:

Hiltzheimer, Jacob. Diaries, 1772-1774. On microfilm at American Philosophical Society; Parsons, Jacob Cox, ed. *Extracts from the Diary of Jacob Hiltzheimer of Philadelphia, 1765-1798*. Philadelphia (1893); *Pennsylvania Gazette*.

REFERENCES:

Tatman and Moss.

49

Walnut Street Jail

South side Walnut Street between Fifth and Sixth Streets, Philadelphia
1773, demolished c. 1835

ALTHOUGH it seems certain that Robert Smith designed the Walnut Street Jail, there is virtually no contemporary documentation. The only reference is that he was among the guests at a party after a "raising supper" for the workmen given by the managers of the project, Joseph Fox and Edward Duffield, on 10 September 1774, after which "they asked a few of their friends to the north-east corner room, where something was provided for them separately." The guest list was select; besides the managers, it included the mayor of Philadelphia, other dignitaries, and Robert Smith (Hiltzheimer diary). Smith's presence indicates that his role was an important one. Writing in 1811, thirty-four years after his death, while the prison still was very much a sight to see in Philadelphia, James Mease declared that "the prison was designed and built by Robert Smith, and is one of the many buildings for which Philadelphia is indebted to that excellent and faithful architect" (Mease, 180).

Construction of the Walnut Street Jail was a long-delayed response to the growing Philadelphia population and the attendant growing rate of crime. From the beginning, Pennsylvania legislative dictates had mandated that each county have a prison. Philadelphia's first solution was a jail known as "The Cage," built in 1682-1683 at the corner of High (Market) and Second Streets. Other jails along High Street were built as the need arose. By the middle of the eighteenth century, the number of prisoners and the requirements for housing them appropriately made the need for a new facility obvious, but it was some years before the legislature acted.

On 26 January 1773, a petition from the "inhabitants of the city and county of Philadelphia" was presented to the Pennsylvania Assembly. It attested to the inadequacy of the existing jail and work house, and requested that "the County Commissioners, Assessors and Justices of the Peace [be given] full Powers to purchase a Lot of Ground, erect a commodious County Gaol, and to dispose of the Ground whereon the present Gaol and Work-House are built" (*Pennsylvania Archives*, ser. 8, 8:6924). At that time, the petition was "ordered to lie on the Table" but it was brought to the fore for discussion again and again. Finally, on 21 October 1773, an act was passed authorizing the city commissioners to purchase the ground and oversee construction of a jail (Mease, 179). In July 1774, Samuel Rhoads, a member of the Committee of Correspondence, "laid before the House" a letter from Benjamin Franklin dated February 2nd with the information that "An Act for erecting a new Gaol" was one of the fifteen Acts of Assembly presented to His Majesty in January (*Pennsylvania Archives*, ser. 8, 8:7093). This notification represented the ultimate authorization of the project.

Samuel Rhoads was a man whose advocacy of civic projects had produced the Pennsylvania Hospital (Catalog #12) and the Almshouse (Catalog #29). He and Smith were well acquainted, and had worked together not only on large scale buildings, but also on Benjamin Franklin's house (Catalog #21). It may have been he who suggested Smith as designer of the prison, although Smith also would have been well known to the managers of the project, Joseph Fox, a fellow member of the Carpenters' Company, and Edward Duffield, active in Presbyterian affairs.

A lot on the south side of Walnut Street, east of Sixth, was "bought partly of the proprietors, Thomas and John Penn, and partly of private persons, for the sum of £3,252," and work must have begun immediately (Mease, 179). This location placed the jail nearly in the shadow of the Pennsylvania State House, one block to the north.

Unfortunately, there are no records covering construction of the jail. Minutes of the "Inspectors of the Jail and Penitentiary House" begin only in 1794, but, as noted, diarist Jacob Hiltzheimer attended a "raising supper" at the jail in September 1774. So it is safe to assume that at least the framework of the roof was in place, and that the building would be covered before winter. The following month, another diarist, Elizabeth Drinker, saw that workmen were very busy at the site, but by December 20th, the Assembly was told of a building only "in part erected," which would require "eleven or twelve thousand pounds more" to complete (Garvan, 125; *Pennsylvania Archives*, ser. 8, 8:7169). "Most of the Tradesmen's Accounts remain

unsettled, not being yet brought in ... [and] paying interest [on the amount to be borrowed] will be a grievous Burthen." Various approaches to financing were discussed, with immediate sale of the old jail being advocated. One solution may have been the issuance of paper currency in April 1775, in denominations of 50 shillings and £5, displaying a picture of the new jail (Snyder, 94). Just what overall course of action was followed is not recorded, but in November the Assembly "Resolved, That it be recommended to the Commissioners of the County of Philadelphia to finish the new Gaol as speedily as may be, and that the Prisoners be removed thither without Loss of Time" (*Pennsylvania Archives*, 8: 7367).

One hundred and five prisoners were moved to Walnut Street in January 1776, when the jail was still unfinished, "and six of them broke jail the night after their transfer" (S&W, 1:305). Whether there was some fundamental weakness in the design or insufficient supervision in the new location remains a mystery. Certainly care had been taken to make the building fireproof, and undoubtedly escape-proof as well. As early as 1771 Benjamin Franklin had written to Samuel Rhoads about practices he had observed in France where, by the use of brick arches and tile floors, the fireproof quality of a building was enhanced. Smith also was well aware of the need for security in a building where those who had been removed from society were to be confined, as illustrated by his care in delineating iron grates for the Public Hospital in Williamsburg (Catalog #43).

Financial problems were obviously not the only factors interfering with completion of the jail while Smith was alive. War with England caused Smith to apply his talents and ingenuity to devising defenses of the Delaware River and building a barracks at Billingsport, New Jersey (Catalog #53). He may have delegated to others oversight of work remaining at the jail, if, indeed, work was to be done. It is probable that work was halted once the prison was occupied in January 1776, because shortly afterwards the prisoners were moved out and Congress requisitioned the building for its own use as a military prison. The British put it to the same use when they captured the city, as did the returning Americans; it was not returned to city and county until 1784 (Sellin, 326).

There is no plan of the prison before 1798, by which time solitary cells and a workhouse had been

So impressive was the Walnut Street Jail in the eighteenth-century Philadelphia landscape, that it was a subject for several artists, even appearing on currency and the cover of a 1778 almanac. Among these depictions was this lively scene that was included in the Birch views published in 1799 and 1800. It shows a board fence along the front of the institution, perhaps to separate inmates using the cellar from passersby. It also suggests that, while the front wall was cut stone, the side walls were laid in rubble. The interesting scene in the foreground depicts a frame building being moved, perhaps the one shown north of the building in an earlier view. Courtesy The Athenæum of Philadelphia.

added at the back of the lot. But three good views from the 1790s survive and provide an excellent idea of what Smith's building looked like. They show a sober tripartite facade, with a slightly projecting, pedimented center section. The hipped roof was topped by a cupola, and punctuated by several chimneys. All in all, the description could have fit Nassau Hall with a few exceptions. The front of the jail was built of cut rather than rubble stone; the central projection was three rather than five bays wide; and the build-ing had only one entrance rather than three, a differ-ence probably prompted by the requirement for greater security. Shallow pilasters marked the corners, and the window in the pediment was a demi-lune rather than an oculus. The building was 184 feet long and 32 feet deep, with wings extending 90 feet back to form three sides of an open court. A guide book published in 1789 described the jail as having "a ground half story, and two stories above it. Every apartment is arched with stone, against fire and force.

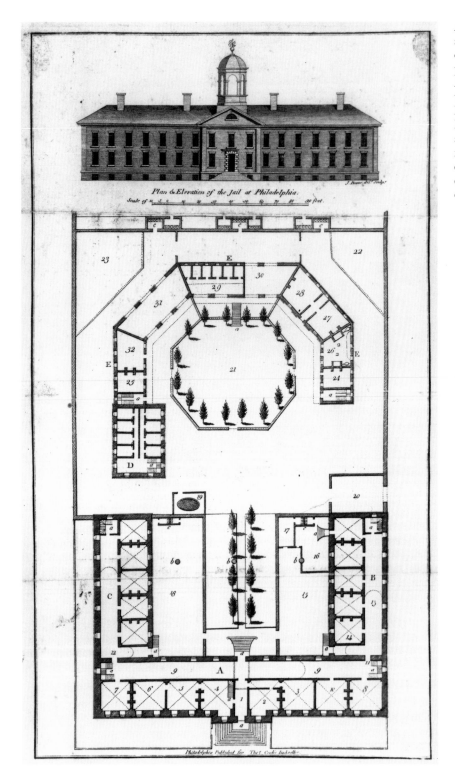

Plan & Elevation of the Jail at Philadelphia.

A front elevation and plan of the jail and its grounds were drawn and engraved by Joseph Bowes, and published in the first issue of the *Philadelphia Magazine* in 1798. By this time a pentagonal structure housing solitary cells and workshops had been constructed behind the jail, as well as a bathing facility at the rear of the north wing. But the engraving also reveals the plan of the original building. Historical Society of Pennsylvania.

It is a hallow [sic] square, 100 [sic] feet in front, and is the most elegant and secure building of the kind in America" (Morse, 331).

An engraving published in 1798 gives a pretty good idea of Smith's design for the interior. The central entry ran through the building to the "hallow square" at the rear. Corridors ran at right angles to the entry along the rear of the front building with stairways and access to the wings at either end. The corridors and the entry could be enclosed by iron gates. The keepers' quarters and offices occupied the front of the building. Cells for the inmates were in the wings, and also in part of the basement, which in addition housed the kitchen, bakery, and dining room.[1]

After the Revolution, reformers began to demand changes in the penal system, calling for separation of the sexes, debtors and criminals, and those who had committed minor or major crimes. A series of laws passed between 1786-1794 were the response to these demands. Among other provisions, the legislation marked the origin of the Pennsylvania System, based on the belief that imprisonment should be not only punishment, but also a means of redemption through solitary confinement and useful labor. These laws and beliefs were responsible for additions to the Walnut Street Jail in Philadelphia, which in part transformed it from a jail into a penitentiary. They included a block of solitary cells and a polygonal structure housing workrooms. This first installation of the Pennsylvania System made the Walnut Street Jail a world-renowned institution. For a period of some thirty-five years, people came from near and far to marvel at what were considered the humanitarian conditions and uplifting, practical programs for rehabilitation. However, with the opening of Eastern State Penitentiary in 1830 and Moyamensing in 1835, the Walnut Street Jail was superseded, and it was razed.

Those viewing the prison in the last decade of the eighteenth century agreed that "upon the whole, it has a handsome and not inelegant appearance more resembling a college than a prison, and is no inconsiderable ornament to the city" (Condie, *Philadelphia Monthly Magazine*).

---

1. Garvan (124) is incorrect in thinking that the basement of Nassau Hall was not used in the same manner. When the building opened in 1756, the buttery, kitchen, and dining room were located there; in 1762 rooms in the basement were finished to accommodate the growing number of students (Wertenbaker, 39).

DOCUMENTATION:

Condie, Thomas. "Plan, Construction and etc. of the Jail and Penitentiary house of Philadelphia." *Philadelphia Monthly Magazine*, 1 (February 1798):97-101; La Rochefoucauld-Liancourt, François-Alexandre-Frédéric. *On the Prisons of Philadelphia By an European*. Philadelphia (1796); Hall, Lieut. Francis. *Travels in Canada and the United States in 1816 and 1817*. Boston (1818); Hiltzheimer, Jacob. Diaries, 1765-1798. Microfilm at American Philosophical Society; Lownes, Caleb. *An Account of the Alteration and Present State of the Penal Laws of Pennsylvania. Containing also, an Account of the Gaol and Penitentiary House of Philadelphia . . .* Philadelphia (1794); Mease, James. *The Picture of Philadelphia, giving an account of its origin, increase and improvements . . . .* Philadelphia (1811); *Minutes of the Common Council of the City of Philadelphia, 1704-1776*. Philadelphia (1847); Morse, Jedidiah. *The American Geography*. Elizabethtown (1789); Niemcewicz, Julian Ursyn. *Under Their Vine and Fig Tree: Travels through America, 1797-1799, 1805*. Newark (1965); *Pennsylvania Archives*. 8th series, Vol. 8. Harrisburg (1935); Scott, Joseph. *A Geographical Dictionary: of the United States of North America*. Philadelphia (1805). Turnbull, Robert J. *A Visit to the Philadelphia Prison . . .* Philadelphia (1796).

REFERENCES:

DePuy, LeRoy B. "The Walnut Street Prison: Pennsylvania's First Penitentiary." *Pennsylvania History*, 18 (April 1951):130-144; Garvan, Beatrice B. "Walnut Street Jail." In *Philadelphia: Three Centuries of American Art*. Philadelphia (1976), 123-125; Jackson, Joseph. "Prisons." In *Encyclopedia of Philadelphia*. Philadelphia (1933), 4:1023; S&W, 1; Sellin, Thorsten. "Philadelphia Prisons of the Eighteenth Century." In *HP*, 326-330; Snyder, Martin P. *City of Independence*. New York (1975); Teeters, Negley K. *The Cradle of the Penitentiary: The Walnut Street Jail at Philadelphia, 1773-1835*. Philadelphia (1955); Wertenbaker, Thomas J. *Princeton: 1746-1896*. Princeton (1946).

Cotter, John L., Bruce C. Gill, Jiyul Kim, and Roger W. Moss. The Walnut Street Prison Workshop. The Athenæum of Philadelphia, 1988.

50

Regulator of Party Walls, Buildings and Partition Fences

Philadelphia
1774

FROM THE BEGINNING, the provincial government sought to assure its citizens that streets, watercourses, and buildings were constructed according to accepted methods. To this end, it provided for the appointment of regulators to inspect building projects. In 1701, the power of appointment was assigned to the Corporation of Philadelphia (Moss [1976], 47). Samuel Powel, known as the "rich carpenter," and one of the first ten members of the Carpenters' Company, was one of the first regulators. The legal status of regulators for overseeing construction of party walls was still in effect in the 1880s when Scharf and Westcott published their *History of Philadelphia* (S&W, 1:201).

The regulators were chosen from a pool of "substantial inhabitants" and their responsibilities included not only the enforcement of building standards, but also hiring workmen for city projects. This highly visible position of regulator represented an endorsement of the individual's mastery of his craft, and offered access to powerful and influential sponsors of public and private projects. It was not considered a conflict for regulators to accept the most profitable work themselves (Moss [1976], 47). Robert Smith was appointed one of five "Regulators of Party Walls, Buildings and Partition Fences" on 25 June 1774 (Minutes of the Common Council, 795).

It is likely that he had served earlier in a similar capacity in the district of Southwark. His name appears in an agreement affirmed 29 March 1769, which resolved "some Controversy... Concerning the Division Line" between two lots. The problem was brought before "Joseph Fox Esqr and John Palmer two of the Regulators for the City of Philadelphia and Luke Morris Robert Smith two of the Regulators for the Sd District Southwark" (Deed Book, I-5:330-331).

DOCUMENTATION:

Minutes of the Common Council. Philadelphia (1847), 795; Recorder of Deeds. Book I-5:330-331.

REFERENCES:

Moss, Roger William Jr. *Master Builders: A History of the* Colonial *Philadelphia Building Trades.* Ann Arbor (1972); ———. "The Origins of the Carpenters' Company of Philadelphia." In *Building Early America.* Radnor, PA (1976); S&W 1.

51

Design and Build a House for the Provost

College of Philadelphia Southwest corner of Fourth and Arch Streets, Philadelphia
1774, demolished

For other projects for the College of Philadelphia, see Catalog #11, Alterations to the New Building, 1755; Catalog #16, Design and Build a Dormitory, 1761)

A THREE-STORY BRICK HOUSE built for Provost William Smith of the College of Pennsylvania stood, although much altered, at the southwest corner of Fourth and Arch Streets until it was demolished to make way for a Holiday Inn.[1] Its construction was triggered by Provost Smith's desire for a house "to put me on at least nearly an equal Footing with Gentlemen in the like Stations in the neighboring Seminaries" (Minutes, 22 February 1774).

Smith had joined the faculty of the institution in 1754, just before its transformation into a degree-granting college under a charter obtained in 1755. Smith was named provost, and, after serving the college for nearly twenty years, asked the trustees to "provide [him] with a House on the College Grounds which now lie vacant" (Minutes, 21 December 1773). Two months later, Smith repeated his request in a letter recorded in the minutes. He commented on "the advanced Price of Necessaries and the growing Expense of a growing Family," which presented a hardship on top of the tedium of several daily trips between the Falls of Schuylkill, where he lived, and Fourth Street. Living on campus, Smith contended, would place him in the middle of things, with the stu-

---

1. Nitzche (12) incorrectly stated that the location was on the southeast corner as did the inscription on a surviving photograph.

dents "immediately under my Eye, upon the Collegiate Plan" (Minutes, 22 February 1774).

Since purchasing the New Building in 1749, the Trustees of the Academy had bought contiguous parcels as they became available (Journal A, 54-55). Among these was the corner lot at Fourth and Arch Streets. In 1765, when two small houses fronting on Fourth Street were acquired, professors were in residence on the campus (Cheyney, 56). Precedent had been set and Provost Smith was persuasive. After receiving his letter at their February meeting:

The Board . . . unanimously agreed to erect a House at the Corner of Arch Street & Fourth Street for the Residence of the Provost of the College; and appointed Mr. Shippen, Mr. Laurence [sic] and Mr. Willing a Committee to prepare and lay before the next Meeting a Plan of the proposed Building, and an Estimate of the Cost of the same.

Three weeks later, on March 15th, the committee presented Robert Smith's plan and estimate for the proposed house.

A Three Story Brick House . . . First Story, Eleven feet in the Clear. Second Do. ten feet; third Story Nine feet high. The Cellar Walls to be of Stone Eight feet high, & of sufficient Thickness to support the Brick Walls above. The East, North and West Walls to be of Brick of the Thickness of Fourteen Inches. The South Wall [the party wall] to be Nine Inches thick. All the Partition Walls to be of Brick Nine Inches thick, except that which forms the smallest Room, part of which from the Chimney to the Front-Wall of the House to be of wood. These Partitions to go three Stories high of Brick. There are to be Fifteen Windows of Twenty four Lights each, Glass 8 1/2 by 11 Inches, for the two principal Stories. The lower Story to have good lined Shutters, and the 2d Story to have single Shutters 1 1/4 Inch Thick—

There are to be eight windows in the 3d Story of Sixteen Lights, and two in the Gable Ends to light the Garrets— A plain Cornice to the Eves of the House & up the Gable End. The House to be well Shingled and Gutters, Pipes &c made of Cedar to convey the Water to the Ground. Stone Steps to the Door, and Red Cedar Cheeks & Sill to the Cellar Door.

There is to be a Brick Kitchen with a Cellar under the whole of one Story above Ground, and a small Piazza in which are to be the Stairs going down to the Cellar, and a small Closet. This Kitchen is to be finished in the Common Way. There is to be a necessary House of Brick, and a Door in by the West End of the Kitchen, and a Fence across the Yard as a Screen to the Necessary; the Yard to be well paved with Bricks -

A good Floor of Inch & Quarter Boards for the lower Story; a plain Cornice to the two large Rooms & Hall, Wash-Boards & Surbase,[2] a small Mantle Cornice to the Chimney with an Architrave under to form the Margin of the Chimneys, which are to be finished with Tiles. Jammboards to the Windows, with a Moulding on the Edge. Doors as in the Plan & Architraves round; good Locks & Hinges to these and all the other Doors. A neat plain Stair Case. The Rooms in Second Story to be finished plain, with Surbase & Wash-boards, Jamm-linings to the Windows, Doors & Architraves, a Mantle Piece to the Chimneys, Closets by the Sides of the Chimneys, good Floors nailed through.

Third Story to have Wash-boards, Closets, Doors and Architraves; Stairs from this Story up to the Garrets—said Garrets to be divided, Wash-boards &c The Whole of the Wooden Work, outside & Inside, to be painted, except the Shingling; and all the Rooms within to be well plaistered; and the whole to be finished in a neat, plain, Workman like Manner, for the Sum of Sixteen Hundred and fifty five Pounds, & I then to pay for that Part of the Dove's Wall that joins this Building——

Signed Robt. Smith

£1655
£   18 for 1/2 Dove's Wall
_____
£1637

N. B. He did not know that the House adjoining was purchased by the Trustees, & the £18 is therefore deducted, when this was told him (Minutes, 15 March 1774).

An insurance survey made 2 May 1776, shortly after the building's completion, lists the dimensions of the house, thirty-four by forty feet, and the kitchen twenty-seven by eighteen feet (Survey, 2 May 1776). William Smith was in residence when Samuel Wetherill, Jr., valued the building, and the description adds a few details to those recorded in the trustees' minutes. Two of the rooms on the first floor were "finisht with Mantle Subbace Skirting & double cornice round." The small room with the wood partition wall, mentioned in the minutes, was Smith's "Library & Study." The second floor was finished like the first, but the third story was "plain." "Open Newell Stairs [were] Ramp't bracketed and [had a] rail against the wall, with Pilasters &c." The double cornices, reflected stair rail with pilasters, and fireplace surrounds were the chief ornamental details in

_____
2. A washboard is what today would be called a baseboard; a surbase, or "subbace"" as appears in a later description, its lowest molding.

The Provost's House survived at the southeast corner of Arch and Fourth Streets until it was demolished for the Holiday Inn that now occupies the site. Like many eighteenth-century buildings in Philadelphia, it had, however, lost much of its dignity, as this early twentieth-century photograph reveals. Courtesy Independence National Historical Park.

The Provost's House was built a little more than ten years after the Maddox Houses (Catalog #22), the only other dwellings for which there is documentation of the terms under which Robert Smith worked set forth in the form of a formal agreement or contract. Comparing the two projects in terms of scale and finishes is not particularly useful because the clients' needs were so radically different. However, it is interesting to compare the payment schedule specified in the Maddox contract with receipts for Smith's work on the Provost's House. Under the contract with Maddox, Smith was to receive a payment on signing the contract, followed by two installments paid on the first of the month. All other payments were to be made after a specified stage of construction was completed—"when the Joists of the Floors of the Houses are laid," for example—with the final payment "when the Whole is finished."

Smith's agreement with the college trustees, on the other hand, stipulated a flat fee without a payment schedule. The college's receipt book simply records the date, who made the payment (generally the college treasurer on an order from the building committee), recipient, and amount, but not what work had been completed. The receipts correspond to entries in Journal A, and total more than the sum agreed upon for constructing the house. Either costs associated with the project increased or Smith was asked to do additional finishing work. Whichever was the case, in March 1776, he "gave in the Balance of his Account . . . [and] the Treasurer [was] directed to pay . . . these Sums in full Discharge of Mr. Smith's Contract for Building the said House" (Minutes, 19 March 1776). The last recorded payment was on April 8th. (Journal A).

In addition to recording standard information, the receipt book documents two things. Smith often received only partial payment on an order ("Forty Pounds in part of an Order for £250," Receipt Book, 2 July 1774), and his son John signed most of the receipts. Does this mean John was "deputized" to oversee the project because Robert was interested and involved in other things, or was he simply relieving his father of a time-consuming business task? Whatever the reason, John's signature suggests a trusted working relationship and connects father and son professionally before their final collaboration on the defenses of the Delaware (Catalog #53).

an otherwise serviceable house of generous proportions. Indeed, the building appears to have been even plainer than the house Smith had built for the president of the College of New Jersey (Catalog #8) twenty years earlier.

Provost Smith's kitchen, however, was the envy of the two professors who lived in the adjoining houses. Just as construction began, they sent a letter to the trustees, which was read at the May meeting, claiming "under-Ground Kitchins fronting the Street [are] so corrupting to Servants, & so inconvenient where there is no other Cellar-Room, that we hope you will pardon our soliciting you, as you are engaged in Building, to grant us Back-Kitchens" (Minutes, 17 May 1774). There is no record of an ensuing discussion or decision in the matter, so it seems safe to assume that "Messrs Davidson & Cannon" had to make do.

DOCUMENTATION:

Archives of the University of Pennsylvania. Minutes of the Trustees of the College, Academy and Charitable Schools. Vol. 2, 1768-1791; Receipt Book College and Academy, 1773-1779, and of the University of Pennsylvania, 1780-1784; Journal A Belonging to the Trustees of the Academy of Philadelphia Anno 1749. Rare Books Coll., University of Pennsylvania Library; Insurance Survey for Policy #1960, 2 May 1776. Philadelphia Contributionship; Notebook of Itineraries. Ezra Stiles Papers. Miscellaneous Papers. Beinecke Rare Book and Manuscript Library. Yale University (microfilm at American Philosophical Society).

REFERENCES:

Cheyney, Edward Potts. *History of the University of Pennsylvania* *1740-1940*. Philadelphia (1940); Nitzsche, George E. *University of Pennsylvania: Its History, Traditions, Buildings and Memorials*....6th edition. Philadelphia (1916); S&W, 3; Turner, William L. "The Charity School, the Academy, and the College." In *HP*, 179-186; Watson (Hazard), 3 (1927); Westcott, Thompson. "Old Academy, Fourth Street." In *The Historic Mansions and Buildings of Philadelphia*. Philadelphia (1877).

52

Proposal for Removal of the Steeple and Erecting a Cupola, Pennsylvania State House [Independence Hall]

Chestnut Street, Philadelphia
1775, not accepted

TWENTY YEARS after master carpenters Edmund Woolley and Ebenezer Tomlinson built the Pennsylvania State House, Woolley directed construction of a brick-faced stone tower, topped by a wooden steeple, and centered on the south face of the building. Woolley's accounts list sundry required materials, describe the scope of work, and furnish a construction sequence (Riley, 17, n79). The tower was completed in March 1753 and on the twenty-ninth of the month Charles Norris wrote to James Wright that "Ed Woolley this day has begun to raise the Belfry" (Riley, 17, n77).

Although Woolley was an experienced builder, he evidently had never erected a steeple before, and this one proved unsound. Its "insecure state" was noted in Assembly minutes as early as 1772 (*Archives*, ser. 8, 8:6714 and 6739). By 1774, its "ruinous condition" was the subject of "some Debate." On January 22nd, the Pennsylvania Assembly passed a motion ordering "the Superintendent of the said House [to] confer with some skilful [sic] Architect . . . on the most proper Manner of rebuilding or repairing the said Steeple . . . ." (*Archives*, ser. 8, 8:7084)

Robert Smith's proposal for the project was contained in a letter presented to the Assembly by "Mr. Rhoads" on 18 March 1775. Smith, described as a "Carpenter," proposed "to take down the Wooden and Brick Part of the State-house Steeple, as low as the Eves of the House, and to erect a Cupola on the Roof of the Front Building" (*Archives*, 8:7220-1). He included "an Estimate of the Expence."

Smith's proposal of a cupola "on the Roof of the Front Building" may have been inspired by his memory of the State House before the addition of the tower and steeple in 1753. More probably he remembered such cupolas on public buildings in Edinburgh. The steeple at Christ Church, and its repairs, had given him experience in steeple construction. But Smith had favored cupolas in his own designs for public buildings: Nassau Hall, the Public Hospital, the Walnut Street Jail, and Carpenters' Hall. A cupola on the front building would have seemed a natural solution to him.

"After some Debate," in April 1774, the issue was set aside for consideration at the next meeting. When the Assembly reconvened in May, no mention was made of the State House. Nor was it discussed in June. The Second Continental Congress met in May and the summer of 1775 ushered in even more pressing matters.

The State House steeple withstood the onslaught of the war years and the occupation of the city by the British. In April 1781, more than four years after Robert Smith's death, the Supreme Executive Council was "authorized and directed to have such parts of the steeple of the State House as are constructed of wood and in a decayed and dangerous condition, taken down, and the remainder sufficiently and effectually covered, in such manner as may be necessary for the preservation of said building" (Quoted in Riley, 24).

Carpenter Thomas Nevell became responsible for the alterations to the State House. A low, sloping hip roof structure, topped with a slender finial, was added to the brick tower. The result provoked a visiting Frenchman to describe the State House as "a building literally crushed by a huge massive tower" (Quoted in Riley, 24).

This stunted appearance remained until 1828, when the present steeple, designed by William Strickland, was erected as a "restoration" of the original. By that time, the technology of steeple construction had improved greatly. Strickland's tower has survived for over 170 years, albeit with major reinforcement in 1963 (Nelson, 295-297).

DOCUMENTATION:

[Pennsylvania Archives] *Colonial Records.* Vol 10. Ed. by Samuel Hazard. Philadelphia (1852); *Pennsylvania Archives.* 8th Series, Vol. 8. Harrisburg (1935).

REFERENCES:

Etting, Frank M. *An Historical Account of the Old State House of Pennsylvania now known as the Hall of Independence.* 2nd ed. Philadelphia (1891); Nelson, Lee H. "Independence Hall: Its Appearance Restored." In *Building Early America.* Ed. by Charles E. Peterson. Radnor, PA (1976); Riley, Edward M. "The Independence Hall Group." In *HP*, 7-42.

53

Defenses of the Delaware River

Chevaux-de-Frise (underwater defenses)
Barracks at Billingsport, New Jersey
1775-1777, demolished

I F ROBERT SMITH had never designed anything else, these wooden "machines" should have made him famous. For a time they helped keep the greatest navy in the world out of the Delaware River, and delayed the British army for weeks on its way to occupy Philadelphia.

In retrospect it is difficult to understand why Sir William Howe, commander of the British forces in America, did not concentrate on taking the Hudson River. This would have effectively split communications between the northern and southern colonies. The plan could not be in put into effect immediately after Washington escaped from the British in New York in the fall of 1776, and fled across New Jersey into Pennsylvania. The British had to pursue him in hopes of engaging him in a decisive battle. But Washington moved more swiftly than the British, escaping across the Delaware into Pennsylvania. He also managed to cross back into New Jersey, and carry out a successful raid against the Hessian garrison in Trenton on Christmas night, bearing prisoners back to Pennsylvania. A few days later he entered New Jersey again, and after skirmishes at Trenton and Princeton, managed to evade the British, slipping away into hilly terrain in Somerset County.

This defeat humiliated Howe, then headquartered in New York. He might have ended the war in the summer of 1777 by sending troops up the Hudson to join those under the command of John "Gentleman Johnnie" Burgoyne, who was coming down from Canada. Instead, he decided to redeem himself for the disastrous New Jersey campaign by taking Philadelphia, the seat of Revolutionary government. He dallied, however, until late July, when he loaded his men into ships, and set sail for Pennsylvania. But knowledge of the defenses of the Delaware made him think it imprudent to attack from that direction. Instead, he came up the Chesapeake, to take Philadelphia through the back door. This was a much longer route, and he did not occupy the city until late September. There was time for Congress to flee westward to safety, and to remove valuable supplies to keep them from falling into enemy hands. The city's bells, including the Liberty Bell, also were moved away: they would not be melted down by the British to make bullets. By this time, it was too late for Burgoyne, who, without reinforcements or adequate supplies, was defeated at Saratoga on October 13th. Although the British managed to overwhelm the Delaware forts, and clear out the chevaux-de-frise by late November, their supply lines were too long, and they were forced to evacuate Philadelphia in June 1778.

Burgoyne's defeat at Saratoga was a turning point in the war. Fighting would continue until 1781, when Washington's Army, with French assistance, defeated Cornwallis at Yorktown. But the threat posed by the capture of the Hudson River never materialized, and communication among the colonies remained open. Although Howe's lassitude certainly was a major factor, the defenses of the Delaware, in which Smith

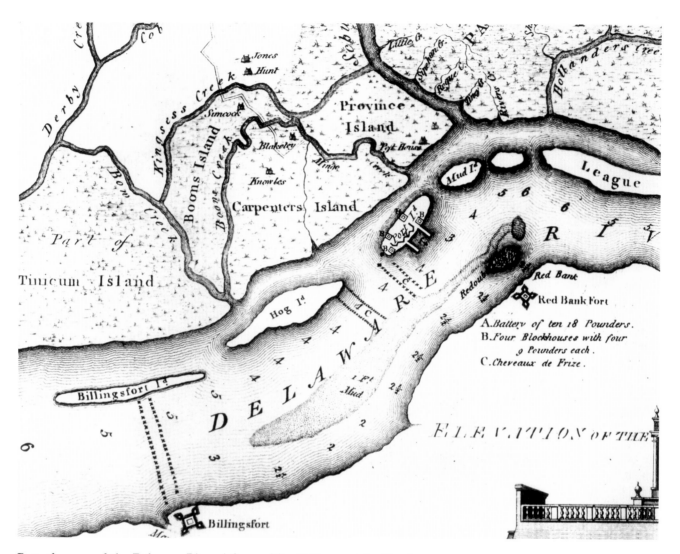

Part of a map of the Delaware River defenses. The Billingsport fortifications,
where Smith did his last work, are at the lower left. Free Library of Philadelphia.

played a vital role, materially contributed to the failure of Britain's grand strategy, and thus to eventual
American victory.

In the fall of 1774, out of town delegates to the
First Continental Congress brought a sense of political urgency to the people of Philadelphia. Most of
the city's Quakers opposed war and the merchant
community saw hostilities as a threat to trade, but
these factions were overwhelmed by radicals willing

to challenge the mother country. Finally the Pennsylvania Assembly was persuaded to appoint a Committee of Safety "for the Defence of our Lives, Liberties and Property." The committee, later called the
Council of Safety, carried tremendous responsibilities
until the spring of 1777 when it was superseded under the new Constitution of Pennsylvania. It first met
on 3 July 1775, and chose Benjamin Franklin as its
president (Jackson, 85). A naval attack by the British

by way of the Delaware River was apprehended, and on July 5th members of the council went down to survey the river and its islands.

To the eye, then as now, the river appeared as a broad and simple sheet of water. But the navigable channels underneath take winding courses. In the eighteenth century sailing ships often were delayed for weeks waiting for favorable winds. Tides regularly complicated the problem, as did ice in winter. Just how to block the ninety-mile river against hostile ships, and still permit the passage of friendly traffic, was no simple problem. At least five different solutions were proposed, some of which bordered on the ridiculous.

From the beginning the council recognized that both boats and "machines" would be needed in a defensive scheme. On 24 July 1775, Robert Smith showed Franklin and the Committee of Safety "a model of a machine for obstructing the Navigation of the River Delaware and explained the Construction of it, which was approved of; at the same time he made an offer of his service in attending and overlooking the Work and building the same Gratis, for which the board thanked him and accepted the offer of his services" (*Colonial Records*, 10:290). Three weeks later Smith also exhibited to the committee a model of a machine "For lowering the raising ballast into and out of the chevaux-de-frise"[1] (*Colonial Records*, 10:299). Smith's design was so well thought of that, in June 1776, Philadelphia carpenters were dispatched to New York City to lay chevaux-de-frise in the harbor. Chevaux-de-frise also were installed in the Hudson River at West Point (Jackson, 376).

These passive defense obstructions were huge and weighty affairs, framed of logs, floored with two-inch planks, and as big as two-story houses. They were armed with diagonal struts tipped with iron spears designed to pierce the bottoms of wooden ships and tear open their cladding. Towed to location, they were loaded down with ballast stones, connected with chains, so they would not shift with currents and

---

1. This French term derives historically from the Frieslanders' early defense of their homeland against invasion by Spanish cavalry. The invention consisted of wooden entanglements, bristling with sharp pointed stakes to baffle both horses and riders. The Frieslanders had no horses. The underwater adaptation at Philadelphia was a "marine" version. In the records, the first use of the term here was on 5 August 1775 (Jackson, 356).

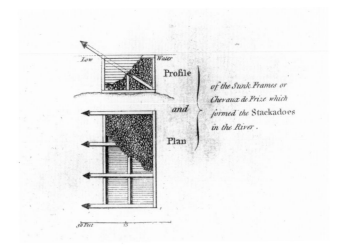

A diagram of a chevaux-de-frise illustrates their construction and shows how stones were placed as ballast inside the timber boxes. Courtesy The Athenæum of Philadelphia.

This engraving of a row of chevaux-de-frise gives some idea of their appearance when they were in place. The barbed logs certainly seem to be formidable impediments for wooden ships. Courtesy The Athenæum of Philadelphia.

tides, and carefully positioned a few feet below low tide, with their armament pointing downstream,

Finding big enough logs for boats and "machines" was the immediate problem. Trees had to be purchased, felled, trimmed, dragged to the Delaware waterfront and there assembled. Even before Smith submitted his plans for chevaux-de-frise, yards on the Gloucester County, New Jersey, shore were very busy. On 11 July 1775 a sub-committee of the Committee of Safety reported that they had viewed a number of pine "loggs." On July 15th the council resolved to "immediately employ all the Carpenters & other Workmen that they think necessary, for collecting materials for building 12 Boats, (including the two already ordered,) and as many Machines as may be thought sufficient for the interruption of the Navigation" (*Colonial Records*, 10:287). An urgent call went out to Philadelphia carpenters and their assistants to hasten to Gloucester County to build boats for the new navy and the "machines" they were to guard.

Assembling these frames on the riverfront was labor-intensive work. Philadelphia carpenter Joseph Govett submitted an account listing the names of seventy-eight workmen. The pay scale varied from 4s.6 to 7s per diem; the days worked per man varied from one-and-a-half to fifty. The work created a veritable industrial village. Nearly half of the workmen seem to have boarded with one Simon Sparks, who kept a tally on food and drink. All was not work. On a lighter note Govett and Joseph Rhoads hosted a celebratory "Barbeque" for them at the expense of £3.15.6 (Govett Accounts).

By 24 August 1775, Govett had built seven frames, Louis Guion four, and two other carpenters four and one respectively. They varied in height to suit the locations intended and were valued accordingly (Jackson, 358). Robert Smith inspected and evaluated the samples and consulted with fellow members of the Carpenters' Company, reporting: "I have taken the opinion of some other persons who are good judges and was Eye Witnesses when they were about to float them off at Gloucester, Viz: Benj'n Loxley, James Worrel[l], Tho's Nevell and Joseph Rackstraw [Rakestraw]" (*Pennsylvania* Archives, ser. 2, 1:754). In September, Robert White and Samuel Morris, Jr., were appointed to supervise launching the first seventeen chevaux opposite Fort Mifflin (Jackson, 363).

Early in 1776, Robert Smith was directed to proceed down to Liberty (Mud) Island with David Rittenhouse, Treasurer of Pennsylvania, to lay out "such works as they shall think sufficient to defend it and to employ the necessary workmen." This was a daunting responsibility and a mark of confidence in Smith's ability both as an engineer and administrator.

The Mud Island fort was the first of the several river forts that had been designed before the war by British Army Engineer Captain John Montresor (1736-1799). (Later—and today—it has been called "Fort Mifflin.") At the time the British believed the threat to Philadelphia was from French and Spanish ships. On 23 April 1771 Montresor presented a plan for a five-star redoubt on Mud Island to be supported on piles. It called for 32 cannon, 4 mortars, 4 royal howitzers, and a garrison of 400 men (Jackson, 60; Dorwart, 14-16). Montresor left his plans with John Palmer, the Philadelphia master mason, whose men worked at constructing stone walls for two years, spending £15,000, before they were stopped. Ironically, Montresor would return in 1777 to plan the attack on the fort he had designed.

By 1775 the international situation had been completely reversed. When construction at Mud Island resumed that year, war against Britain had become certain. A large complex of gun emplacements, barracks and supporting structures were hastily put up; tiers of chevaux-de-frise were planted in the waters adjoining; and a swarm of newly launched water batteries, row galleys, gondolas, fireships and other craft were assigned to protect them.

Smith, however, having gotten the work at Mud Island started, was asked to proceed further down the river. In June 1776 he was ordered to have chevaux-de-frise sunk opposite Billingsport on the Jersey shore (*Colonial Records*, 10:601 and 603). The intent was to build a fortification at Billingsport to protect the new "machines." On 15 June 1776 the Committee of Safety had written to General Washington asking for "an Engineer to view the Ground and furnish plans for carrying the same into execution" at Billingsport. He responded by engaging the celebrated Polish patriot, Thaddeus Kosciuszko, just arrived from France, who drew plans [now lost] for which he was paid £50 (Dorwart, 34). It is not known whether they were executed.

Whatever the plans were to be, a site had to be acquired. The day after the Declaration of Independence was signed (5 July 1776), George Clymer and Michael Hillegas, Treasurer of the Thirteen United Colonies, paid £60 Pennsylvania currency for ninety-six acres of farmland at Billingsport on which to build the fort. This was the first piece of real estate acquired by the new American government. The sellers were to remove a dwelling house and kitchen and "Buildings Joining," already on the site. The fort to be built there was later referred to as "the four gun Battery at the mouth of the Great Mantua Creek." It was an elevated site forty feet above the river at its narrowest point (Stewart, 109, 170).

Smith's first concern was the logistics of sheltering and feeding his workmen. Only a week after the purchase of the site, Robert Smith the carpenter paid another Robert Smith, a sailmaker, £25.18.0 worth for "awnings" for making tents (*Colonial Records*, 10:641). His son John had joined him at Billingsport and Smith employed him as a messenger to convey his plans to the Committee of Safety.

Bellengsport [sic], July 13th, 1776

Gentlemen:

I should have waited on you had not the business here required my constant attendance. I have been collecting materials this week for the shades [tents] to accomodet the Labourers on the Fort Ground; the whole is not arrived here, but I have reason to expect they will as soon as they are wanted. Next week, I think I shall be able to muster sixty or seventy Carpenters, part of which will begin on Monday morning to work on the Barracks, and I think if the weather favor us we can lodge 150 in three or four days, and as many more in the same time after or by the middle of the week after next. How the Com^tee intends to vitual those labourers I know not. If they shu^d think fit to employ Joseph Cassin the person I have employ^d to provide for the Carpenters, I make no doubt he would give satisfaction as he does here . . . I shall have six of the frames ready for raising by the middle of next week, but they are only of the small sizes, for want of larger and more suitable timber, which comes in very slow; If it were not for Mr. Morris, who spares no pains to collect Logs, I should be unable to proceed. My son waits on the Com^tee with this letter because I could not. The Com^tee, I hope, will please to direct him to receive such a sun of money as they may Judge sufficient to go on with, finding and paying the Carpenters, &c., the sum of £200 I have received will not answer for next week.

I have the honor to be, Gentlemen, Your very humble Servant, Robt. Smith

(*Pennsylvania Archives*, ser 1, 4:784)

Smith spent several weeks building barracks, but did not work on fortifications (Jackson, 60). The first order of business was to place some sixty chevaux-de-frise in the river. The problems in positioning these "machines" may have required a great deal of skill and patience. Smith described the difficulties at Billingsport to the Committee of Safety.

I am now ready to raise A Number of frames. But the depth of the water opisite to where we have framed them is Not sufficent to bear them off we must go lower down, The water there is deeper but we have not room enough on the Beach to raise them. I wo.d therefore propose that A Number of Labourers should be set to work at A Gul-ly that has been made in the Bank by the rains that has falen from time to time, to inlarge this Gap that we may have room to lay the floors at a sufficent distance from the water till we can errect the upper works in order to add weight that the tide may not carry them off before we have finish.d the frame. Mr. Hicks tells me that he cannot imploy the Labourers under his care at the fort, before they are discharged. Suppose you should order him to set twenty five or thirty of those People on this Service, and put him in A way how they used to be vitual.d there is Lodging ready near the place for 312 men where they may sleep. I Beg Gentlemen that this may be attended to otherways I shall be hindered much, and the public business will be behind. I am Gentlemen Your Most Obedient Servant Robt Smith (*Pennsylvania Archives*, ser. 1, 5:8).

Meanwhile, on 13 March 1776, Arthur Donaldson, master ship's carpenter, had been authorized to launch the chevaux and James Coburn to deliver and sink them (*Colonial Records*, 10:513). A list of the equipment and supplies ordered for such a job is suggestive:

2 Anchors from 11 to 13 or 1400 weight each; 2 cables about 11 inches each; 4 Buoy Ropes about 6 inches & 20 fathoms long; 2 Hedges Anchors 150 to 300 wt. & 2 Towlines of 6 Inches, & 1 towline of 7 1/2 Inches to Heave off by, each 100 to 120 fathoms long; 2 large long Boats with Windlass's & David's [davits], & a Sheave forward in each; 1 Six or Eight Oar'd Barge; Sundry Coils of Rigging 2 1/2 to 3 Inches & 30 or 40 Good Water Cask & Two Shallop (Quoted in Jackson, 361).

A summation of Robert Smith's recompense for work at Billingsport can be found in the manuscript Revolutionary Papers in Harrisburg. On 19 June 1776, he received £200 from John Nixon, treasurer of the Committee of Safety. The continuing account, terminated in December, totaled the large sum of £2,558.15.2. The last Smith letter preserved in that collection was signed by him on December 5th. On 11 February 1777 he died at home in Philadelphia. The minutes of the Council of Safety make no mention of his passing, but he was succeeded by his carpenter son John who was appointed "to take the management and direction of building, finishing and Launching of the Chevaux-de Frizes" (*Pennsylvania Archives*, ser. 2, 1:89). From March 1st to August 26th John was paid "for his own & the pay of a number of Ship and house Carpenters, timbers, Victuals &ca" over £3,200. According to the financial accounts his new brother-in-law, William Williams, also there, was advanced £400. Those expenditures marked the end of the first building campaign at

Billingsport. Williams was soon absorbed into the patriot army, where he served with distinction.

In their campaign to take the Delaware, complete by 21 November 1777, the British removed enough chevaux-de-frise to bring naval vessels up the river.

When the Americans reoccupied Philadelphia, they were still fearful of another attack, and sank additional ones. But after the war was over, the chevaux-de-frise became a nuisance.

The Memorial of the Merchants of Philadelphia by their Committee That the Chevaux de Frize planted in the River Delaware as an obstruction to the approach of an Enemy, are no longer either necessary or useful for that Purpose, but that they are found by Experience to be highly injurious to the Trade of this City, by impeding the Navigation, delaying Vessels in their Passage, Endangering the navigable Property of the Merchants, insomuch that notwithstanding the Utmost Care, heavy Losses frequently happen by accidents occasioned by the said obstruction (*Pennsylvania Archives*, ser. 2, 1:757).

Finally, a partnership of Levi Hollingsworth, Philadelphia merchant, and Arthur Donaldson, who had sunk many of the enormous boxes, contracted to raise or destroy sixty-three of the machines. This was done by sweeping the river bottom, assisted by divers, for which they billed the Supreme Executive Council £7,400 on 20 October 1784 (*Pennsylvania Archives*, ser. 2, 1:758-760 and 773). Still, fragments remained in the river to be recovered and put on display in the twentieth century, some at the Whitall House, a state-owned site at National Park, a town on the Jersey side of the river, and some at Fort Mifflin.

Looking back, the American defense strategy was successful for a time. While the chevaux-de-frise had been widely publicized when they were sunk, their exact locations were kept secret—known only to ten captains of pilot boats specially licensed to escort friendly vessels through them (S&W, 1:339). Although eventually all the American river defenses were overwhelmed, they contributed to the tardy arrival of General Howe's troops in Philadelphia, forcing them to take a long, roundabout route coming up through the Chesapeake Bay. Washington's great strength as a commander was that he knew when to run away, so that he could return to fight another day. The Delaware River defenses allowed time for Congress to follow the same strategy, escaping from Philadelphia, along with vital supplies needed to carry on the war. Furthermore, the British had to expend so much energy in capturing the river forts that no troops could be spared to relieve Burgoyne. The crucial role of Robert Smith's chevaux-de-frise, backed by the "Pennsylvania Navy" and the river forts, can hardly be overstated.

DOCUMENTATION:

Joseph Govett Account, 1775. Copy (original now missing). Peterson Files; *Minutes of the Provincial Council of Pennsylvania. Colonial Records.* Vol. 10, 1771-1776. Ed. by Samuel Hazard. Harrisburg (1852); *Naval Documents of the American Revolution.* Vol 10. Washington (1996); *Pennsylvania Archives.* Ser. 1, vols. 4, 5 and 10. Ser. 2, vol. 1; Revolutionary Papers. Vols 2a, 4, 4a. Pennsylvania State Archives, Harrisburg; Stauffer Collection. Vol. 7. Historical Society of Pennsylvania.

REFERENCES:

Dorwart, Jeffrey M. *Fort Mifflin of Pennsylvania: An Illustrated History.* Philadelphia (1998); Jackson, John W. *The Pennsylvania Navy 1775-1781.* New Brunswick NJ (1974); Simpson, Hazel Burroughs. *The Byllings Point Saga.* (1971); Stewart, Frank H. *Notes on Old Gloucester County.* Vol 3. Woodbury, NJ(1937); Weigley, Russell F., ed. *Philadelphia: A 300-Year History.* New York and London (1982).

INDEX

Unless otherwise noted, all buildings and places are in Philadelphia.

Pages where illustrations appear are identified by italics.

ROBERT SMITH: *Architect, Builder, Patriot* 1722-1777

was designed by Klaus Gemming, Carrboro, North Carolina.
The text was set in Stamperia Valdonega's original film version
of *Imprint* (VAL), a typeface cut in 1912 for the periodical
of the same name, the first original book type to be designed
especially for mechanical composition. It is modeled on
William Caslon's *Old Face* (1734).

The illustrations were reproduced in fine-line duotone and printed
by Stamperia Valdonega, Arbizzano, Verona, Italy, on 100-pound
acid-free Bodonia, made by Cartiere Fedrigoni.

The book was bound by Legatoria Torriani in Brillianta cloth
by Scholko, with Nettuno endpapers by Fedrigoni.
The entire production was supervised by
Martino Mardersteig of Stamperia Valdonega.

The Athenæum of Philadelphia